Exploring Kyoto

京都

Exploring Kyoto

On Foot in the Ancient Capital

Judith Clancy

Stone Bridge Press • Berkeley, California

Published by
Stone Bridge Press
P. O. Box 8208
Berkeley, CA 94707
tel 510-524-8732 • sbp@stonebridge.com • www.stonebridge.com

This is a revised and updated edition of *Exploring Kyoto*, originally published in 1997 by Weatherhill, Inc., New York and Tokyo.

All Japanese words except common place names have been romanized with long vowel signs.

Text and photographs © 2008 Judith Clancy.

Cover design by Linda Ronan, incorporating an image of Fushimi Inari Shrine.

Printed in the United States of America.

2012 2011 2010 2009 2008   10 9 8 7 6 5 4 3 2 1

LIBRARY OF CONGRESS CATALOGING-IN-PUBLICATION DATA

Clancy, Judith.
  Exploring Kyoto : on foot in the ancient capital / Judith Clancy. – Rev. ed.
      p. cm.
  Includes index.
  ISBN 978-1-933330-64-8 (pbk.)
  1. Kyoto (Japan)—Description and travel. 2. Walking—Japan—Kyoto—
Guidebooks. 3. Kyoto (Japan)—Guidebooks. I. Title.
  DS897.K84C57 2008
  915.2'1864045—dc22

                    2008005317

CONTENTS

Introduction 7

Exploring Kyoto

INTRODUCTION

The city of Kyoto nestles in a basin traversed by several rivers and surrounded on three sides by mountains. To the south, it opens onto the Osaka plain. To the northeast is Mt. Hiei (848 meters), in the northwest is Mt. Atago (910 meters), and to the north Mt. Kurama (699 meters), beyond which wave after wave of mountains extend to the Japan Sea.

The Ancient Capital

From the fifth to eighth centuries, the Hata clan, a large family of Korean descent, occupied much of the future site of Kyoto, then known as the province of Yamashiro ("the back of the mountains"). They raised silkworms, controlled the imperial weaving industry, and enjoyed great prosperity. The Hata founded the Fushimi Inari and Matsuo Shrines at which prayers were offered for abundant rice harvests and silk production. They were also responsible for building Kōryūji in 603, well before Kyoto's founding, to enshrine an image given them by Prince Shōtoku (572–621).

In 784, the imperial court was relocated from Nara to Nagaoka, now a suburb in southwestern Kyoto. However, a number of deaths, including that of the crown prince, caused the emperor Kammu to consider the Nagaoka site inauspicious and to move the capital again. Invited by the Hata to use their land for hunting expeditions, the emperor was impressed by the beautiful scenery, the natural protection offered by the surrounding mountains, and the many rivers that flowed through the basin. In 794, Heiankyō, the Capital of Peace and Tranquility, was established.

The new capital was laid out on a grid pattern modeled on that of the ancient Chinese capital of Chang'an (present-day Xi'an). The grid cut the city into large square divisions called *chō*, a feature preserved to this day in central Kyoto. Heiankyō was 4.46 kilometers east to west and 5.18 kilometers north to south, with the imperial palace in the center of the northernmost part of the city.

Suzaku Ōji, an eighty-five-meter-wide thoroughfare lined with willows and pines running south from the palace, divided the city into Sakyō and Ukyō, or Left and Right Wards. From east to west ran a set of numbered streets, which along with the broad north–south avenues like Suzaku, formed a street grid that can still be seen on a modern map. Ichijō to Kujō Dōri (First to Ninth Streets) have run along the same roadways for more than a thousand years. At the southern end of Suzaku Ōji stood the main gate to the city, Rajōmon (also know as Rashōmon). Unlike Xi'an, which was surrounded by a fortress-like stone wall, no wall was built around Kyoto, though documents indicate that a small wall extended to the right and left of the Rajōmon. The gate itself, more decorative than defensive, was a two-story structure almost thirty meters high and sixty meters across, painted a bright cinnabar red. Today, the only indication of its site is a single stone marker in a cramped playground. (A replica one-eighth of the original size is stored in the Municipal Art Museum.)

In 794, the capital boasted 80,000 dwellings and a population of 80,000 (today's population is about 1.5 million). By the time it was complete in 818, another 40,000 dwellings had been added and the population had increased to 120,000, making it one of the world's largest cities at that time.

Near the site of present-day Kyoto Station were the East and West Markets, where a variety of shops sold silk, brocade, and damask, cotton for stuffing, ramie, thread, dyes, needles, leather, oil, metal goods, and oxen. One market was open the first half of the month; the other the latter half. Administration offices were located in each market marked by large, distinctive towers. Both markets were fronted by grounds spacious enough to accommodate the citizens who gathered to exchange gossip, buy new

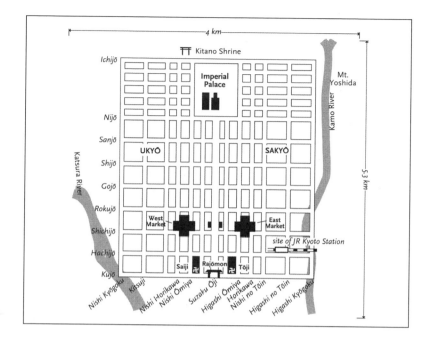

HEIANKYŌ

remedies from hawkers, or offer alms to mendicant monks. For reasons that are not clear, the East Market thrived, whereas the West Market closed in 825. Today, Kyoto's central food market is located very close to where its predecessor, the East Market, once stood.

Two large official temple complexes, Tōji (East Temple) and Saiji (West Temple), were built on either side of the Rajōmon in the Right and Left Wards of the capital. Tōji became a temple of the Shingon sect when it was granted to the priest Kōbō Daishi in 823. Not much is known about Saiji, other than it may have functioned as an administrative site for the various Nara schools of Buddhism. Centuries later, a smaller Saiji became a Jōdo temple, but when it fell into ruins, it was not rebuilt. While Tōji still exists, the site of Saiji is now a park with a small mound, atop which stand two large hackberry trees. A sign in the park shows the original layout of the temple, which was the mirror image of Tōji.

Today, **Tōji**, designated as a World Heritage Site, offers visitors a glimpse of what a 1,200-year-old temple complex looked like. The Homotsukan museum [Open 9 to 4:30, spring and fall. Admission ¥500. Tel: 691-3325] contains many fine examples of Buddhist sculpture, as do the Kōdō and Kondō, which can be entered with an additional ¥500. The Miedō, to the west of the Homotsukan (no admission) conducts daily services to the temple's founder, Kōbō Daishi, every morning between 6 and 7.

Originally, Heiankyō was oriented slightly to the west of the present center of Kyoto, and the Kamo River marked its eastern limits. However, much building took place east of the Kamo starting in the Enchō period (923–30), at which time the western district went into a decline and reverted to rice fields, many of which still remain. The old capital's west boundary, Nishi Kyōgoku Dōri, no longer exists except as the name of an area in the southwest corner of the city near the Katsura River. The temples and homes that once stood here are long gone. As the west remained undeveloped, the increasing eastward development turned Suzaku Ōji (present-day Sembon Dōri) into the capital's western boundary. Teramachi formed the eastern boundary, and Kuramachi and Kujō Dōri respectively became the northern and southern limits.

Over the centuries, fires, wars, and earthquakes changed the face of the city, and repeated rebuilding gradually moved the city closer to the Kamo River. It was in the late sixteenth century that Kyoto assumed its present shape, thanks largely to the patronage of the warlord Toyotomi Hideyoshi (1536–98). In the Tenshō era (1573–91), Hideyoshi discarded the Right and Left Wards, redividing the city into Kamigyō and Shimogyō, the Upper and Lower Capitals. Hideyoshi relocated many temples to Teramachi (Temple District), where they may still be found today, along with shops selling religious items such as incense, altar furnishings, candles, prayer beads, and statuary. Wide streets were narrowed and the space filled in with houses—believed by some to discourage unruly crowds from massing. With the loss of its broad boulevards, the Kyoto of the original planners vanished, and the grand dimensions that made it a ninth-century marvel disappeared.

Perhaps the most remarkable project of this time was the construction of an earthen defense embankment, called Odoi, around Kyoto. Building began in the early spring of 1591 and was completed seventeen months later in May of 1592. The speed with which this was done testifies to both Hideyoshi's powers of organization and the size of the labor force at his disposal. It also reveals that the capital was in such a ruinous state after more than a century of civil war that the erection of the embankment did not have to be delayed by the displacement of large numbers of citizens.

The **Odoi** was approximately nine meters wide. Bamboo, the root system of which would strengthen its earthen composition, was planted on top. Moats were dug on one and sometimes both sides. Where the Odoi was bordered on one side by a river, such as the Kamo, no moat was constructed. Openings in the embankment allowing access to and from the city were called *kuchi*, or "mouths," and the roads issuing from them were named after the districts outside the capital to which they led. The contemporary place names Kuramaguchi, Awataguchi, and Tambaguchi are reminders of these openings in the Odoi. The area inside the Odoi became known as Rakuchū (Inner Capital) and the outside Rakugai (Outer Capital). Besides the nine main *kuchi*, there were other openings in the Odoi. These small passageways, probably left unguarded, helped facilitate the flow of food and goods into the capital from nearby farms.

Although documents show that the Odoi was intact more than a century after its construction, natural disasters eventually demolished many sections, which were not rebuilt. The most central and accessible intact portion of the Odoi forms the east border of Rōzanji temple on Teramachi Dōri midway between Marutamachi Dōri and Imadegawa Dōri (see Teramachi walk, page 115). The longest and most beautifully preserved portion is located between the Kitano and Hirano shrines (see Kitano walk, page 52), where bamboo interspersed with various large trees shade the plum-lined Kamiya River as it runs along the outer embankment of the Odoi.

Kyoto retained its sixteenth-century layout until the introduction of the railway in the Meiji period (1868–1912). Canals that until then had been used for the transport of goods were abandoned, filled in, and rails were laid, preparing Kyoto for its development as a modern industrial city.

Touring the Modern City

The foresight of Japan's ancient rulers in choosing this location for the imperial capital of Heiankyō continues to benefit Kyoto residents. The hills on three sides form a scenic backdrop for its temples, gardens, and homes. Easily accessible, these hills are marked with well-traveled paths offering plenty of opportunities for hikers, while the city proper is relatively flat, ideal for cycling and walking. The banks of its four major rivers, the Takano, Kamo, Katsura, and Uji have been landscaped and are lined with paths. Public transportation is extensive; subway stations, bus stops, and taxis are abundant.

Crisscrossing the original street grid that still provides the backbone of the central city are hundreds of tiny alleys, curving paths that follow canals, and streets that lead to large temple precincts, bustling markets, small playgrounds, and tiny parks unmarked on tourist maps. Kyoto is a jumble of architectural styles, and scattered among its modern and traditional homes and businesses are fifteen hundred Buddhist temples (*tera*) and Shintō shrines (*jinja, taisha*), many with famous gardens and works of art.

One of Kyoto's distinctive structures is the townhouse or *machiya*, a long, narrow, wooden row house. A simple lattice window and door open to dark inner rooms. Small skylights let in some sun, as does an inner garden (*tsubo-niwa*). A single stone lantern, a ground-cover of moss, and one or two plants may be all that constitute the garden, but this small plot of green

A bridge spans the pond in the garden of Sentō Gosho.

gives air and color to the interior rooms, making them seem larger. Rows of these townhouses are found in several downtown areas. Because of their depth and narrowness, they are referred to as "eels' nests." The simplicity of their dark-stained wooded fronts, a tantalizing glimpse of the beauty of their inner rooms, and their quiet ambience are a particular Kyoto attraction. A fine example of a merchant's townhouse is the **Horino Kinenkan** [Open 10 to 4. Closed Mondays, Obon, and New Year holidays. Admission ¥300. Tel: 223-2072], three blocks south of Marutamachi Dōri on the west side of Sakaimachi Dōri.

For centuries, the presence of the imperial court in Kyoto attracted the country's best artists. The city has always had many ateliers for ceramics, painting, dyeing, and weaving. Craftsmen, always in great demand, usually displayed their wares on the street in front of their homes, which doubled as their workplaces. Old screens depicting daily life in the capital show the streets teeming with activity: artisans busy at their work, festivals in progress, shoppers going to market. These ateliers and workshops, in contemporary guise, are still scattered amid residential areas.

Because homes and businesses look much alike, a split curtain (*noren*) is hung in the doorway of a shop or restaurant giving the name of the establishment and the nature of its trade. If no *noren* is hung out, the shop is not open for business. (Bathhouses have their own distinctive curtains, emblazoned with the symbol for hot water, the name of an advertiser, and a seasonal motif.)

Festivals are held all year round, though the majority are held in spring and fall. Neighborhood festivals, although often not included in the formal calendar of events, are well known to residents. Every neighborhood has its shrine. Once a year, the enshrined god is paraded through the streets in a black lacquer box-like palanquin glittering with gold fixtures. Special offerings of food and drink are set out on neighborhood altars, and colorful banners decorate the shrine precincts. The mood is friendly, sometimes playful, as when people momentarily step beneath a large red passing umbrella, believing that by doing so they will be granted good health for the ensuing year. Onlookers are welcome and are often urged to participate.

There are other less publicized annual events. Many temples that have valuable objects in their storehouses, such as hanging scrolls, tea utensils, and Noh masks, have a set date for airing these precious possessions. Admission is charged, and the public can view these seldom-displayed treasures. Famous gardens may also be opened for viewing only at special times. The **Tourist Infor-**

mation Center [Open 9 to 5 Monday through Friday; 9 to 12 on Saturday. Closed on national holidays. Tel: 343-6655], located on the ninth floor of the Isetan Department Store at Kyoto Station, posts notices of special openings and provides maps and assistance.

The religious services that take place in temples are not weekly occurrences as in Christian churches. Moreover, many temples are reliquaries of antiquity, and visitors usually are allowed to view the buildings and treasures. Representative of a variety of architectural styles, many buildings have been designated National Treasures, or Important Cultural Properties. Temple gardens receive many visitors for their seasonal flowers, but also for the wooden plaques or stones inscribed with poems by famous persons.

Kyoto has a mild but humid climate with four distinct seasons, and a rich variety of flowers associated with each season. When cherry trees bloom or maples turn a brilliant red, it is a national event covered by the media. Camellias blossom throughout the winter months, and many other non-deciduous trees and shrubs keep the cityscape green even in January and February. Starting with plums festivals in February, Kyoto is bedecked with flowers: cherry blossoms, rhododendron, azalea, peonies, wisteria, irises, hydrangea, lilies, assorted wildflowers, scarlet amaryllis, bush clover, chrysanthemums, maples, and the early-blooming sazanqua camellias. The city offers a spectacular show of flora set amidst some of the world's greatest gardens and stateliest architecture.

This book is for those who enjoy exploring at an unhurried pace. The walks begin with the Imperial Park in the center of the city and move in two counterclockwise circles around the inner city and the outer city. Because there are fewer buses, trains, and subways to outer city destinations, transport information is given in the text, while it is not for the inner city walks. One consideration in arranging the walks was economy. Most places can be reached by a single bus or subway ride there and back, reducing transportation costs. And enough admission-free sights are included in each walk to allow the reader a full day of leisurely and inexpensive sightseeing.

Detailed maps show streets now usually traveled by the tourist. Even if you lose your way or venture in another direction, you can do so without worry, for Kyoto streets are as safe as they are interesting. Local police boxes are marked by a globe-like red light and frequently display maps of the area. Anyone may enter and ask directions. To make phone calls, the area code in Kyoto is 075.

Although a morning or afternoon bus tour ensures seeing many major attractions, it does not allow the visitor to experience Kyoto life, nor to browse in the neighborhoods and shops surrounding famous sights. Those inclined to window-shop will find enough galleries, traditional shops, boutiques, and restaurants along the way to satisfy their curiosity. Some temples have nursery schools and kindergartens, and serve as neighborhood gathering places for local residents. There is always a surprising amount of activity around Kyoto's famous sights, and it is worthwhile spending the time to discover the real Kyoto—a city that encompasses both the latest technology and centuries-old traditions.

Transportation

Kyoto can be reached from all major cities by Japan Railways (JR). Three private railways, Keihan, Hankyū, and Kintetsu, operate between Kyoto, Osaka, Kobe, and Nara. Two smaller private lines, the Keifuku and the Eizan, serve the western and northeastern parts of the city, respectively. The Kyoto subway has one north–south line and one east–west line. Within the city numerous bus companies operate: City Bus, Kyoto Bus, Keihan Bus, JR Bus, and Hankyū Bus.

The Raku Bus (numbers 100, 101, 102) allows you to see major sites explaining these places en route. All buses leave from

Kyoto Station. Pamphlets in English, Chinese, and Korean are available at the information counter on the ground level of the underground Transportation Center at Kyoto Station and Karasuma Ōike Subway Station.

A one-day bus pass (*ichinichi basu ken*) for City Bus users costs ¥500 and may be purchased on the bus. Another, more comprehensive day pass includes use of City Bus, Kyoto Bus, and the subway. It is called Kyoto Sightseeing One-Day Bus Pass (*Kyoto kankō ichinichi basu ken*) and costs ¥1,200 for adults and ¥600 for children. These passes as well as maps of bus and subway lines are available in Kyoto Station at kiosks and ticket vendors marked Kōtsū Annai (Transport Information); at the Tourist Information Center mentioned above; at the Shijō Karasuma, Ōike-Karasuma, and Keihan subway stations; at Kitaōji Bus and Subway Terminal; and at major hotels.

Commercial bus tours provide those with limited time a brief glimpse of the city's highlights. Taxis also can be hired for a few hours or for the day. On request, four companies, **Kyoren** [Tel: 221-1210], **Rakuto Group** [Tel: 593-1112], **Yasaka Jidōsha** [Tel: 841-6261], and **MK** [Tel: 721-2237] will arrange for English-speaking drivers.

A free monthly publication, *Kyoto Visitors' Guide*, available at hotels and Tourist Information Centers, provides a map of the city, a simple transport map, and a listing of monthly events.

Traditional Culture

The city boasts a number of excellent museums and galleries, led by the **Kyoto National Museum** [Kokuritsu Hakubutsukan. Open 9 to 4. Closed Mondays. Tel: 541-1151] at Shichijō Dōri and Higashiōji Dōri, with its outstanding permanent collection and regular special exhibitions of Japanese and Western art.

The **Museum of Traditional Crafts** (Fureaikan) is located in the basement of the **Miyako Messe Exhibition Hall** [Open 9 to 5.

Closed Mondays. Tel: 762-2633]. This complex, located in the Oka-zaki district of the city, displays crafts and videos that explain craft techniques and processes in both Japanese and English. Another convenient place to purchase and get a comprehensive view of lo-cal crafts is the **Kyoto Handicraft Center** [Open 10 to 6. Tel: 761-5080] on Marutamachi Dōri, one block east of Higashiōji Dōri.

The **Archaeological Museum** [Open to 5. Closed Mondays] is located on Imadegawa Dōri, several blocks west of Horikawa [Tel: 432-3245. Admission ¥300]. Displays of Kyoto's original pit dwell-ings, shards of pottery, and metal unearthed during the construc-tion of the subway in the 1990s can be viewed.

The **Kampō Museum** exhibits calligraphy and houses a fine collection of inkstones [Open 10 to 4. Closed between exhibitions and over the New Year. Admission ¥600. Tel: 771-7130].

Demonstrations of weaving are given at the **Nishijin-ori Kai-kan** [Open 9 to 5. Tel: 451-9231], a block south of Imadegawa Dōri on Horikawa Dōri. *Yūzen* (paste-resist) dyeing can be seen at the **Kodai Yūzen Museum** [Open 9 to 5. Tel: 823-0500] on the south side of Takatsuji Dōri, west of Horikawa Dōri. Admission is ¥500, and for an extra ¥1,700, visitors may try their hand at dyeing a handkerchief using traditional stencils [www.kodaiyuzen.co.jp]. Indigo-dyed articles are on sale at **Aizen Kōbō** [Open 9 to 5:50. Tel: 441-0355]. The shop is a traditional-style workplace on the south side of Nakasuji Dōri, west of Ōmiya Dōri.

Contemporary exhibitions of dyed work are held at the **Musée de Some Seiryū** [Open 10 to 6 November to March; 11 to 7 April to October. Closed Mondays. Admission ¥300. Tel: 255-5301]. The museum is on the east side of Muromachi, north of Nishiki Kōji.

Ikenobō [Tel: 321-2838], the oldest school of flower arrange-ment, has its headquarters in Kyoto on Karasuma Dōri, three blocks north of Shijō Dōri. All other major schools have branches in Kyoto where lessons are given. Flower exhibitions take place mainly in the spring and autumn, often in department stores.

Posters and newspapers announce major shows. Direct descendants of the tea master Sen no Rikyū (1520–91) head two major schools of the tea ceremony: **Urasenke** [Tel: 431-6474], located on Horikawa Dōri north of Teranouchi Dōri, and **Omotesenke** [Tel: 432-111], on Ogawa Dōri north of Teranouchi Dōri.

Japan has had a long love affair with illustrations. The comic book museum features comics from around the world. The ¥500 admission allows one to enter and leave throughout the day. **Kyoto International Manga Museum** [Open 10 to 7:30. Closed Wednesdays. Tel: 254-7455] is north of Ōike Dōri on Karasuma Dōri.

The performing arts were embraced and patronized by the court and flourished. The Kanze and Kongo schools of Noh drama both have theaters here and give frequent performances [**Kanze Kaikan**, Tel: 771-6114; **Kongō Nōgakudō**, Tel: 441-7222]; another Noh venue is the **Kawamura Nōbutai** [Tel: 451-4513]. Kabuki, once a rambunctious distant cousin to Noh, evolved to become the refined drama it is today. Performances are given several times a year at **Minamiza** [Tel: 561-1155]. In the spring and fall, the geisha districts give performances of traditional dance [**Gion Kobu Kaburenjo**, Tel: 541-3391; **Pontochō Kaburenjo**, Tel: 221-2025; **Miyagawachō Kaburenjo**, Tel: 561-1151; **Kamishichiken Kaburenjo**, Tel: 461-0148].

International Community House [Kokusai Kōryū Kaikan. Closed Mondays. Tel: 752-3010] on Niōmon Dōri, south of the zoo, offers lessons in tea ceremony, Japanese zither (*koto*), calligraphy (*shodō*), ink painting (*sumi-e*), and Japanese language. Visitors are welcome to observe or participate, and English is spoken. Lessons depend on the number of teachers available.

Japanese love to shop and many visit at least one flea market a month, whether intending to buy something or just to meet friends and stroll the temple or shrine gounds. Items from antiques to *zōri* sandals can be found among the hundreds of stalls set up at temple fairs. Bargaining is welcome, perhaps even expected, but more as a friendly exchange than intense haggling.

Tōji: Open the first Sunday of the month [Open 7 to 4] and on the twenty-first, which is the largest monthly "Kōbō-san" market day [Open 7 to 5]. Located at Kujō and Sembon Dōri.

Chionji: Known for hand-crafted items [Open 8 to 4]. Located on the northeast corner of Imadegawa and Higashi-ōji.

Kitano Temmangū Shrine: Kyoto's second-largest market, known as "Tenjin-san" market [Open 7 to 5]. Located on Imadegawa between Nishiōji and Sembon Dōri.

Much smaller and newer markets are at Myōrenji on the twelfth, Kami Goryō Shrine on the eighteenth, and Kamigamo Shrine on the fourth Sunday.

YWCA: A twice-monthly flea market on the first and third Saturdays [Open 11 to 2. Tel: 431-0351]. South of Shimodachiuri Dōri on Muromachi Dōri.

Japanese Etiquette

Observing a few simple rules of behavior at the places you visit will make your sightseeing experience more pleasant.

Shrines When visiting a shrine, you might like to follow Japanese custom and ladle water from the basin over both hands, then rinse your mouth with the water flowing into the basin. Approach the main shrine building, toss a coin into the offering box, pull the long, thick hemp rope twice to sound the bell, bow, then clap your hands twice and make a wish or say a prayer and bow again. A shrine attendant will assist you if you wish to purchase votive prayer plaques (*ema*), small amulets (*omamori*), or fortune slips (*omikuji*). If no one is in sight, press the buzzer where these items are on sale, and someone will come to help you. Onlookers are welcome to watch the blessing of a newborn baby or a wedding but are not allowed to enter the inner shrine where the ceremony takes place. Photography is permitted as long as you do not disturb the ritual or are specifically asked not to take a picture.

Temples Remove your shoes before entering the Main Hall of a temple unless otherwise indicated. Slippers are often available, but if not, proceed in your stocking feet (bare feet are discouraged). When the exit differs from the entrance, plastic bags may be provided to carry your shoes in.

Flash pictures are usually not allowed. If you are not sure, hold up your camera and point to it. The attendant will let you know.

The large brocade cushion placed in front of the altar is for the priest who conducts services. You should not go beyond that point unless others are doing so, such as when there is a special viewing of images or scrolls.

Sticks of incense and candles are usually for sale next to a coin box with a sign on it indicating the price of the donation. When in doubt, put in ¥50 for a small candle or stick of incense.

Religious images in most temples should not be touched or approached too closely. In addition to being objects of veneration, they often are valuable sculptures of historical importance. Occasionally, a statue of Binzuru, a disciple of the Buddha associated with healing, is found seated on a raised chair outside or just inside the Main Hall and is rubbed as a charm for healing. Other images that may be touched are the large stone or bronze deer or cows found in some shrine precincts. These are patted or rubbed in whatever places the petitioner wishes a cure.

Tea Ceremonies Kyoto has a long association with tea. Occasionally, formal tea ceremonies are held outdoors or in temples with well-known tearooms. If invited to a tea ceremony, watch the other guests and imitate what they do. On entering the tearoom, bow or acknowledge others in the room, take a place alongside another guest, but do not sit directly in front of the alcove (*tokonoma*), which is the seat of honor. Kneel, sitting on your heels. Do not sit with crossed legs unless invited to do so. Eat the sweet when it is served, or discreetly wrap it in tissue and put it in your pocket; do not leave it. Some Japanese sweets come wrapped in a leaf, which is not eaten. Drink the tea in three neat sips, wipe the edge of the bowl, and replace it on the floor. Remain seated and enjoy the ceremony until the actions of the other guests signal that it is time to leave. Return all bows with a bow.

Public Restrooms When entering a public restroom, knock before opening the door. It is a courtesy for the person inside the stall to respond to a knock with a knock, signaling that it is occupied.

Entering a House or Shop Most homes have doorbells, but older, traditional shops and homes, such as the *machiya*, do not. Slide open the front door and say "*Gomen kudasai*" before stepping into the entryway. Wait there until someone appears.

Bathing One of the great pleasures of visiting Japan is partaking in its tradition of communal bathing. Other nations may sit around the table and talk the night away—Japanese will indulge while relaxing in a deep tub of hot water. Hot springs abound throughout this volcanic land and within the city a number of "super-spas" have opened. If you aren't too embarrassed to try, the experience will be a delightfully memorable one.

When entering a public bath (*onsen*), remove your shoes and place them in a locker. Sometimes ¥100 is needed for the locker, but this will usually be returned when you leave. Pay for the bath at the reception counter or buy a ticket at the machine nearby (someone will help you). Change where indicated after locking your valuables in a locker. Once in the bath, wash off and rinse well, then submerge yourself in a tub. (Towels are not to be put in the tubs so some patrons will fold them neatly and put them on their heads while soaking.) Return to the faucet and wash and shampoo while seated, being careful not to splash anyone nearby.

Towel off lightly before returning to the changing room. Be sure to drink something because you can dehydrate quickly. Hair dryers and other amenities are supplied. Most of the super-spas have body soap and shampoo in bottles for customers' use so all you must bring is a small washcloth and bath towel.

Onsen to Try

- **Nizaemon** [Open 10 a.m. to 12 a.m. Admission ¥800. Tel: 393-4500]. A free shuttle bus service leaves from Katsura Hankyū Station.
- **Tenzan no Yu** [Open 10 a.m. to 12 a.m. Closed the third Monday; if a holiday, closed the following day. Admission ¥1,000. Tel: 882-4126] is a three-minute walk from the Arisugawa Keifuku Station near Arashiyama.
- **Yamato no Yu** [Open 10 a.m. to 1 a.m. Admission ¥ 800. Tel: 813-2611] is located west of Sembon Dōri and Matsubara Dōri (southwest of Shijō Ōmiya).
- **Makoto no Yu** [Open 8 a.m. to 11 p.m. Admission ¥1,000. Tel: 351-4084] is in the Shimabara district, a seven-minute walk from the JR Tamaguchi Station.
- **Takenosato Onsen** [In the Hotel Kyoto Eminence. Open 10:30 to 9:30. Admission ¥1,000. www.k-eminence.com] is located in Rakusai New Town, a fifteen-minute walk from Chikurin Kōen and City Bus Nishi 1, Nishi 2, and Nishi 5, Sakaidani Ōhashi bus stop to Hankyū Katsura Station.

Acknowledgments

Tourist sites in Kyoto are marked with a plethora of signs giving local lore, poems, and historical information—in Japanese. After years of living in Kyoto, I finally began to translate a few of them and these efforts gradually grew into a book. This required the help of many friends who willingly gave their time and advice, and whom I wish to thank.

Hiromi and Naomi Okunishi searched their encyclopedias for facts behind legends and superstitions. Yoshiko Taue found complex Chinese characters not in ordinary dictionaries. Sadako Kotani, Hideko Nozaki, and Michi Oki helped correct my translations and shared their knowledge of history and popular culture.

Tomohide Ashida, consultant to the Granvia Hotel, offered suggestions and guidance on the needs of visitors. John Hart Benson Jr., then editor of *Kyoto Visitor's Guide*, encouraged me to write a series of monthly articles on walks around Kyoto; his good humor remains intact even after editing those early efforts. Karl Heinz Shultz and Masataka Hayami tested the accuracy of the maps and suggested alternative routes that enriched them. Hiroko Matsuo, a Nishijin-based photographer, generously provided a beautiful selection of photographs. Betsy Sterling Benjamin, Janice Brown, Joshua Popenoe, Edith Shiffert, and Dr. Eiko Tomoyoshi always showed interest in my latest episode of fact gathering. Lois Karhu, along with friends from Women's Network and fellow Reiki practitioners offered much support and encouragement. Rebecca Teele generously offered to read and correct the manuscript. John Goodman helped edit new additions. Catherine Ludvik's expertise of Mt. Hiei and Benzaiten answered the many questions I had about religious practices on that mountain.

It is to Patricia Yamada that I owe my greatest thanks. Her editorial skills and her knowledge of Buddhism and of Kyoto's history were invaluable in bringing clarity and accuracy to the text, and her friendship sustained my faith in this project.

I am very appreciative of the time and information given by the countless priests, temple employees, gardeners, and restaurant and shop owners who answered my many questions and shared their wealth of knowledge with me.

Finally, I wish to thank the publisher Peter Goodman, the editor Nina Wegner, and the staff of Stone Bridge Press for their capable and gracious support in making the revised edition possible.

Exploring Kyoto

京都

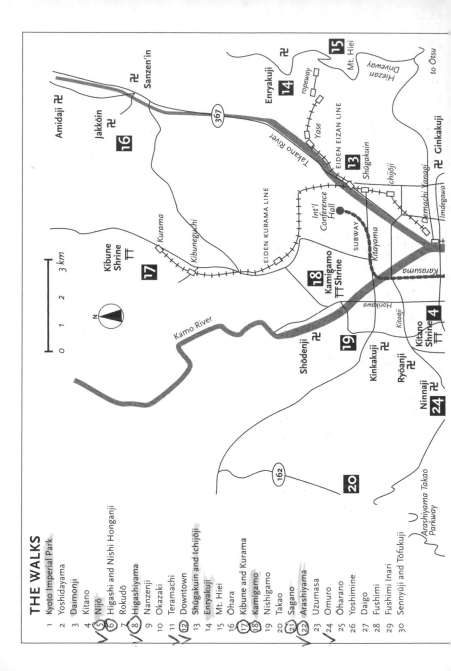

THE WALKS

1. Kyoto Imperial Park
2. Yoshidayama
3. Daimonji
4. Kitano
5. Nijō
6. Higashi and Nishi Honganji
7. Rokudō
8. Higashiyama
9. Nanzenji
10. Okazaki
11. Teramachi
12. Downtown
13. Shūgakuin and Ichijōji
14. Enryakuji
15. Mt. Hiei
16. Ōhara
17. Kibune and Kurama
18. Kamigamo
19. Nishigamo
20. Takao
21. Sagano
22. Arashiyama
23. Uzumasa
24. Omuro
25. Ōharano
26. Yoshimine
27. Daigo
28. Fushimi
29. Fushimi Inari
30. Sennyūji and Tōfukuji

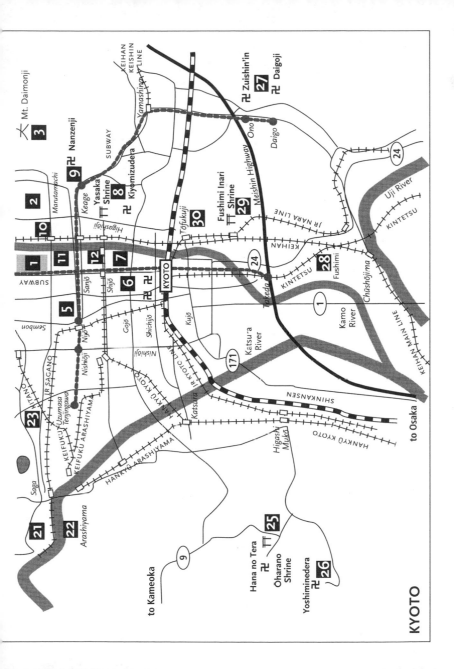

KYOTO

SITES

卍	Buddhist temple
开	Shintō shrine
🌲	pagoda
🔔	bell
🇹🇹	gate
👤	stone image
🔺	stone marker
⊥⊥	graves
示	imperial mausoleum
∬	waterfall
	spring
▲	mountain
●	commercial establishments and other points of interest

LOCAL FLORA

	camellia (Nov–April)
⣿	plum (Feb–early April)
✴	cherry (April)
	azalea (April–May)
	iris (late May–June)
	hydrangea (June–July)
	water lily (June–July)
	lotus (July)
	bush clover (Sept)
🍁	maple (late Oct–Nov)
	pine
	other trees
WHS	World Heritage Site
♨	hot springs/onsen

TRANSPORTATION AND SERVICES

••••••	route of walk
═══	road, street, highway
++▭++	rail line and station
S	subway station

♀	bus stop
P	parking
⊗	police station
〒	post office

KEY TO MAPS

KYOTO IMPERIAL PARK 京都御苑

Kyoto Gyoen　京都御苑
Kyoto Gosho　京都御所
Sentō Gosho　仙洞御所

As you step into Kyoto Gyoen, the park that surrounds Kyoto Gosho, the former imperial palace, you are likely to be met by the swish of a frisbee or barking dogs, their tails wagging as they appraise other canines out for a walk; this a far cry from the sounds one might have expected to hear just a little over a century ago. Until the 1860s, more than two hundred estates of retired emperors, court nobles, and aristocrats were located within this enclosed patch of green. Then the swish you might have heard would have been that of the silk garments of nobles on their way to court, while the barking might have come from the guns of imperial troops as they fought those defending the collapsing Tokugawa shogunate. Vestiges of that era, marked by scattered boulders and sign posts, offer a glimpse of Kyoto's past.

Originally, **Hamagurimon** ("Clam Gate;" the suffix "-mon" means gate) was always kept closed. However, a great fire swept through the city in 1788, and, as the flames neared, it opened, like a clamshell tossed on the fire—presumably to allow people to escape—and has remained open ever since.

The end of the Edo period (1600–1868) was a time of great political upheaval, ending in the destruction of the shogunate, the restoration of the imperial rule, and the relocation of the capital to Tokyo. In the midst of this turmoil, feuding clans and factions tried on more than one occasion to force their way into the palace to petition the emperor directly. In one such clash, which took place in the late summer of 1864 and became known as the Hamaguri Go-

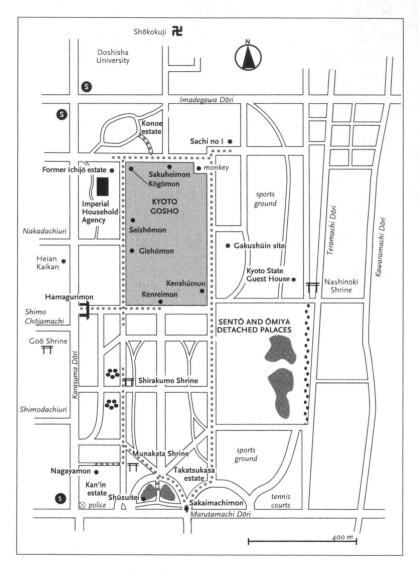

KYOTO IMPERIAL PARK

mon Incident, invading forces from the domain of Chōshū were repelled by troops from Satsuma and Aizu defending the imperial court. The gate is still scarred with the bullet marks left by their struggle. Small round indentations can be found at eye level.

A large expanse of gravel surrounds the outer wall of **Kyoto Gosho**, the old imperial palace. Close by the wall, an imposing *muku* tree (*Aphananthe aspera*) spreads its limbs like a massive fan. The tree was once a part of the Shimizu residence. Today, three hundred years later, it is marked with a sign that explains that it witnessed the fighting at the Hamagurimon in 1864, and is the spot where Lord Kijima Matabei was killed while fighting on the side of the imperial guards. South and west of the giant *muku* is a long stand of peach and plum trees. There are five or more varieties planted here; they begin to bloom in late February and continue to display their flowers into early April.

In the middle of the palace's south outer wall is the magnificent gate known as the **Kenreimon**. This gate, which may be used only by the emperor, is a fine example of Japanese architectural aesthetics. The quiet beauty of unpainted cryptomeria wood and bark-shingled roof lend a distinctly Japanese flavor to this royal entranceway.

The **Gishūmon** admitted princes, princesses, and royal peers to the imperial palace. The **Seishōmon** is used by visitors who have applied for and received permission to enter the palace compound itself. (Twice a year, for five days in the spring and fall, the palace is open to the general public from 9 to 3, during which time visitors enter through the Gishūmon.) The third and last gate on the west side is the **Kōgōmon**, and opposite it is a simple wooden pillar that designates the site of the former Ichijō residence.

The **Sakuheimon**, the only gate in the north wall, was used by consorts and ladies-in-waiting. Across from it, one of the small paths to the north leads to a rather overgrown area with a sign marking the site of the former Konoe estate. The Konoe were among the highest-ranking aristocrats associated with the court, and for over a thousand years they served as regents and chief advisors to the emperor. Today, very little is left of their garden, although yellow wagtails, kingfishers, and a number of other feathered visitors find their way to the secluded pond. West of the pond stood a mansion that served as a temporary imperial residence. A sign indicates that one emperor composed a poem while viewing a treasured cherry that grew here.

A wide graveled road leads out of the north gate of the park. Just to the right, before the exit, is a walled-in area that was once the Katsura residence. Today this compound provides housing for the employees of the park and palace.

Japanese consider the northeast direction so unlucky that the outer wall of the palace was built without a proper corner. (This superstition is so pervasive that a bed will not be laid out with the head facing north, nor are traditional houses constructed with northeast-facing entrances.) However, tucked up under the eaves on the eastern side is a caged wooden monkey wearing a nobleman's hat and carrying a Shintō wand with paper strips. Legend has it that this rascally monkey caused so much trouble at court that he was consequently assigned to the northeast corner to pester and scare off whatever evil spirits found their way into the palace grounds. He was allowed out at night to patrol the area, but was kept in his cage and out of mischief during the day. Today, the netting which enclosed him is intended more to protect him from prying hands than the other way around.

In the northeast corner of the park is a wooden pillar and a black wooden fence that surround a stone well called **Sachi no I**, or "Well of Divine Protection." The water from this well was used to give the infant Emperor Meiji, born to a concubine within this compound, his first bath. In former days, most of the water used in the palace ground was provided by deep wells.

Slightly southeast of this spot is one of Kyoto's favorite bird-watching locations. Regular bird watchers are often found patiently waiting with camera and tripod to catch some of the migrating species that gather near a natural spring. Very near here, tucked into a wooded area is a tiny self-service library. If it is open, just pull up the shutter, select one of the books on the local flora and fauna, have a seat at a picnic table, and read up (in Japanese) on the trees and birds that can be found nearby.

South of this area, the **Kyoto State Guest House** (Kyoto Geihinkan) was opened in 2005 for visitors of state.

South of here among the pines is a sign that marks the site of the original **Gakushūin**, the Peers School. Although many residences originally occupied this site, a space was cleared and a school building constructed in 1847 to instruct nobles and palace employees in history and in the Chinese and Japanese classics. The Gakushūin still exits, but is now a modern university, located in Tokyo. (One of its graduates, Kawashima Kiko, married Prince Aya, the second son of the present emperor.)

The gate historically used by the empress, **Kenshūmon**, is a massive structure constructed of cryptomeria wood. Southeast of it is the Sentō Gosho, which along with Katsura Rikyū and Shūgakuin Rikyū, is one of Kyoto's three detached palaces. Enclosed by a tile-roofed earthen wall (peach-shaped tiles mark the western entrance), the **Sentō Gosho** has one of Kyoto's most impressive gardens. Advance permission from the Imperial Household Agency is needed to enter. The tour through this garden, which takes one hour, is given only in Japanese, but that should not deter you from taking it. The magnificent beauty of these grounds requires no explanation.

The southern edge of the Sentō Gosho marked the southern limits of the palace grounds until the great Temmei Fire of 1788. After that, land was cleared to Marutamachi Dōri and new imperial residences added. Now, a public tennis court and baseball field occupy the southeastern corner of the park.

Opposite **Sakaimachimon**, a marker and several scattered boulders indicate the former Takatsukasa residence, and a little farther to the west on the left is the former site of the Kujō estate, another favorite bird-watching spot. From the old bridge, you are sure to see at least five kinds of birds within minutes. Besides the ever-present pigeons, crows, brown-eared bulbuls, and sparrows, you may spot wagtails, grey starlings, dusky thrushes, tits, Oriental greenfinches, Japanese grosbeaks, white-eyes, Indian tree pipits, Japanese green pigeons, and perhaps hear the elusive bush warbler. Depending upon the season, waxwings, Siberian blue robins, Siberian bluechats, blue-and-white flycatchers, and goldcrests may be spotted migrating through. The teahouse **Shūsuitei** mirrored in the pond is still used for tea ceremonies [Open 9 to 4. Admission ¥200]. Stone pillars from the dismantled Gojo Bridge were used in the construction of the bridge that spans the pond.

The tiny shrine seen from the bridge was built in the twelfth century by Taira Kiyomori, who dedicated it to his mother, Lady Gion. When the Kujō family acquired this land after the Hōei Fire of 1708, they continued to maintain the shrine. The gently sweeping top portion of the stone *torii* is in the ancient Chinese style, making this one of Kyoto's three most unusual *torii* (the other two are at the Konoshima and Kitano Temmangū shrines).

The view north from the pond's bridge extends all the way to the Kenreimon. At the midpoint off to the right stands a large mound of earth from the top of which a black pine soars—a dignified substitute for a huge stone lantern which once stood there.

The Ministry of the Environment Kyoto Gyoen National Garden Office is housed on the grounds of the former **Kan'in estate** [Open 9 to 4. Closed Mondays, holidays, and December 29 to January 3. Tel: 255-6433; http://www.kyotogyoen.go.jp/english.html], which was built in the eighteenth century. Of the many residences that graced these grounds, only this one retains much of its original layout. The former mansion, a storehouse, and the garden are

The muku tree at the southwest corner of the Imperial Palace marks the spot where Lord Kijima Matabei died.

in typical Edo-period (1600–1868) style, as is the compound. Long structures like this one contained stalls for horses, as well as storage rooms. Admission is free and visitors are welcome to enter the grounds and former estate that housed four households. Inside are photo displays of the local flora and fauna and archeological sites in the park area. The inside and surrounding gardens are spacious and modern in feeling with a grass, not moss, ground cover.

Nearby are **Munakata Shrine**, which was patronized by the Fujiwara clan, and two hundred meters farther north, **Shirakumo Shrine**, which is dedicated to the goddess Benten. Local people will stop at either shrine for a moment of prayer on their way to work, or to fill containers with the well water from Munakata Shrine.

It is a short walk from this corner of the park to the intersection of Karasuma Dōri and Marutamachi Dōri, with its subway and bus stops. A number of coffee shops and good restaurants are located in the area. Japanese restaurants are found in the Heian

Kaikan on Karasuma Dōri north of the Hamaguri Gomon. The grounds were part of the old Nagase estate and views of this beautiful garden can be seen from the restaurant or the coffee lounge in the lobby. The Garden Park Hotel and the Palaceside Hotels have Japanese and Western-style restaurants respectively and are reasonably priced.

Entrance to Kyoto Gosho, Sentō Gosho, Katsura Rikyū, or Shūgakuin Rikyū requires permission from the **Imperial Household Agency** [Kunaichō. Open 8:45 to 12 and 1 to 4, Monday through Friday. Tel: 211-1211; http://sankan.kunaicho.go.jp] located in the northwest part of the Kyoto Imperial Park. (The Kyoto Gosho is open to the public without prior permission for one week in April and another in October.) While Japanese citizens must apply by mail months in advance, foreign visitors have been extended the courtesy of more immediate entry. To apply, call or appear in person at the agency with a passport or alien registration card. All the tours are conducted in Japanese.

Times are as follows:

Kyoto Gosho: 10 and 2 (one-hour tour)
Sentō Gosho: 11 and 1:30 (one-hour tour)
Katsura Rikyū: 9, 10, 11, 12, 1:30, 2, and 3 (75-min. tour)
Shūgakuin Rikyū: 9, 10, 11, 1:30, and 3 (75-min. tour)

YOSHIDAYAMA 吉田山

Yoshida Shrine 吉田神社
Saijōsho Daigengū 斎場所大元宮
Shinnyodō 真如堂
Tōboku'in 東北院
Kurodani 黒谷
Okazaki Shrine 岡崎神社
Kyoto Handicraft Center
　　京都ハンディクラフトセンター

Yoshidayama, at 102.6 meters, is the only "mountain" to be found within the central area of this relatively flat city. Scattered along its sloping, winding roads there are many temples, cemeteries, and shrines—providing visitors with an opportunity to explore Yoshidayama's hilly back lanes, many of which are staired or too narrow for cars. Along the winding streets is the temple Shinnyodō with its famous painting of the dying Buddha; the temple and cemetery of Kurodani, as unpretentious as its founder, Hōnen; and two local shrines that are among the city's oldest: Yoshida Shrine and Okazaki Shrine. There are two main approaches to Yoshidayama: from the north off of Imadegawa Dōri; and from the west off of Higashiōji Dōri.

Near the start of the northern route, just east of a small triangular patch of greenery, stand two large stone images of Dainichi Nyorai, known as the **Kitashirakawa Stone Buddhas**. One is rumored to be the Taikō Buddha. The story goes that in the late 1590s, the warlord Toyotomi Hideyoshi (his honorific title was Taikō, or imperial regent) took a liking to it and had it installed on the grounds of his estate. One night, it was heard crying to be returned to Kitashirakawa, and was promptly brought back to this spot.

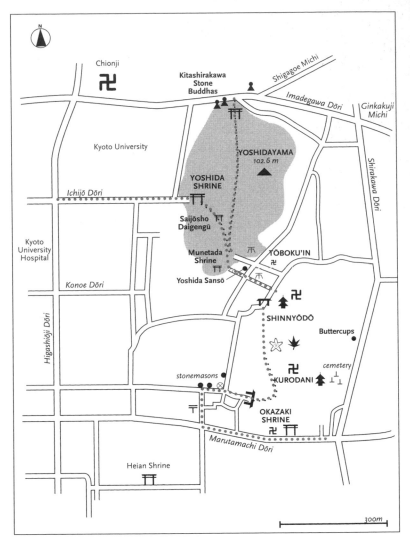

YOSHIDAYAMA

A little to the east, on the north side of Imadegawa Dōri at its intersection with Shigagoe Michi, is a massive stone image of Amida Nyorai from the Kamakura period (1185–1333). Long ago, this image stood at Kojinguchi, one of the exits leading out of the city toward the village of Shirakawa. This district is still home to a number of local women known as *Shirakawame* who prepare and sell the small bouquets of flowers used to adorn home altars and Jizō images. This Amida image is considered their patron, protecting them as they wend their way through the busy city streets.

The main approach to **Yoshida Shrine** is a three-minute walk east of the intersection of Higashiōji Dōri and Higashi Ichijō Dōri, and runs by Kyoto University, one of Japan's top two universities. In 859, the tutelary god of the powerful Fujiwara clan, originally enshrined in Nara, was moved to Kyoto. The nobleman Fujiwara Yamakage (824–88) offered to build a new shrine for his clan's deity. The god cooperated, reportedly arriving on the back of a deer to take up his residence in Kyoto. Today, a bronze statue of a deer memorializes this deity's totemic animal. To the right of the statue, a wide path leads up the mountain. A little way up on the right is a small shrine dedicated to Yamakage. He is the patron of cooks and bakers, and many practitioners of the culinary arts come here to pray.

Farther up on the left is the shrine **Saijōsho Daigengū**. A beautiful example of Shintō architecture, it is one of the most interesting structures in the complex. Built in 1484, this eight-sided structure topped by a thatched and crossbeamed roof memorializes the deities in the Grand Shrines of Ise. Just beyond is **Munetada Shrine**. Built in 1826, it is dedicated to the founder of one of Japan's new religions, a Shintō sect called Kurozumikyō.

The stairs down from the shrine pass through a residential area and lead directly to the temple **Shinnyodō** [Open 9 to 4. Admission ¥500. Tel: 771-0915]. The approach to the temple gives the impression of much urban development. Until seventy years ago, most of the houses belonged to people associated with the shrines and temples on Yoshidayama. A period of development followed in which much of the natural scenery of the hill was sacrificed for new dwellings and roads. Today, building is greatly restricted in this area.

Shinnyodō, like many other Kyoto temples, is an offshoot of Enryakuji, the Tendai temple complex on Mt. Hiei in the northeast of the city. In 984, the priest Kaisan came down from the mountain and built a thatched hut on this site. Over the centuries, grander buildings were constructed. About 350 years ago, the founder of the Mitsui industrial dynasty became the temple's chief patron, and ever since, members of that family have been buried here.

In March, from the fifteenth to the end of the month, an enormous painting of the death of the historical Buddha, Shakyamuni (*nehanzu*) is displayed inside the Main Hall. Finished in 1707, this several-meter-long painting shows more than a hundred human disciples and creatures assembled in grief around the reclining holy man. Admission is ¥600 during this two-week period.

In the garden, designed in 1990 to complement the *nehanzu*, four boulders set in a mound of moss symbolize the body of the historical Buddha. The grouping of rocks in the right foreground symbolizes the cloud-borne retinue of heavenly beings carrying an elixir for the dying Buddha. The garden incorporates a view of Higashiyama, the city's Eastern Hills, a landscaping technique known as *shakkei*, or "borrowed scenery." On the south side of the garden is what is said to be the oldest stone lantern in Kyoto. Believed to be about six hundred years old, it resembles those found in Nara's Kasuga Shrine.

Several imperial tombs are located around Shinnyodō. Their regal pines and geometric stone masonry make them some of the most elegant pieces of real estate in the area. A rather forlorn little temple to the northwest of Shinnyodō, called **Tōboku'in** is reputed to have been the hermitage of the poetess Izumi Shikibu, who

Cooks and bakers offer their thanks and prayers to their tuletary god at Yamakage Shrine.

lived almost a thousand years ago. When in bloom, the fragrance of the two daphne bushes and a cluster of lace hydrangea outside the gate announce the temple's whereabouts in a manner more befitting this ancient court lady than does the dilapidated gate itself. An old gnarled tree inside the compound is said to be a descendent of the poetess's favorite plum.

Around the corner to the west is the elegant old Japanese inn, **Yoshida Sansō** [Tel: 771-6125]. The garden is a masterpiece of hillside real estate and visitors are welcome to stroll up the driveway to the main building. Beyond is a tea salon [Open 11 to 5], which serves beverages with a slip of paper on which the proprietress has written a poem.

Back past Shinnyodō, the street leading south turns to gravel after it passes through a large wooden gate. It and the road to the right, which is paved, lead to the Jōdo (Pure Land) Konkai Kōmyōji, more popularly known as **Kurodani** [Tel: 771-2204]. The Pure Land sect, an offshoot of Tendai Buddhism, offers salvation through faith in the Buddha Amida, practiced by chanting a mantra known as the *nembutsu*. This sect grew quickly from the thirteenth century onward and is today one of Japan's largest.

Inside the Main Hall there is an interesting ornamental canopy above the altar. Such canopies usually are made of metal, but this one is wood and painted in a traditional color-gradation technique popular nine hundred years ago (though the present canopy is only sixty years old).

Kurodani was established in 1175 by Hōnen, founder of the Pure Land sect. Today, there are nineteen subtemples on its grounds. The large cemetery that lies to the east is crowned by a three-storied pagoda built in 1633. All of its graves face west, the direction of Amida's Pure Land paradise. Many of them are without headstones, having been vandalized by Aizu opponents who believed that by damaging their enemies' gravestones, they also defiled their spirits.

It is customary to spruce up the family grave three times a year: at the spring and autumn equinoxes and the mid-August Obon holiday. At those times, there is much activity in the cemeteries as family members gather to sweep up fallen leaves and put out fresh offerings, which often include food and even *sake*. For this purpose, two small buildings at the edge of the cemetery hold buckets, brooms, flowers, incense, candles, and water for those who come to tidy up the family grave.

The road that runs in front of the main gate passes the shops of several stonemasons. South of here is Marutamachi Dōri, from which a few minutes' walk brings you to **Okazaki Shrine** [Tel: 771-1963], one of Kyoto's four most ancient shrines. Founded in 704, it guarded the eastern side of the capital.

The main building, rebuilt several times, is a gem, rich in ornamentation and polished to a shine. This may have something to do with the large wedding hall adjoining it, which ensures a steady flow of supplicants. The two main deities enshrined are Susanoo no Mikoto and Kushiinada Hime no Mikoto, husband and wife, who share the space with their three daughters and five sons. Thus, for young couples, it is considered an auspicious place to marry.

From here, it is a five-minute walk west to the Kyoto Handicraft Center [Open 10 to 6. Tel: 761-5080] and from there another five minutes south to Heian Shrine. There is plenty of public transportation on both Higashiōji Dōri and Marutamachi Dōri. Most westbound buses go to Shijō-Kawaramachi from here.

A minute east, at the intersection with Tennōchō, is a Japanese restaurant and a coffee shop. A twelve-minute walk north from here past the bus yard on Shirakawa Dōri will bring you to **Buttercups** [Open 10 to 10. Closed Tuesdays. Tel: 751-9337], a reasonably priced eatery serving espresso and a variety of homemade sandwiches and desserts. There is a chalkboard menu in Japanese and English.

DAIMONJI 大文字

Hakusa Sonsō 白沙村荘
Ginkakuji 銀閣寺
Mt. Daimonji 大文字山
Jōdoin 浄土院
Tetsugaku no Michi 哲学の道
Hōnen'in 法然院
Ōtoyo Jinja 大豊神社

Until the last century, the area of Kyoto that hugs Higashiyama (the Eastern Hills) was considered rural and remote. It attracted artists and wealthy city dwellers who considered these lush foothills an ideal place to build their ateliers and villas. The Hakusa Sonsō estate combines a gallery with an extensive garden. Mt. Daimonji provides hikers with good trails leading up Higashiyama, while the path known as Testugaku no Michi (Philosopher's Walk) is popular among those out for a leisurely stroll southward to the many temples located along the shady banks of the canal that runs beside much of it. It was here, too, in about 1480, that Yoshimasa, the eighth Ashikaga shogun, chose to situate his villa, the famous Ginkakuji, or Silver Pavilion.

The approach to the Silver Pavilion, **Ginkakuji Michi**, runs along the canal lined with cherry trees, one of Kyoto's popular blossom-viewing spots. On the south side of the canal are several inexpensive restaurants with a wide variety of rice and noodle dishes, a European-style place called **Noa Noa** that features spaghetti with a Japanese touch, and lots of stalls selling food, sweets, and souvenirs.

Next to Noa Noa is the lovely garden of **Hakusa Sonsō** [Open 10 to 5 daily. Admission ¥900, students ¥800. Tel: 751-0446], for-

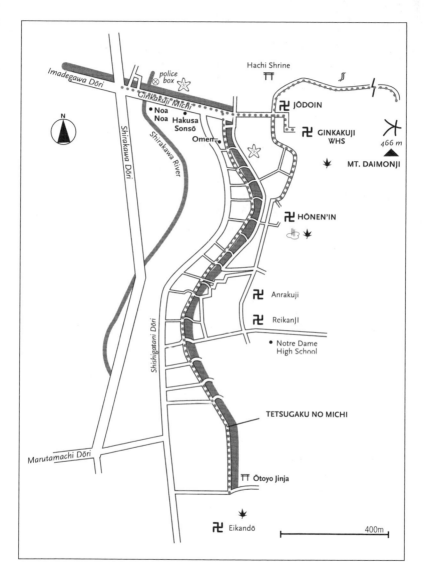

DAIMONJI

merly the atelier of Hashimoto Kansetsu (1883–1945), a famous Nihonga painter. (Nihonga are paintings on paper or silk using water-soluble inks and mineral pigments. Although the basic techniques originally came from China, this style of painting has evolved in Japan since ancient times, and the name means "Japanese painting"—in contrast with the Western-style painting introduced to Japan in the Meiji period.)

Several years ago, an American newspaper featured a story entitled "Japanese Paying Thousands for Rocks." The article explained that the rocks were not diamonds, just ordinary rocks, and that a good-sized stone of appropriate shape and color would fetch up to $75,000 in Japan. As incredible as it may seem to foreign readers, any Japanese who owns enough land to accommodate large stones can certainly afford them, and though they are not diamonds, they are just as valuable in the eyes of the Japanese.

Hakusa Sonsō has many such rocks. One is large and flat enough to be used as a miniature stage, while others bear tiny Buddhist images, or have been skillfully carved into representations of *rakan*, disciples of the Buddha. Many also serve as steppingstones in the pathways that wind through the grounds. The estate's main building reflects traditional villa architecture, complete with fin de siècle glass lampshades and lattice-work windows decorated with wobbly panes of glass. In contrast, the Japanese aesthetic concept of *wabi* (rustic simplicity) is evident in the teahouse and in the small thatched pavilion opposite it. On the grounds is a gallery that houses some examples of Hashimoto's own work, along with a number of fine Persian miniatures and delicate pieces of Chinese glass collected by the artist on his travels.

Exit Hakusa Sonsō, turn right, and cross at the traffic signal. The road straight ahead narrows and becomes a pedestrian-only thoroughfare during the day. Cross the canal and follow the crowds headed uphill toward **Ginkakuji** [Open 8:30 to 5. Admission ¥500. Tel: 771-5725].

The late fifteenth century was a time of almost unremitting civil strife, culminating in the Ōnin War of 1467–77, which left much of Kyoto in ruins. Despite the fact he played a central role in igniting the conflict, shogun Yoshimasa removed himself from the city and his responsibilities as a leader, and busied himself constructing buildings to be used for the pursuit of such diversions as tea and incense ceremonies and moon-viewing parties. He created his own world, one unconcerned with the fate of his war- and famine-ravaged subjects, and in doing so Yoshimasa incurred the wrath of commoners for centuries to come. Like his grandfather, Yoshimitsu, who built the Kinkakuji (Golden Pavilion), Yoshimasu selfishly determined to leave a legacy of beauty and refinement rather than one of wise statesmanship. After his death in 1490, the complex was converted into a Zen temple, Jishōji. For today's visitors, this temple, better known as Ginkakuji, is a repository of exquisite architecture and gardens and is now a World Heritage Site. The buildings seem so unpretentious, however, that it is hard to believe that they represented great wealth and opulence five hundred years ago, when they were built.

The impressive entrance to the temple consists of three components: stone, bamboo, and hedge. The size of this wall denoted great wealth and separated the inhabitants within from the commoners outside as effectively as any moat. The first view of the garden is through a graceful cusped window. Framed within is a glimpse of raked gravel, and beyond that, in the shadows of Higashiyama, a less formal stroll garden. Visitors may sit on the extended porch of the Hondō, or Main Hall, to view the dry "sea and mountain" garden that on moonlit nights inspired poets of yore. Originally, Yoshimasa had intended to cover his villa with silver leaf as his grandfather had covered Kinkakuji with gold leaf. Though that was never accomplished, one can imagine the smooth and weathered roof shingles turning silvery on moonlit nights, making the pavilion worthy of its name.

The stroll garden was inspired by Yoshimasa's admiration for the moss garden at Saihōji in western Kyoto. Shaded by maple trees, several varieties of moss carpet the area. One path ends at a cool, clear spring known as the "Well for Tea," while the slim waterfall near the path on the way up is known as the "Moon Washing Falls" because the rippling water "washes away" the reflected moonlight. If you are lucky, you might spy a brilliant kingfisher awaiting his next meal near the pond. The nearby forested mountain provides a habitat for many species of birds, and you are likely to see the Japanese pygmy woodpecker, several kinds of tits, Daurian redstarts, Japanese white-eyes, and Oriental greenfinches.

Ginkakuji lies at the foot of **Mt. Daimonji** (466 meters), which bears on one side of the mountain a giant wooden structure of the Chinese character *dai*, meaning "great" or "large." Originally, the temple of Jōdoji occupied much of this area before a great fire destroyed all but a few of the temple buildings over a thousand years ago. However, legend claims that the temple's image of Amida Buddha was found miraculously unharmed higher up on the mountainside. In 808, when Kyoto was suffering from plague and famine, the famous priest Kūkai is said to have built a huge bonfire on the site where the image was found to ask Buddha's help. Kūkai's prayers were answered, and his act of faith became a custom that continues to the present. Even today, pilgrims make the climb to pay their respects to Kūkai for the part he played in enlisting Buddha's help to abate the plague. Every August 16, at the end of Obon, an occasion to honor the spirits of the ancestors, the *dai* structure on Mt. Daimonji is set ablaze after sunset to guide the souls of the departed back to the world of spirits. For the few moments that the *dai* is aflame, the city dims its lights in order that this beautiful religious spectacle can be better appreciated.

Jōdoin is to the north of Ginkakuji. Only this tiny hall remains to mark the spot where the huge temple complex of Jōdoji once stood. The thirty-minute hike up the mountain is on a wide and

A view of the garden at Ginkakuji framed in a cusped window.

easy path (though appropriate shoes are recommended). Pass Jō-doin, turn right just before you reach a small shrine, and follow a road that leads past an assembly of small Buddhist images and a car park for Ginkakuji. Bamboo grass and ferns line the trail, and the mountainside is so thick with trees that you won't catch a glimpse of the city until you reach the top. After five minutes, look for a stream of water splashing out of a pipe beside a tiny Buddhist image. Lots of residents stroll up to fill containers with the tasty water.

A little farther along, the path divides. Cross the stream and continue upward. This is a favorite hike for many Kyotoites, and you are apt to see even elderly folks, cane in hand, prayer beads around their wrists, slowly but surely hiking up the trail. In Japan, fellow hikers share a camaraderie that makes any outing a pleasure. Do not be surprised if you are greeted with a robust "*Kon-nichiwa.*" Responding in kind is sure to be met with a smile.

From the top, the view of the city is magnificent. It is not difficult to pick out the Kyoto Gosho, the Kamo and Takano rivers, and the Shimogamo and Kamigamo shrines. Kyoto is an easy city in which to get your bearings, and this bird's-eye view will show you why. If it is a warm day and the weather is clear, this is a fine place to watch the sunset, which should occur between 5 and 7 depending on the time of year. Do not linger long in the winter, however, for the mountain gets dark quickly and the path is unlighted.

The image of Fudō Myōō (a Buddhist guardian deity, one of the five "Kings of Light"), now housed in a concrete shrine at the top, was supposedly placed there by Kūkai himself (posthumously known as Kōbō Daishi). The *dai* itself covers a large triangular area bare of trees or bushes and is easy to identify. There are many trails down from it. In fact, paths run along the ridge of Higashi-yama, branching down to many of the temples that lie along Philosopher's Walk. One of Kyoto's popular restaurants, **Omen** [Open 11 to 10. Closed Thursdays. Tel: 771-8994], is in the area. *O* means honorable and *men* means noodles, but this shop offers a lot more than that. Built in the traditional style, the rustic interior provides warmth, conviviality, and good cooking—a perfect post-hike repast. Besides the standard fare, there are seasonal specials, and an English menu is available upon request.

If weather does not permit the hike up Mt. Daimonji, the landscaped **Tetsugaku no Michi** (Philosopher's Walk), named after the philosopher Nishida Kitarō (1870–1945), who lived nearby, makes an excellent alternative. Take an immediate left after leaving Ginkakuji, and stroll through a quiet residential area to the temple compound of **Hōnen'in** [Open 7 to 4. Free admission. Tel: 771-2420]. Walk past the temple's driveway entrance and enter at the main gate a little farther south. In late winter and early spring this approach is brightened by hundreds of red camellia blossoms interspersed with the delicate maple trees that shade the walk up to the thatched temple gate. The large, old stone marker standing at the entrance announces that visitors who eat meat or imbibe alcohol may not enter, a reminder of the strict dietary requirements adhered to by Buddhists long ago. The rustic gate indicates that this area was once farmland far outside the city limits. It is also a suitable reflection of the character of the temple's founder, the Buddhist saint Hōnen (1133–1212). Still in active use as a monastery, the inner buildings are not open to the public except on specially announced occasions, but enough of the grounds and garden can be viewed to make a visit worthwhile.

Retrace your steps to the canal that runs beside Philosopher's Walk. At the south end of the walk on the east side of the path is **Ōtoyo Jinja**, a tiny shrine with a thousand-year-old history. Instead of guardian dogs, this shrine has two rats in front of its main altar, both considered to have saved locals from a forest fire, thus making this a well-visited shrine during the year of the rat. It is also noted for the great variety of winter- and spring-blooming camellia bushes that populate its grounds.

A left turn at the end of the canal and another ten minutes of walking will eventually bring you to the temple complexes of Eikandō and Nanzenji. A turn to the right leads back to Ginkakuji Michi. Philosopher's Walk is well trod throughout the year: dog walkers; students taking the long way home; residents out for a stroll; joggers; and tourists who come to enjoy the camellias in winter, the cherry blossoms of spring, the kingfishers and swallows in summer, and the gorgeous autumn tints of the cherry trees. Shops offering Japanese-style sweets or coffee and cake, located every few blocks, provide visitors with many chances to refresh themselves.

北野

KITANO 北野

Kuginuki Jizō 釘抜地蔵
Sembon Emmadō 千本えんま堂
Sembon Shakadō 千本釈迦堂
Kitano Temmangū 北野天満宮
Odoi 大土居
Hirano Shrine 平野神社
Tōjiin 等持院

Curiously, the major temples of Kyoto offer a look at historically important architecture and world-famous gardens but do not usually acquaint visitors with the religious practices that make them sacred places. There are, however, many smaller and less distinguished but active places of worship throughout the city. Kuginuki Jizō, Sembon Emmadō, and the Kitano Temmangū shrine are examples, offering satisfying glimpses into the spiritual life of Kyotoites. The other stops on the walk, Sembon Shakadō, Hirano Shrine, and Tōjiin, feature some excellent Buddhist statuary and one of the loveliest gardens in the city.

Kuginuki Jizō, also known as Shakuzōji [Open 8 to 4:30. Tel: 414-2233], is a few minutes' walk north of the Sembon-Imadegawa intersection on the east side of Sembon Dōri. The temple is identifiable by a row of red lanterns hanging over its entrance. Jizō is the bodhisattva revered for rescuing sinners from hell and guiding children safely through childhood. He is also the patron of pregnant women, aborted infants, and travelers. Jizō is one of Japan's most popular deities, and wayside shrines with his stone image are found throughout the country. Colorful bibs inscribed with prayers are offerings from his supplicants, as are the pieces of candy, soft drinks, and other treats often placed at his feet. Neighborhood associations take charge of cleaning the

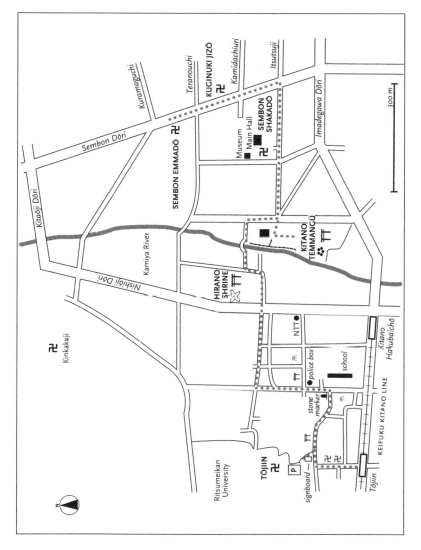

KITANO

shrines and setting out fresh flowers on a regular basis to honor the deity.

Many of the Jizō images in the city have specific powers attributed to them, one if which Kuginuki Jizō. This Jizō is a legendary healer, and his devotees can be seen circling the Main Hall a prescribed number of times in prayer, stopping to touch a small rectangular brass plaque mounted on the back of the hall, and offering candles and incense.

Kuginuki means "nail-puller," and on the left side of the entrance and in front of the Main Hall are large, standing sets of pliers and nails festooned with colorful bibs like those found on images of Jizō. The lanterns also carry the nail-and-plier motif, and the walls of the Main Hall are covered with wooden plaques to which two long nails and pliers are attached. The plaques are inscribed with the name and age of the person for whom a cure is desired, and sometimes the name of the donor.

There is, of course, a story behind all this. Shakuzōji was founded in 819, but it was later that this Jizō's healing ability became widely known. In 1556, a forty-year-old man who lived near the temple suddenly suffered crippling pain in both his hands. He prayed to this Jizō for relief, and when Jizō appeared to him in a dream, learned that in a former life he had pierced the hands of an effigy he had made to represent someone he hated (a practice not uncommon in medieval Japan). The spirit of the hated person was seeking revenge by inflicting similar pain. As an act of atonement for his past misdeed, he offered a set of eight-inch nails and a pair of pliers to Jizō, asking forgiveness. His crippling pains disappeared, and word soon spread throughout the city of the healing power of this Jizō. His offering of nails and pliers has been a tradition ever since, even for healing quite different ailments.

Although the healing Jizō image in the Main Hall is not on view, you can see other statues behind the Main Hall that also receive prayers for cures. On the left is a new, standing image of Jizō, beside which is a small enclosure with a stone image of Amida Buddha, an Important Cultural Property, dated 1225. The lotus pedestal, body, and halo of the Amida are carved from a single stone and it is one of the oldest and most attractive images of its kind. (The crack in the statue's midriff occurred during a move.) In a separate structure on the right is an image of Kannon, the Goddess of Mercy.

A few minutes' walk north of Kuginuki Jizō on the west side of Sembon is Injōji, better known as **Sembon Emmadō** [Open 9 to 5. Free admission, but ¥300 to enter the inner hall. Tel: 462-5866], a Shingon temple founded in the early eleventh century. Entering the grounds, the first image you will encounter, in the center of the entrance enclosure, is that of Binzuru, one of the original disciples of Shakyamuni, the historical Buddha. This stark-looking wooden statue is so worn from the touch of supplicants seeking Binzuru's help and healing power that its extremities are almost worn away. The walls of the enclosure are decorated with four large panels covered with faded pictures of hell. As a result of fire damage in the 1970s, only the figures of Emma, King of Hell, and his assistants can be identified—in the upper left of the panels on the north side.

The interior of the Main Hall may be viewed from this enclosure. Its beams are still charred from the flames of the fire, inadvertently providing this massive (2.5-meter) image of Emma with a realistic setting. Unlike many other Buddhist images, whose garments are of Indian origin, Emma and his assistants wear the distinctive robes and headgear of ancient Chinese officials, which makes them easy to identify. Emma's amber eyes bulge as he listens to the assistant on his left read out the sins of the newly dead. After Emma has pronounced judgment, the assistant on his right directs the soul to the appropriate hell, different hells being allotted to different types of sins.

Present-day Sembon Dōri was part of Suzaku Ōji, the main

thoroughfare of the original Heian capital. There are two theo-
ries as to how the street got its name, Sembon, which means "a
thousand" (accompanied by a counter used in Japanese for long,
thin objects). A millennium ago, it was possible to see all the way
down to the Rajōmon gate from atop Mt. Funaoka (120 meters),
which was at the north end of the avenue, behind the palace. The
seven-kilometer thoroughfare was lined with pine trees (some say
willows) and seen from atop the mountain, it seemed as though a
thousand trees lined the boulevard. Others claim that the street's
name comes from the many wooden grave tablets found on Mt.
Funaoka, a site where funerals were conducted.

The land west of Mt. Funaoka was called Rendaino (Field of
the Lotus Pedestal), which refers to the lotus pedestal upon which
the Goddess of Mercy carries a dead soul to paradise. Many names
in this area are associated with death, and perhaps because of this,
stone images of Buddhist deities (mostly of Jizō), many of them
gravestones, were placed around the Sembon area, some out of de-
votion, others in hopes of quelling evil spirits. These images have
been gathered together behind the Main Hall. The temple is most
active during the festival of Obon (August 7–16), when Kyotoites
hold memorial rights for ancestral spirits.

To reach Daihōonji, popularly known as **Sembon Shakadō**
[Open 9 to 4:30. Tel: 461-5973], walk south past Kuginuki Jizō and
then west on Itsutsuji Dōri. In five minutes or so, you will see a
sign in English with the name of the temple written on it. Opposite the entrance is one of the many shops that repair and supply
loom equipment.

The Main Hall of Sembon Shakadō is one of Kyoto's oldest
structures. This is also a museum that houses an important collection of Buddhist images. The ¥500 fee provides entrance to both.
Unfortunately, there is no information posted in English in this
impressive exhibit of Buddhist images, many of which have been
designated National Treasures or Important Cultural Properties.

Along the wall facing the entrance is one of the museum's distinctive images, an elfin figure of the Buddha as an infant that stands with one hand pointing upward, the other downward, symbolizing the expanse of his domain. This Heian-period (794–1185) figure is made of bronze. Along the right wall are six magnificent wooden images of Kannon, the Goddess of Mercy, each a little over two meters tall, dating from 1224. The woodcarvings of peacocks and dragons were once part of upright drum stands and also date from the Heian period. The two massive wheels come from a carriage belonging to the shogun Ashikaga Yoshimitsu (1358–1408).

The Main Hall, completed in 1227, is a National Treasure and has survived fires, earthquakes, and the Ōnin War (1467–77), a particularly devastating series of battles fought over right of succession to the Ashikaga shogunate—a war which destroyed most of Kyoto, depleted its resources, and from which the city took years to recover. The enormous pillars in front of the altar bear evidence of the fierce fighting, for they have been disfigured by the slashes and punctures of swords, spears, and arrows, softened over the centuries by the touch of curious fingers.

According to legend, the Main Hall has withstood the vicissitudes of time because it is so well constructed. The credit for this is given to the head carpenter and his wife, Okame. When building first began, the head carpenter miscalculated the length of the hall and made the central pillar too short. He was so beside himself with worry that he asked his wife for advice, an act considered undignified for a man. She suggested that he lengthen the pillar by fitting it with another piece, which he did, and construction proceeded. However, before the ceremony for placing the pillar, Okame took her own life as a way of atoning for the loss of face her husband suffered by seeking her advice. Filled with remorse that his beloved wife had not lived to see this ceremony, the carpenter carved a mask of her face, to which he attached a prayer, and hoisted them up on the pillar. To this day, carpenters secure a mask of Okame (usually of papier-mâché) on the central pillar of a building under construction and pray that their efforts will be as successful as those at the Shakadō.

Otafuku is the name of a Shintō deity, but the word also means "mumps," a condition in which one resembles Okame, who is famous for her full, plump cheeks as well as for her conjugal loyalty. Perhaps this is why the names of Okame and Otafuku are used interchangeably. Both are associated with successful construction, happy marriage, easy childbirth, and easing life's aches and pains, and, as seen from the collection of Otafuku dolls along the corridor at the east side of the Mail Hall, fertility.

Walk west on Itsutsuji Dōri to the east entrance of **Kitano Temmangū** [Tel: 461-0005], a shrine known to many visitors for the comings and goings of sharp-eyed shoppers and even sharper-eyed hawkers who make its flea market, held monthly on the twenty-fifth, a nationally known event. Kitano Temmangū is a shrine principally known as the place to ask for success in school entrance examinations—from those of elite kindergartens to those of colleges and universities. During the winter "examination hell," long lines of youngsters and their relatives wait patiently to have their lucky charms, which cost four or five thousand yen, blessed by the shrine's priests.

The deity enshrined is the ninth-century scholar and court noble, Sugawara no Michizane (845–903) a victim of court intrigue who was unjustly exiled to distant Kyushu, where he died. Michizane was later deified to appease his angry spirit, which his supporters maintain was responsible for a series of natural catastrophes and epidemics that followed his death. Shrines to Michizane are extremely popular and are found throughout Japan. When a shrine's name ends in Temmangū, this scholar is the enshrined deity. In Kyoto, this shrine is also referred to affectionately as Kitano Tenjin or Tenjin-san (Tenjin literally means "Heavenly Spirit").

The Main Hall, a National Treasure, was rebuilt in 1607 in the *gongen* style of shrine architecture, in which the two main buildings are joined by a corridor that is considered a symbolic link between this world and the next. Every fifty years the cypress roof is reshingled; the last time in 2002.

Because it is also home to approximately two thousand plum trees considered sacred to its deity, Kitano Temmangū has become synonymous with this flower, and a decorative plum motif adorns its lanterns, tiles, and woodwork. Its thousand-tree plum orchard is

Binzuru at Emma Shakado has been worn smooth over the centuries by the hands of supplicants.

open from the end of January to mid-March. (The ¥500 admission fee includes a sweet and a packet of slightly salty instant plum tea that you mix with hot water provided in thermoses set out on benches.) However, it is not necessary to enter the orchard to see the plums, because another thousand trees are scattered about the shrine grounds.

The trees at Kitano yield a fine crop of plums that are picked and dried in the open air in early June. They then are pickled until tart and tasty, packaged, and sold at the shrine. Within the inner shrine there are two fenced-off trees, a pine on the east and a red plum on the west, both associated with Sugawara Michizane. Their special significance derives from the fact that the scholar's first and last poems were about plums, and the pine is said to have been planted by persons directed to do so by Michizane's spirit.

There are bronze and stone images of seated cows along the main approach and within the shrine's precincts to honor this animal that collapsed and died while pulling Michizane's corpse. Also, Michizane was born in the year of the cow, so these creatures receive attention from those seeking relief from pain and worry. People gently rub the part of the cow that corresponds to their own aches and pains.

Visitors pass under three large stone *torii* to enter the main precincts, and on the west side of the path, between the second and third *torii*, is a small subshrine dedicated to Sugawara's mother Tomoji. The small stone *torii* of this shrine, made in the Kamakura period (1185–1392), is regarded as one of Kyoto's three most unusual *torii* because of the lotus petal bases of its pillars, which impart a Buddhist flavor to this Shintō symbol.

To the west of the Main Hall, outside the shrine's inner courtyard, is a heavily shaded stairway that leads to a view of a good portion of the earthen embankment, known as the Odoi, built by the warlord Toyotomi Hideyoshi in 1591 as a defense surrounding the city. The section here is the largest and best preserved. During the spring plum blossom and fall maple seasons, admission (¥600) is charged and visitors are allowed access to a walk that runs along both sides of the Kamiya River, which is on the west side of the Odoi. At the northernmost point of the walk is a red arched bridge and a large stone monument on which the characters for Odoi are carved.

The nearby **Hirano Shrine** [Tel: 461-4450] is west of the north entrance of Kitano Temmangū. It was founded by Emperor Kammu in 784, very near its present location. The Main Hall is built in a style unique to this shrine; it consists of a pair of matched buildings sitting side by side, facing east. The roofs of the twin halls resemble the gracefully spread wings of a pair of alighting birds. Rebuilt in the 1600s, the Main Hall is an Important Cultural Treasure. The beauty of the shrine compound is enhanced by a huge four-hundred-year-old camphor tree whose spreading limbs give the entire complex a dignified serenity.

To the south of the shrine there is a grove of five hundred cherry trees. In mid-April, when food stalls and seats are set up throughout the grounds under the blossoming trees, Hirano Shrine becomes the site of boisterous partying. The yearly cherry blossom festival, held on April 10, dates from 985, and is one of Kyoto's oldest celebrations.

Tōjiin [Open 8 to 4:30. Admission ¥500. Tel: 461-5786] is a ten-minute walk farther west through a quiet residential area. Cross Nishiōji Dōri at the traffic light in front of Hirano Shrine and walk west to the next light. Turn left, or south, and walk three blocks; on the left you will pass an ultramodern-looking structure, a subsidiary shrine of Kumano Shrine.

Another block south, a stone pillar on the west corner, or right side of the street, has the name Tōjiin carved on its south side. Turn right and follow the curving street past Rakusei Shrine until you come to a large, square, white sign with the Japanese characters for Tōjiin painted in black. The path leading north passes a cemetery with the graves of members of the family and descendants of the first Ashikaga shogun, Takauji (1275–1351).

Tōjiin was founded in 1341 by this ruthless shogun, whose successors filled their lives with pleasure at the expense of their downtrodden subjects. Over the centuries, these rulers came to be hated, and long after their deaths people paid to enter the temple and strike their statues, which are preserved here. In 1863, the temple was stormed by a group of samurai who rushed in and beheaded three of the statues, then displayed the heads on the bank of the Kamo River at the Sanjō Bridge. Their deed was an act of defiance against the then-ruling Tokugawa shogun. The six samurai responsible for disfiguring the statues were immediately captured and decapitated. The heads of the statues were returned to the temple and the statues restored. The complete set of the wooden figures of the Ashikaga shoguns can be viewed in the hall on the east side of the temple grounds.

Today, most visitors come to view the temple's gardens, which were designed by the Zen priest Musō Soseki (1271–1346), better known by his posthumous title Musō Kokushi. This priest also founded Tenryūji in Arashiyama, the Zen temple with which Tōji-in is affiliated.

The garden is both for viewing and strolling; slippers are provided at the foot of the stairs leading to it. On a quiet vantage point overlooking the garden from the north is the beautiful thatched-roof teahouse, Seirentei ("Teahouse of Clear Rippling Waves"). The densely shaded, moss-covered eastern section of the garden was once a part of the nunnery, Shinnyoji, from which it was incorporated. South of the Hōjō, or Abbot's Quarters, is a large, dry landscape garden, as light and open as the other garden is green and dense. This is a lovely temple to enjoy powdered green tea and a sweet, available for ¥400.

From Tōjiin Station on the Keifuku Railway, westbound trains go to Arashiyama and eastbound ones to the terminal at Imadegawa-Nishiōji (an intersection also called Hakubaichō). You can also walk back to Nishiōji Dōri, where there are frequent buses to Kyoto Station or downtown.

NIJŌ 二条

Nijō Castle 二条城
Nijō Jin'ya 二条陣屋

By the beginning of the seventeenth century, the Tokugawa shoguns, who ruled from their new seat of power in Edo (the old name for Tokyo), had imposed a strict class system on Japan, dividing society from top to bottom into four main groups: samurai, farmers, artisans, and merchants. The respective activities of the four classes were closely regulated. In Kyoto, Nijō Castle served as a symbol of shogunal power, reminding citizens that the Tokugawa house, and not the imperial court, really ruled Japan. Another reminder is Nijō Jin'ya, the private residence of a dispossessed lord who became a member of the merchant class.

In contrast to the court nobility, who valued the understated and refined, the military leaders of the Tokugawa clan spared no cost in exhibiting their power and taste in bold, almost intimidating ways. Built only for administrative functions (no shogun after Iemitsu, Tokugawa Ieyasu's grandson, visited Kyoto), **Nijō Castle** [Nijōjō. Open 8:45 to 4. Admission ¥600. Tel: 841-0096] never served as a fortress. Its large rooms were designed to hold great numbers of official visitors, who were seated separately according to rank. The carved wooden transoms and wall carvings that adorn theses rooms are some of the largest ever made. No part of the Nijō Castle is left undecorated; everywhere the display is ornate and obvious. Splendidly painted sliding doors, some of the largest paintings executed by the artists of the famed Kanō school, decorate the castle's inner rooms.

A walk through the garden does not produce a similar sense of aesthetic continuity. When viewed in segments, framed by doorways and windows, the grounds are lovely. Taken overall, however,

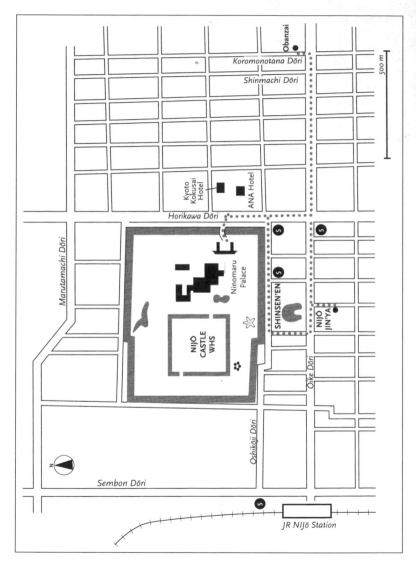

NIJŌ

they seem rather barren, an impression due perhaps to the absence of large shade trees. In the southwest grounds, there are a number of fine rocks set in moss, which create an appropriate feeling of strength.

For those not in the imperial line or of the shogunate, the seventeenth to nineteenth centuries were a time of harsh rule, characterized by a mass of social regulations and sumptuary taxes imposed by the Tokugawa clan in an effort to maintain its power. All displays of affluence were regarded as foolhardy and dangerous. However, this did not deter wealthy merchants from wearing beautiful inner garments and lining their simple kimono with silk woven and dyed in the latest technique and fashion. Perhaps it was at this point that Japan became something other than it seemed—a land where things were hidden from public view—thereby gaining itself a centuries-old reputation for being "inscrutable."

Nijō Jin'ya [Small tours start at 10, 11, 2, and 3. Admission ¥1,000. Tel: 841-0972], one of the most intriguing examples of Edo-period architecture to be found anywhere in Japan, epitomizes its era. Built about 330 years ago, it is a house of hidden places and false impressions, a masterpiece of subterfuge.

Children under fifteen years of age are not admitted, and since Nijō Jin'ya is still a private residence of the Ogawa family, reservations are necessary. Foreign visitors who do not understand Japanese are requested to bring a guide who can interpret for them. The **Tourist Information Center** [Tel: 344-3300] on the ninth floor of the Isetan Department Store at Kyoto Station will help arrange volunteer student guides. Please apply in person by 4:30 the day before (by 11:30 on Saturdays). The guides are free, but you are expected to pay for their meals, admission fees, and all transportation expenses.

Ogawa Hiraemon, builder of Nijō Jin'ya, came to Kyoto from the neighboring province of Ōmi (present-day Shiga Prefecture) and started business in 1670 as a rice dealer and money lender.

Hiraemon's father had been a *daimyō* (feudal lord) on the island of Shikoku, but was dispossessed of his property and castle by Tokugawa Ieyasu—the penalty he paid for having originally sided with Ishida Mitsunari, Ieyasu's rival, at the decisive Battle of Sekigahara in 1600.

As a way of keeping an eye on the *daimyō*, the shogunate made it a rule that they had to spend alternate years in residence in Edo. This created a demand for suitable accommodation for the lords and their retinues as they made their way to and from Edo. As it was conveniently located near Nijō Castle, and since the owner himself had many *daimyō* connections, Hiraemon's house gradually established a reputation for itself as an inn at which *daimyō* from western Japan stopped on their travels to and from the shogunal capital. The name *jin'ya*—meaning a type of official residence—indicates this. As the number of his guests increased, Hiraemon began to enlarge and fortify his property—first against fire, then against the possibility of political intrigue. These changes took thirty years to complete; great care and thought were given to each room.

The deception begins even before you enter. Viewed from the outside, this unobtrusive residence appears to be a one-story dwelling, but it actually has three floors, although the third floor only contains two rooms. Inside ceilings are purposely low—to deter any display of swordsmanship. Intentional or not, they also serve to make the house rather dark and cool.

The corridor around the fifteen-mat main room is covered with *tatami*, an unusual flooring for a corridor. By removing the sliding doors, however, the room could be increased to the size of twenty mats, a convenient means of bypassing the stipulated room size for those of Hiraemon's rank. The *tatami* corridor is not flush with the outer veranda, which is lower, to insure against rain from splashing inward.

Not all features are practical: a number reflect the taste of the

The stillness of the pond reflects the arched bridge in Shinsen'en garden.

house's owner. One such is a tiny cabinet decorated with lacquer, bits of ivory, and pieces of glass, a precious commodity in the seventeenth century. Ceramic covers made of Kutani ware hide nails in this room, while a wooden transom between rooms is cut with designs in the shape of the Ogawa family crest.

One of the salient features of the main rooms is a skylight, beyond which lies a hidden passage where a guard could wait in concealment. The adjoining room has solid wooden floors and was used for performances of Noh drama. An understanding of acoustics existed in the seventeenth century; the paper doors have cedar panels that slide down to act as amplifiers. Since the panels also direct sound upwards, they would have facilitated eavesdropping on conversations from above.

The corridor that leads from these rooms is divided down the middle into two sections, one for use by *daimyō*, the other for their retainers. At the end of this hallway, slightly extended beams in the corner provide footholds that would allow a guard to scale the wall and disappear through a tiny angled hole in the ceiling.

Well-tended gardens can be viewed from several rooms, and the second garden shown on the tour has a notably large, square stone well. Kyoto's history has been marked by terrible fires, the scourge of those residing in wooden dwellings. Hiraemon was aware of this and dug strategically placed wells to guarantee easy access to water. These, together with its thick plaster walls, helped Nijō Jin'ya survive the great Temmei Fire of 1788, which virtually destroyed the city. These wells also served as hiding places for valuables.

The next rooms on the tour are a tiny tearoom with two slender lengths of bamboo embedded in the wall to mark the *tokonoma* (ornamental alcove), and a storage room for tea utensils that could also serve as a convenient hiding place or escape route.

In the hallway, a concealed stairway is lowered to enable visitors to reach the second floor. The first room shown on the second floor gently slopes downward. Remarkably, this is the only room that clearly shows its age. It is named the Boat Room—not (as I first assumed) because of its sinking appearance, but because one must step down into it. The ceiling and windows are also in keeping with the boat theme. The pulley at the window served the dual purpose of bringing up well water and allowing for a quick escape.

The second floor is even darker than the first, and this is intentional. Heavy "earthen" windows slide close over narrow slat-like openings to protect the building from flames, but the darkness they create was also intended to lead the uninvited astray. The false stairway has only two steps and would easily send a hapless intruder tumbling into the dark void beneath.

A popular pastime in those days was the tea ceremony, which may explain why about a third of the twenty-six rooms are equipped with sunken hearths. One of the second floor tearooms boasts a bamboo wall beam shaped like an ink brush, a decorative touch amid the protective features. Another purely decorative aspect of the house can be found on this floor, namely sliding doors painted with scenes of Japan's most famous places, Mt. Fuji being the most easily recognized. In general, practical considerations take precedence over artistic ones throughout the *jin'ya*. One of the house's most delightful features combines both. It is a large round paper window located over the stairway nearest the exit. Known as the clock window, it uses the shadows of the sun cast by the lattice stays to tell the hour.

The area offers plenty of coffee shops and eateries. **Heihachi Shinsen'en** [Open 11 to 9 daily. Tel: 841-0811], a restaurant near Nijō Castle on the grounds of Shinsen'en, the original site of the imperial palace, has *tatami* rooms that offer views of a 1,180-year-old garden. Meals start at ¥3,000, and a menu with photos of the courses is available. Sushi restaurant **Jōmon** [Open 11:30 to 2 and 5 to 9. Closed Wednesdays. Tel: 231-5188], just south of the ANA Hotel, also has Japanese-style meals from ¥1,300 and an English menu is available. If you have just left the Nijō Jin'ya and wish to enjoy lunch in the company of Kyoto's modern-day merchants, try **Obanzai** [Lunch from 11 to 2; tea-time 2:30 to 5; dinner from 5 to 9. Tel: 223-6623], a natural-food restaurant on Koromonotana Dōri just north of Ōike Dōri that features brown *(gemmai)* or half-polished *(haigamai)* rice. The buffet-style lunch is about ¥1,000.

HIGASHI 東本願寺
and NISHI HONGANJI 西本願寺

Kikokutei 枳穀低
Higashi Honganji 東本願寺
Dendōin 伝道院
Nishi Honganji 西本願寺
Shimabara 島原
Sumiya Museum 角屋
Sumiyoshi Shrine 住吉神社
Umekōji Locomotive Museum
　　梅小路蒸汽機関車館
Midori no Yakata みどりの館
Inochi no Mori 命の森

Located close to JR Kyoto Station, the imposing temples of Higashi (East) and Nishi (West) Honganji are easy to find due to their sheer size. Both belong to Jōdo Shinshū, the True Pure Land sect, Japan's most popular branch of Buddhism. As built-up as this area is, it boasts two spacious gardens: Kikokutei and Midori no Yakata. In between these green isles is another kind of isle, the once moat-enclosed pleasure quarter of Shimabara.

Beginning in the thirteenth century, Jōdo Shinshū grew quickly among the common people by asserting that salvation cold be attained merely by chanting the invocation *Nam'Amida Butsu* ("Hail to Amida Buddha"). By the early seventeenth century, its power was great enough to threaten the new Tokugawa shogunate. Tokugawa Ieyasu (1542–1616) believed in a policy of divide-and-conquer, and that is what he did,

東本願寺 西本願寺

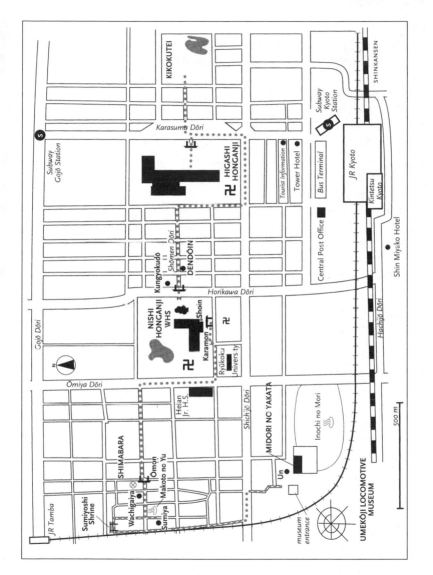

HIGASHI and NISHI HONGANJI

encouraging a succession dispute within the sect to develop into an outright schism by allowing the establishment of Higashi Honganji in 1602. (Nishi Honganji had been established on its present site, as head temple of the sect, about a decade earlier.) Today, the two Jōdo Shinshū branches sponsor different universities and differ in philosophy. Recent differences have further divided their followers. Ieyasu would no doubt be pleased.

The temples and their neighborhoods are rich in items of interest, both secular and sacred. A good place to begin exploring this area is **Kikokutei** (meaning "the estate of the trifolate orange"), a garden belonging to Higashi Honganji. Known formally as Shōseien [Open 9 to 4. Admission ¥500. Tel: 371-2961], this large parklike garden lies directly east of Higashi Honganji's main gate.

In 1641, this land was given to Sennyo (1604–58), thirteenth abbot of Higashi Honganji, by the Tokugawa shogunate. He and Ishikawa Jōzan (1583–1672), builder of the Shisendō, designed the garden. Various buildings dot the grounds, the largest being the residence in the northwest corner built for Sennyo's retirement. A graceful example of early Edo architecture, its veranda extends over a little pond and its glass doors glimmer with light reflected from the water beneath. The raised islands in the pond are remnants of the Odoi, a part of its southeastern earthen embankment. Destroyed by fire numerous times, the buildings have been faithfully reconstructed in the original style. The spacious grounds encircle a pond inhabited by carp, some of remarkable size. Several varieties of ducks—spotbills, mallards, pintails, and green-winged teals—are winter visitors. Unlike Kyoto's more formal gardens, you can walk everywhere, even over the tiny arched bridge and through the elegant covered one. Its lack of pretension is part of its charm.

Walk straight west to **Higashi Honganji** [Open 6 to 5:30 daily; 6:20 to 4:30 in winter. Free admission. Tel: 371-9181] and its massive gate and grounds, through which hundreds of out-of-town parishioners and visitors pass every week. There are roughly ten million followers of this branch of Jōdo Shinshū worldwide. The temple, however, does not function as a local place of worship, and regular services are not a part of the daily schedule. Most visitors enter the Main Hall, say a prayer and leave; everyone is welcome. There is a curious item in the corridor between the Founder's Hall and the Amida Hall—a large coiled rope made from the tresses of female devotees. It is a custom for parishioners to contribute to the rebuilding of temples. Lacking financial means, women in the past contributed one of their most precious possessions, their hair. This rope, used to hoist the temple beams into place, was made in the 1890s. The one-ton rope is enclosed in a sturdy glass case.

Besides out-of-town followers and assorted tourists, another group of natives has made this a stop: pigeons. It is against Buddhist law to take life; consequently, active means of banishing the pigeons have not been taken. In fact, small bags of beans to feed the winged occupants of the massive entrance gate can be bought from the vendors at the entrance, who also sell assorted religious items.

Exit Higashi Honganji and walk south, then west along Shichijō Dōri. Turn north for two blocks on the street that runs along the temple complex, then west on Shōmen Dōri. *Shōmen* means "facing," and in this case the street faced an immense image of the Buddha at Hōkōji, a temple in the foothills of Higashiyama. Hōkōji burned down in 1943, though its grounds still remain and Shōmen Dōri still runs from its grounds to both Honganji temples.

The walk along Shōmen Dōri passes shops which sell all manner of accessories for home altars: silk brocade cushions for bells, glittering ornaments, statues, prayer beads, and portable altars can all be found here. Along the street, one building especially stands out. Built of unusual masonry, topped by a mosque-like roof, and surrounded by mythical creatures atop stone posts, it marks the southeast corner of Aburanokōji Dōri and Shōmen Dōri. Built in 1912, the **Dendōin** was designed by Ito Chūta, a member of an expedition the Nishi Honganji sent to Tibet and western China and reflects components of Western, Chinese, and Central Asian architecture as interpreted by Ito. Originally, it housed a life insurance company that catered exclusively to members of Jōdo Shinshū. Now it houses temple-related offices.

At Horikawa Dōri is another massive gate. The second shop to the north of it on Horikawa is the well-known incense shop **Kungyokudō** [Open 9 to 7. Closed first and third Sundays. Tel: 371-0162]. The original building served temple-goers for four hundred years before being replaced by an ultramodern stone-and-glass structure. Besides the usual varieties of incense, scented sachets, and candles, the shop's specialty is a fragrant round pellet of incense called *kunkō*.

Nishi Honganji [Open 5:30 to 6 daily; 6 to 5 in winter. Free admission. Tel: 371-5181] has been more fortunate than its sister temple. Although Higashi Honganji has burned down repeatedly, Nishi Honganji was completely destroyed by fire only once, in 1617, and today is a World Heritage Site.

Founded in 1272, Nishi Honganji was moved to its present location in 1591. The Amida Hall, complete in 1760, enshrines a one-meter-tall statue of Amida Buddha carved in 1611. Next to the Amida Hall, and connected to it by a covered walkway, is the Founder's Hall. As in the Amida Hall, the expansive *tatami* seating area here has been worn to an almost velvety smoothness by thousands of feet. (As a comfort to the increasing age of its followers, folding chairs are being used for formal ceremonies.) Both buildings are decorated with elaborate wood carvings and Kanō-school wall paintings typical of the Edo period (1600–1868).

Subsequent fires have ravaged parts of the complex, but the gnarled and sprawling gingko tree in the southeast part of the courtyard always survived. The tree has been accorded special care since the fire of 1864, when the rest of the area was in flames. The story goes that this tree "sprayed" the main building with moisture and "saved" it.

The elaborate Chinese-style gate Karamon stands sentry at Nishi Honganji.

South of the temple's office building is the **Shoin**, a sweeping cedar-roofed building that is thought by some scholars to have originally been part of warlord Toyotomi Hideyoshi's Fushimi Castle. Others believe it was built on its present site for a visit of the third Tokugawa shogun. With its sumptously painted *fusuma* doors and intricate double-faced carved transoms, the Shoin is a magnificent example of the architectural style and decorative techniques of the Momoyama period (1568–1600).

Unfortunately, permission to enter must be applied for in advance, and the procedure takes time. If interested, have someone call in Japanese to find out when the Shoin is open. Then, on a return postcard (*ōfuku hagaki*), state the preferred date of your visit and mail it to the temple (Nishi Honganji, Hanayachō-sagaru, Horikawa Dōri, Shimogyō-ku, Kyoto, 600-8358). The temple will inform you via mail as to when you may visit.

For those who do not have enough time to do this, there is a consolation: just south of the Shoin is the resplendent **Karamon**, or Chinese gate. Brought from Fushimi Castle, this ornate and beautiful structure has been designated a National Treasure. Long ago, it was popularly known as the Higurashi no Mon, or "Day-Spending Gate," because by the time a visitor finished looking at the intricate carvings, the day was over. West of the Karamon is an exit from the temple complex that faces a long two-storied building that is on the grounds of Ryūkoku University, a school affiliated with Nishi Honganji. Built in 1879, it was renovated to restore its nineteenth-century appearance.

Walk west from the Karamon to the end of the temple complex, turn right, and walk north to Hanayamachi Dōri (Flower-Shop Street). The traffic light marks the entrance to the Shimabara Shopping Street. This thoroughfare caters to the more secular aspects of life, offering workmen's footwear, ladies' cotton undergarments, and household hardware. It is also a step into a world with a very different kind of history. Continue to the next traffic light and cross the street. Pass the flower shop on the corner, the only one that remains from long ago when shops in this area supplied the temples and worshippers with bouquets. The street jogs just a little to the left, enough to slow down traffic passing through the gate that used to lead to the first licensed pleasure quarter in Japan: **Shimabara**. Three other such quarters existed: one each in Nagasaki, Osaka, and Tokyo. All have been destroyed by fire.

The weather-beaten East Gate, also known as Ōmon (Great Gate), was rebuilt in 1867 after the devastating fire of 1854. A sign in Japanese and English stands to the side, as does a lone willow tree (the willow is a symbol of courtesans, graceful yet resilient). Shimabara was surrounded by a moat and wall, and the gates were the only means of entering and leaving, so the women who had been sold into bondage here perished tragically in that fire.

Shimabara was never completely rebuilt, but two of its famous establishments remain, now preserved as Important Cultural Assets, and still function as places of entertainment. **Wachigaiya**, on the first side street north, opened in the Genroku era (1688–1704) and was the place where high-ranking courtesans lived while undergoing training. Today, it is open for guided tours and occasional social events. A minute's walk away is the elegant **Sumiya** (founded 1781), where the courtesans entertained their clients. Skilled in feminine graces, courtesans were talented performers who could entertain the clientele with wit as well as song. More than the pleasures of the flesh were attended to within these walls, though. Toward the end of the Edo period, the pro-emperor merchants of Kyoto reportedly met here to plot the overthrow of the shogunate. The present building, which dates to the nineteenth century, is a masterpiece of late-Edo architecture. The **Sumiya Museum** [Tel: 351-0024. Closed midsummer, midwinter, and Mondays. Closed on Tuesday if Monday is a national holiday. Admission ¥1,000; ¥800 extra for the second floor] displays a collection of paintings and artifacts related to Shimabara history, housed in one of the only remaining examples of Ageya architecture.

One recent addition to this district is the large bathhouse **Makoto no Yu** [Open 8 a.m. to 11 p.m. Admission ¥1,000. Tel: 351-4084]. Although drinking and carousing were activities connected with this district even a hundred years ago, today's Japanese love sitting and chatting in a hot bath, often followed by good food and drink, so appropriately enough, a restaurant and hotel are also on the premises.

Next to the site of the West Gate to Shimabara is the tiny **Sumiyoshi Shrine**. The shrine is dedicated to the fox spirit, a symbol of fertility—a curious choice considering its location, since the ladies in residence would normally not have wanted to become pregnant. The West Gate was toppled by a truck in the 1970s, and the old willow tree that stood beside it was replaced by a stone marker, which displays a picture of the old gate and an outline of the quarters.

Opposite Shimabara's west entrance are the JR elevated train tracks, and beyond that is Kyoto's central food market. A five-minute walk south along the elevated tracks leads to Shichijō Dōri. Cross at the light, and follow the sound of locomotive whistles to the Meiji-era train station. This is the entrance to the **Umekōji Locomotive Museum** [Umekōji Jōkiki Kanshakan. Open 9:30 to 4:30. Admission ¥400 for adults, ¥100 for children. Tel: 314-2996]. The museum features an original railroad turntable and several old-fashioned steam locomotives filling the stalls, along with photographs of well-known trains and various memorabilia. One interesting exhibit is a replica of the control room of the Shinkansen. Its windshield is a video screen that shows the engineer's view from the bullet train as it approaches stations and passes scenery along its route.

The modern structure to the west of the locomotive museum is one of the city's newer gardens, **Midori no Yakata** [Open 9 to 5. Closed Mondays. Admission ¥200. Tel: 352-2500], built in 1994 to mark the city's twelve-hundredth anniversary. The nine-thousand-square-meter garden centers on a five-tiered shallow pond constructed of lustrous black Indian marble. Surrounding the pond are softly formed hills covered with grass, moss, and bamboo grass, accented with seasonal plantings of colorful flowers. About fifty kinds of trees and shrubs line the winding paths. Boulders brought from Okayama Prefecture form a waterfall, in which all the water is drawn from an underground spring. A stroll through the adjoining park, **Inochi no Mori** (Woods of Life), is free and a welcome respite for those in a need of a bit of greenery in this area.

The popular Japanese restaurant chain **Un** [Open 11 to 10. Closed Mondays. Tel: 343-6520] has a branch here to the right of the garden's entrance.

ROKUDŌ 六道

Rokuharamitsuji 六波羅蜜寺
Saifukuji 西福寺
Rokudō no Tsuji 六道の辻
Rokudō Chinkōji 六道珍皇寺
Otowa no Taki 音羽の滝
Toribeno 鳥辺野
Nishi Ōtani 西大谷
Kawai Kanjirō Kinenkan 河井寛次郎記念館

Rokuharamitsuji, Saifukuji, and Rokudō Chinkōji, though tiny compared to the many large temple complexes found elsewhere in Kyoto, nevertheless play a large part in the city's most important religious holiday, Obon. This festival, which takes place in early August, is when the Japanese have traditionally welcomed back the spirits of their departed ancestors by means of a variety of religious observances. One readies the family altar for Obon, which means replacing all of its offering dishes, and this practice has encouraged the enterprising potters of the Kiyomizu district to establish a pottery fair (tōki ichi). August 7 to 9, from 8 a.m. to 10 p.m., both sides of the Gojō Dōri from the Kamo River to Higashiōji Dōri are lined with stalls displaying almost every kind of ceramic ware produced by local potters. The residence and studio of the famous potter Kawai Kanjirō is a place where one can get a glimpse of the long, sloping wood-fired kilns that used to dot this area. Also included in this walk are stops at Kiyomizudera, one of Kyoto's most famous sights, and several other small but charming temples in the vicinity.

Rokuharamitsuji [Open 8 to 5. Admission ¥600. Tel: 561-6980] is one of Kyoto's oldest temple buildings, and in early August, a center for Obon preparations. Take the Keihan Railway to Kiyo-

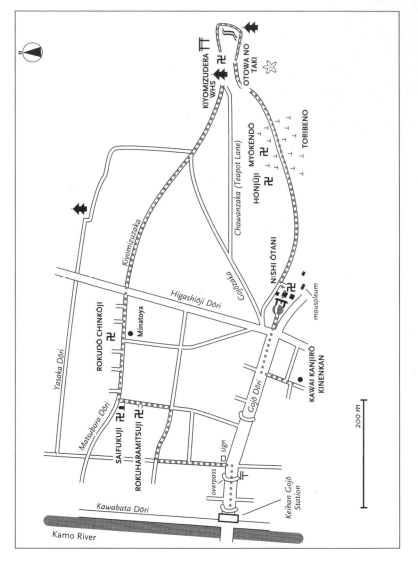

ROKUDŌ

mizu Gojō. Both the stairway and escalator of Exit No. 4 emerge on the north side of Gojō Dōri. Walk east five blocks from the exit to a sign that points in the direction of Rokuharamitsuji and Ebisu Shrine. After two blocks, turn right and pass the elevated school playground. Turn left, and the temple compound is on the left.

The Main Hall of Rokuharamitsuji is one of the oldest structures in the city, dating from 1174, and the temple has several statues designated Important Cultural Properties, exhibited in the Treasure Hall just behind the Main Hall. Rokuharamitsuji is also the seventeenth temple on a thirty-three-temple pilgrimage in western Japan dedicated to Kannon, the bodhisattva of compassion. The monks inside the Main Hall are often busy inscribing scrolls carried by visitors making this popular pilgrimage. You too can have a calligraphic inscription done, provided you purchase a book or the pre-stamped paper sold at these temples especially for this purpose. Most temples charge ¥300, and the beautiful calligraphy makes a lovely memento. Hair dryers are provided for the busy pilgrim who can't wait for the ink on his or her scroll to dry naturally.

The entrance to the Treasure Hall [Admission ¥500] is at the back of the Main Hall. One of its most remarkable images is that of the temple's founder, the itinerant monk Kūya, from whose mouth emerge six tiny Buddhas representing the six syllables of the mantra of the Pure Land sect: *Nam'Amida Butsu*. This *nembutsu*, as it is called, is a simple prayer by which the supplicant puts his or her faith in Amida's saving grace. Kūya spread this sect among the common people by chanting this prayer while dancing and beating a gong as he roamed the streets of Kyoto and far-distant villages helping and praying with the peasants.

Most of the statues are from the Kamakura period (1185–1333). In this period, joinery was used extensively in sculpture, with several blocks of wood employed in the construction of a single image, a method that produced more natural torsos and limbs. Sculptors also inset eyes of painted crystal in the statues for realistic effect. A mirror placed beside the seated statue of Taira no Kiyomori, a famous warlord whose headquarters was in this area, reflects the overhead lights into his eyes, enhancing their lifelike quality.

A standing statue, called Katsura Jizō, holds a length of black hair, said to have belonged to a young woman who unexpectedly lost her mother. Too poor to pay for a funeral, she was on the verge of despair. A monk appeared and generously offered to perform the service for her mother. Having nothing else to give, the young girl decided to offer her hair as a token of appreciation. The next day, she cut it off, wrapped it in paper, and went looking for the monk. Instead, she found this statue and left her hair next to it with a prayer of thanks. The locks of hair on the small stand at the foot of this Jizō have been left by supplicants in thanks for prayers fulfilled, or as petitions for favors. To the north of the Main Hall is a new building which contains a water trough and images of the guardian deity Fudō Myōō and the bodhisattvas Kannon and Jizō, over which people ladle water. Long ago, a deep well on the grounds was thought to reach all the way down to the other world. People who have lost a relative come to pour water over the figures in hope of assuring the spirit a safe journey to paradise.

One block north of Rokuharamitsuji is **Saifukuji** [Tel: 551-0675]. At the corner, a stone marker reads Rokudō no Tsuji, the Crossroads of the Six Realms of Rebirth. Long ago, the Rokuhara area was the entrance to Toribeno, a public burial ground, and it had many temples especially for conducting funerals. For the premodern Japanese, the Six Realms (those of heavenly beings, warring titans, humans, animals, hungry ghosts, and creatures of hell) were more than a figure of speech. Spirits were considered real, capable of causing misfortune, bringing disease, and creating other calamities. It was from this unimposing marker that the dead spirit was believed to begin its journey to a world of rebirth after being judged by a tribunal of the Ten Kings.

Saifukuji receives many visitors during early August. To the left of its entrance, there are rows of small stone images draped with colorful bibs that have babies' cups filled with water set before them. Most also have paper-thin plaques (*sotoba*) of wood with the names of couples written on them. The images are of Jizō, the bodhisattva who is the special protector of small children and unborn infants. The offerings of food, soft drinks, and toys seen here are for the spirits of aborted, miscarried, or stillborn babies. During Obon, visitors come to pray as well as to view the hanging scrolls depicting the Six Realms and their various inhabitants. (A small offering is requested to enter the Main Hall and view the scrolls.)

East of this temple is **Rokudō Chinkōji** (also known as Rokudō Chinnōji). Most of the year, half of the temple's compound serves as a parking lot, but on August 7–10, the grounds are crowded with stalls selling branches of *koyamaki*, a type of yew, which is said to assist the spirits of the dead in returning to this world for Obon. This belief grew out of a story about Ono no Takamura (808–52), a statesman-scholar whose wooden statue, along with one of Emma, King of Hell, is preserved in a building to the right of the entrance. Considered exceptionally wise and learned, Ono was commanded while still alive to appear before Emma to help decide into which of the six realms the dead should be reborn. He is said to have journeyed to and from Emma's court along the branch of a yew tree that grew next to a well beside his study (now on the temple's land).

On entering the temple, people purchase thin wooden plaques and present them to the monks to inscribe the names of the dead persons to be memorialized. Holding the name plaques, they then line up to ring the temple bell—thereby "pulling" the spirit back to this world. Because spirits of the dead are considered capable of bringing with them disease and misfortune, the name plaques are purified by waving them through the smoke of burning incense, then set in a trough on the west side of the grounds, and water ladled over them to further purify the spirit. The atmosphere is not a mournful one; it is calm and friendly, and onlookers are welcome.

On August 7–10, Matsubara Dōri is lined with stalls selling goods for home altars: incense, candles, unpainted wooden shelves, and small white ceramic dishes and vases—everything needed for the Obon observances. A sweet called *yūrei ame* or "ghost candy," reflects the area's association with burials. The wrapper tells the story of a pregnant woman who died during childbirth and was buried in Toribeno. Although she had died, her child had not, and cried out in hunger. The loving spirit of the mother could not rest, and searching for something to give her crying child, she came down from the cemetery to a candy store on this street just as it was closing. The owner sold her some candy with which she fed her baby. The woman's pitiful appearance aroused the curiosity of the owner and on the third evening, he followed her to Toribeno where she disappeared. It was then that he heard the cries of a baby, which led him to the newly dug grave. Frightened by the events of the evening, he ran to a nearby temple and told his story to a priest. Together, they returned to the grave, dug it up and rescued the living baby. The child was raised in the temple and the mother's spirit was never seen again. This old-fashioned brown sugar "rock" candy is still sold on this street at **Minatoya**.

Cross Higashiōji Dōri at Matsubara Dōri and follow the winding street uphill toward what is considered by many to be Kyoto's best-loved temple, Kiyomizudera (see Higashiyama walk, page 88). The shops lining this street sell the famous Kiyomizu pottery (*Kyōyaki*) and souvenirs of all sorts. At the top of the street, instead of entering the temple, take the path to the right, and continue past the pillar-supported Main Hall to **Otowa no Taki**, or "Sound of Feathers Fall," where water pouring forth from the mountain is channeled into three streams that fall into a pool below. The long-

Supplicants pray for their deceased relatives at Chinkōji during Obon.

handled dippers in the ultraviolet sterilizer can be used to sample this tasty water.

The southern part of the temple's grounds is surprisingly wooded. Places to sit have been provided and there are several refreshment stalls scattered in this part of the precinct. A hot drink of sweet *sake* flavored with ginger (*amazake*) is available during the cold months, and a syrup-flavored shaved ice *(kakigōri)* is sold in the summer at stalls where you will see blue-and-white banners bearing in bright red the Chinese character for ice.

A less-traveled route passes between the two restaurants south of the falls. After a few meters, the path enters a quiet, forested dale that leads to **Toribeno**, one of the largest and oldest cemeteries in Kyoto. Stonemasons and caretakers selling buckets, incense, and flowers set up shop near the 23,000 graves, about 90 percent of which are actively attended to by relatives of the deceased.

Past the cemetery are several small temples on the right:

Myōkendō, which has a small raised platform on its grounds of similar construction to the platforms at Kiyomizudera, and **Honjūji**, with an attractive six-sided structure on its grounds and an umbrella-shaped white pine.

The north entrance to **Nishi Ōtani** temple is on the left side of the downward-sloping road. This is a modern mortuary temple built to house the ashes of the dead (Buddhism brought the custom of cremation to Japan), and it is dedicated to the founder of the Jōdo Shin sect, Shinran Shōnin (1173–1263), a man to whom Kannon appeared in a dream and said that celibacy was not required of a priest. It is affiliated with the Higashi Honganji temple complex located near Kyoto Station. The grounds are always open. The easternmost building on your left is Meichōdō, dating from 1661, where services are held for the founder. Across the large rectangular courtyard is a memorial hall dedicated to the war dead and beyond that, a building that contains the ashes of deceased members of the sect. More than twenty thousand small "locker-type" family crypts contain ceramic jars filled with ashes.

Buddhist memorial ceremonies are held on the forty-ninth day after a person's death and on the first, third, seventh, thirteenth, seventeenth, twenty-third, twenty-seventh, thirty-third, and fiftieth anniversaries. (After the third memorial, many people stop conducting services.) It is to temples like this one that families come for these services, and the reason that a number of visitors are dressed in black. The Main Hall in the center of the grounds enshrines an image of Amida. The Higashiōji entrance to the ground is attractively marked with two very large lanterns and an arched stone bridge spanning a pond surrounded by shrubs and trees.

Exit the temple, and cross to the south under the elevated highway. Turn right, cross Higashiōji, then walk west. At the first narrow street, turn left and walk south to the traditional-looking residence of one of Japan's most famous potters, the **Kawai Kanjirō**

Kinenkan [Open 10 to 5. Closed Mondays and August 10–20 when the family observes Obon. Admission ¥900. Tel: 561-3585].

Kawai Kanjirō (1890–1967) was a leader of the Folk Crafts Movement of the 1930s, whose philosophy encouraged the making of beautiful, simple, everyday utensils. Nowhere is his personal philosophy more evident than in this finely crafted house, which was brought from Nara Prefecture, and the furnishings it contains. In the back of the compound is his studio and two kilns: a small one for low-fired items, and a long, climbing-type one (*noborigama*) of the sort that used to dot this area. (Pollution laws no longer allow kilns to be fired within the city limits.)

HIGASHIYAMA 東山

Yasaka Shrine　八坂神社
Maruyama Kōen　丸山公園
Chōrakuji　長楽寺
Ōtani Sobyō　大谷祖廟
Bashōdō　芭蕉堂
Entokuin　円徳院
Kōdaiji　高台寺
Ryōzen Kannon　露山観音
Yasaka Kōshindō　八坂庚申堂
Yasaka no Tō　八坂の塔
Sannenzaka　三年坂
Ninenzaka　二年坂
Kiyomizudera　清水寺
Jishu Shrine　地主神社
Otowa no Taki　音羽の滝

From ancient times, the mist-shrouded slopes of Higashiyama, the hills bordering Kyoto on the east, have inspired generations of poets and artists. These thirty-six peaks are home to many temples, restaurants, traditional inns, and tea shops, all picturesquely located along narrow winding streets. Here, too, are two of Kyoto's most famous landmarks, Yasaka Shrine and Maruyama Kōen, the park behind the shrine. One of Kyoto's most beloved and eclectic temples, Kiyomizudera, lies at the end of this walk. Along the way are other delights, some not as well known, such as Chōrakuji, Ōtani Sobyō, and Yasaka Kōshindō. The landmark pagoda Yasaka no Tō is in the heart of this district, and many a heart has found its way to Jishu Shrine in search of love. Ninenzaka and Sannenzaka are marvelous streets for browsing shops full of traditional pottery and crafts, though be careful not to slip and fall victim to the superstitions surrounding their names.

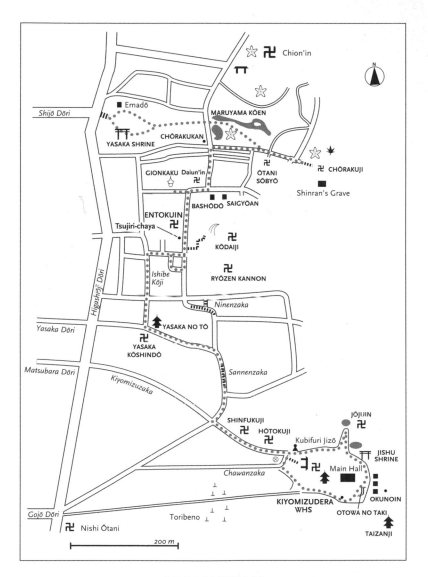

HIGASHIYAMA

Until 1868, **Yasaka Shrine** was called Gion-san or Gion-sha by local people, after which it was officially named after the eight hills
in this area (*yasaka* means "eight hills"). Originally, it enshrined a
god of healing and was connected to the Tendai sect of Buddhism.
Now it is a Shintō shrine.

The brillliant two-story red gate at the east end of Shijō Dōri
houses two wooden guardians seated at attention on stools with
sleeping tiger motifs. Beyond the gate, the paved walk divides. On
the right are stalls selling treats and souvenirs. To the left, the walk
goes past the Emadō, a structure raised on pillars whose roof protects large votive plaques (*ema*) painted with various figures from
Japanese mythology and history. Raised shrine structures such as
this reflect an ancient and native building style, unlike the ground-
level, Chinese style of construction that accompanied Buddhism
to Japan.

The main building, which dates from 1654, was built in what
is known as *Gion-zukuri*, or Gion-style construction. Most shrines
have two sacred buildings: the *honden* (Main Hall) where the tuletary god resides, and a connected *haiden* (Worship Hall) in which
a bell is suspended by a large straw rope. The Worship Hall is located in front of the Main Hall, usually separated from it by a narrow path or corridor. At Yasaka Shrine, the Main Hall is contained
within the Worship Hall—the only shrine building of this type in
Japan. A massive cypress-shingled roof sweeps down in a graceful arc, revealing highly decorated upturned eaves with an elaborate underside of gold- and red-tiered struts. To accommodate the
many visitors at Yasaka, three thick straw ropes hang from the
bells so that supplicants can ring one and catch the attention of
the resident god, Susanoo no Mikoto. Brass cylinders in front of
the booths manned by priests contain numbered sticks that can be
shaken out and traded for a ¥100 slip of paper on which a fortune
is written.

Maruyama Kōen, directly east of the shrine, was designated a public park in 1886, but existed before this official recognition. The park's most famous feature is an enormous weeping cherry tree that stands enclosed by a low bamboo fence in the middle of the park. The tree is spotlit at night when it is in full bloom in April, and hundreds of visitors come to stand in awe of its delicate beauty. (As the tree matures and ages, another is being cultivated as its eventual replacement.)

Chōrakuji [Open 9 to 5. Closed Thursdays. Admission ¥500. Tel: 561-0589] is located in the southeast part of the park at the end of a long set of alternately high and low steps. Founded in 805 by the monk Saichō (767–822), this temple originally belonged to the Tendai sect. The approach to the Main Hall is so steep that, seen at this sharp angle through the boughs of an overhanging maple, the hall appears as remote as a mountain hermitage and is appropriately picturesque. Visitors can enter the slate-floored hall wearing their shoes. The three statues—Amida Buddha flanked by the bodhisattvas Kannon and Seishi—date from the Heian period (794–1185). Unlike larger temples, here one can get so close to this delicate trinity of Buddha and bodhisattvas that it seems as if they take a personal interest in those who stand before them. In the back on the left is an eight-hundred-year-old soft-fired clay statue of Hotei, one of the Seven Gods of Good Fortune. The grounds are filled with cherry and maple trees; hence the temple, ordinarily closed on Thursdays, is open every day in the spring from April 1 to May 10, and in the autumn from October 20 to November 31. During these periods it charges ¥650.

Paths lead to a new building housing a number of Important Cultural Properties (shoes may be worn inside). The left side is lined with an excellent display of life-sized Buddhist statuary, and on the right are displayed two glass-enclosed items that bring this temple's past into the vibrant present: a scroll and a Buddhist ritual banner. In 1185, after her clan was annihilated in the Battle of Dannoura, Kenreimon'in, the mother of the child-emperor Antoku, was sent to this temple and took the tonsure. During the battle, fought at sea, she had tried to drown herself, along with her mother who was holding her eight-year-old grandson. The others perished but she alone was pulled from the sea by her enemies and taken back to the capital. From Chōrakuji she moved to the isolated hermitage of Jakkōin far in the northeast of Kyoto, where she lived out the rest of her life praying for her dead son and relatives. Her portrait, mounted on the scroll, was purposefully darkened so that it would appear to be of no consequence to those who wished to destroy all traces of Kenreimon'in's clan. Next to it is a silk banner made from her son's robes, which she gave to the temple when she became a nun.

The building across from the entrance has a thermos set out so that visitors can help themselves to tea while enjoying a view of the garden from the *tatami* room.

A bark-shingled gate on the left of the stair leading away from Chōrakuji is the north entrance to **Ōtani Sobyō** [Open 6 to 5. Daily services at 8:30 and sutra chanting at 2:30. Tel: 561-4167]. This temple preserves the mausoleum of Shinran Shōnin (1173–1263), founder of Jōdo Shinshū, as well as the graves of successive abbots of Higashi Honganji. The three-hundred-year-old Main Hall enshrines a statue of Amida Nyorai, which sits on an altar sumptuously decorated with gold ornaments and rich, colored brocades. Ōtani Sobyō is one of the most active temples in this area. Visitors are welcome to join the groups of out-of-town parishioners as they are guided through the premises. The mausoleum is up the stairway east of the Main Hall, behind an elaborately carved gate, a fine example of Momoyama period (1568–1600) architecture. The tomb was moved here from Nishi Ōtani in 1870, and took fourteen years to reconstruct.

The nearby coffee shop and restaurant called **Chōrakukan**, a European-style building completed in 1909, is designated a historical landmark. The temple Daiun'in is not usually open to the public, but is well known for its distinctive tower, the **Gionkaku**, rising thirty-six meters above its surroundings. In 1928, a prominent businessman, Ōkura Kihachirō, had a tower built of steel and concrete resembling one of the floats used in the Gion Festival. Originally, it was housed on his estate, but was later moved here.

Bashōdō stands on the next corner south. This thatched-roof hut was built in 1786 by the haiku master Takakuwa Rantō to honor the memory of the famous poet Matsuo Bashō (1644–94). Inside is a small statue of Bashō carved by one of his pupils, Morikawa Kyoroku. Takakuwa chose this site because of its proximity to the site of the house of the Heian-period poet Saigyō (1118–90), who was greatly admired by Bashō. The thatched-roof house east of Bashō's memorial is the **Saigyōan**. Used as a meeting place for pro-imperial forces at the time of the Meiji Restoration, the structure was rebuilt in 1983.

Walk west and then south to reach **Tsujiri-chaya**, a sweets shop famous for its powdered green tea desserts. Next to this shop, a little to the north is the luxurious Momoyama period (1568–1600) moss and rock garden designed by Kobori Enshū. **Entokuin** [Open 10 to 4:30. Admission ¥500. Tel: 525-0101] shows Enshū's originality and distinctive use of rock placement, the three stone bridges giving movement and strength to the layout. During the spring and fall viewing, the garden is lit up and hours are extended to 9:30 p.m.

Almost directly across the street is a long stone staircase that passes through a narrow tile-roofed gate. This is the entrance to **Kōdaiji** [Open 9 to 4:30; 4 in winter. Admission ¥500. Tel: 561-9966]. Built in 1605 for Kita no Mandokoro (1549–1629), the widow of the warlord Toyotomi Hideyoshi (1535–98), its construction was financed through the largess of his successor, Tokugawa Ieyasu (1542–1616). The architecture is typical of the Momoyama period (1568–1600), a period during which, at Hideyoshi's command, artisans throughout the capital were kept busy repairing, rebuilding, and rejuvenating the many temples that had deteriorated through decades of war and poverty. The city owes much of its present shape and its heritage of beautiful temples to the efforts and vision of Hideyoshi.

The Main Hall has many excellent examples of richly decorated lacquerware, including images of Hideyoshi and his wife. One especially impressive piece is a miniature shrine, the doors of which are open to reveal delicate hanging ornaments and rows upon rows of tiered Buddhist images.

The Kaisandō (Founder's Hall), built in 1605, has a sumptuously detailed interior, every surface of which is painted or covered with elaborate pictures. The ceiling is made of panels taken from Hideyoshi's flagship and from his wife's carriage. The undulating covered stairway is aptly named "Recumbent Dragon," and connects the Founder's Hall with the mausoleum above.

Two teahouses designed by the famous tea master Sen no Rikyū (1520–91) sit in the uppermost part of the complex. The inside roof of the "Umbrella House" on the left arches up like an open umbrella with bamboo ribs and interwoven branches. As a humorous rejoinder, it is complemented by the two-storied "Rainshower" teahouse. Beyond the parking lot in front of Kōdaiji, a gigantic thirty-meter-tall image of the bodhisattva of mercy, called the **Ryōzen Kannon**, is visible. It is a memorial to soldiers who died in World War II. Cut through the parking lot, take the stairs down, and turn left and walk in the direction of the five-storied pagoda.

Look for a narrow stone-paved street on the right, in the direction of the city. Known as **Ishibe Kōji**, this charming passageway is lined with fine restaurants and inns. At the west end of Ishibe Kōji, turn left and walk toward the bright red gate of the temple popularly known as **Yasaka Kōshindō**. A set of the three see-no-evil monkeys are perched atop the outside gate and another set sits in front of the inside altar. Long strings of hanging monkeys of all sizes and hues form a colorful backdrop. *Kōshin no Hi*, the

At Jishu Shrine, foxes answer prayers for good crops and many children.

Day of the Monkey in the traditional calendar, is said to be the day when evil spirits are afoot and try to enter the bodies of sleeping humans. Staying up all night or buying a charm helps stave off the invaders. Besides the usual charms on sale, this temple has odd-shaped painted clay figures which resemble fingers. The priest explained that these are good luck charms for *koto* players, pianists, calligraphers, abacus-users, and other people whose livelihood depends on their fingers.

Outside the gate to the right is the stately **Yasaka no Tō** [Open 10 to 4. Admission ¥400. Tel: 551-2417], a pagoda on the grounds of **Hōkanji**. The temple is believed to have originally been erected in the seventh century, based on a plan similar to that of Shitennōji in Osaka, and rebuilt in 1440 by the sixth Ashikaga shogun, Yoshinori. The pagoda is a structure that developed from the Indian stupa, built to enshrine relics of the Buddha or house Buddhist images. Hōkanji's pagoda supposedly contains some of the

Buddha's ashes beneath its single massive central pillar. Five Buddha images sit on a raised platform around this pillar, the smallest among the scrolling clouds that face west. The interior of the pagoda is painted in an artistic tradition that prĕdates the structure's reconstruction in 1440.

Exit the pagoda grounds and follow the gently sloping hill east toward the mountains. The cobbled street here is known as the **Sannenzaka**, the "Three-Year Slope." To the north is the **Ninenzaka**, or "Two-Year Slope." Both streets were paved with stone in about 808, and they may be the most continually trod-upon streets in the whole capital. According to a local superstition, if you slip on one or the other, you are liable for two or three years of bad luck, which can be dispelled by the purchase of a gourd. Sannezaka, an alternate name for Nannenzaka, means "the slope of easy childbirth," and from ancient times, pregnant women wound their way through these streets to seek the intercession of Kannon, the bodhisattva of mercy, whose image is enshrined in nearby Kiyomizudera. A statue of the benevolent Kannon is said to have been worshipped by the pregnant wife of the Nara-period (710–94) Emperor Shōmu. Today, several exquisite images of the deity are still housed in this temple.

Over the centuries, millions of pilgrims have passed along these streets, stopping to buy a charm, sip a cup of tea, or purchase a piece of the local porcelain and earthenware, collectively called Kyōyaki. Consequently, shops line the streets, but however crowded it is, the mood is convivial and relaxed. The shops and houses built at sloping angles make the area architecturally unique. This was one of the first places in Kyoto to be designated a Historic District.

Tucked in between the shops are two small temples on the north side of the street. The raised shutters of **Shinfukuji** reveal an inner altar with several Buddhist statues and farther east, the equally small **Hōtokuji** specializes in selling charms to ward off the misfortune that may befall men at the unlucky ages of twenty-five, forty-two, and sixty-one, and women at nineteen, thirty-three, and thirty-nine.

At the first set of wide steps leading toward the Main Hall of Kiyomizudera are two interesting images that are part of the temple complex. To the left (north) of the steps is a new, forty-centimeter-high stone image known as **Kubifuri Jizō**, or "Head-swiveling Jizō." (The original of this image is enclosed directly behind it.) Legend says that if one points the face in the direction concerning one's wish or desire and says a prayer, it will be granted. The building behind these two images is the Senjudō, which houses a splendid, fine-featured, gilt image of a thousand-armed Kannon.

Kiyomizudera [Open 6 to 6. Admission ¥300. Tel: 551-1234] is a temple that actually predates the founding of Kyoto. In 778, Enchin, a priest of the Hossō sect of Buddhism, came from Nara and built a hermitage on Mt. Otowa that houses an image of Kannon, the bodhisattva of mercy. The image still enshrined at the temple today is believed to be the original and it is considered so sacred that it is only on view for a short time every thirty-three years (next in 2024). Kiyomizudera is the sixteenth temple on a thirty-three-temple circuit pilgrimage dedicated to Kannon.

The Niōmon, which houses the two temple guardians, dates from 1478, making this gate one of the oldest structures in the complex. A fire destroyed most of the temple buildings in 1629, and they were rebuilt in 1633 under orders of the shogun Tokugawa Iemitsu. Past the three-tiered pagoda on the left is an unpainted building, the Sutra Hall, built to store the temple's Buddhist scriptures.

A path to the left leads north, past a Benten shrine in the middle of a pond to a subtemple, **Jōjuin** [When open, admission is ¥600. Tel: 561-5783]. Its garden is famous for the many stone basins, lanterns, and steppingstones given by Toyotomi Hideyoshi. It is also justly famous for its garden, using the technique known as *shakkei,* or "borrowed scenery." A view of the densely wooded hills behind it is incorporated in the design, expanding the garden in a generous manner. The placement of two lanterns, one in the garden proper, the other in a clearing on the opposite hillside, also helps blur the distinction between the end of the formal garden and the beginning of the "borrowed" scenery.

Retrace your steps to the main path. The admission booth for Kiyomizudera is across the path from the dragon fountain spout. The first item of interest is an enclosure to which are chained a pair of iron staves and iron *geta* (clogs). Children of all ages and many adults vie to see how high or how long they can lift these items before losing their grip. Japanese legend relates the extraordinary feats of strength and fierce loyalty of the priest Benkei, a retainer of the twelfth-century warrior Minamoto no Yoshitsune. One story tells of how Benkei had similar footwear and weapons made, but in doing so, his overconfidence brought him defeat. These replicas were fashioned in Benkei's honor by a blacksmith who lived about a century ago.

The overall structure of the Main Hall is difficult to appreciate while standing directly under its massive roof or on its pillar-supported veranda, but for centuries, pilgrims have delighted in this building's height, feeling of weightlessness, and superb view. Lit only by the light of day and a few candles, the cavernous interior of the Main Hall is sunken and on a floor of stone sits the altar that holds the temple's thousand-armed Kannon.

Beyond the Main Hall is the entrance to the popular **Jishu Shrine** [Open 9 to 5:30. Free admission. Tel: 541-2097]. Although this shrine is said to be as old as Kiyomizudera, it is not now a part of the complex. The shrine's appeal has much to do with match-making. There is a statue of Daikoku, one of the Seven Gods of Good Fortune, almost completely submerged in red and white square tags. Those wishing for romance should write their name on one tag and the would-be lover's name on a second, then tie them together and drape them on the statue.

On the uppermost level two squat rocks, each bound with a sacred rope and cut papers, are a focal point. If supplicants can walk with their eyes closed from one rock to the other while thinking of their sweethearts, their love will succeed. Printed on slips of paper and mounted on the inner shrine's fence are the names of those whose wishes came true.

Exit the shrine, returning to the Kiyomizudera ground, and continue toward the mountain. A set of stairs leads to a higher level where five buildings stand facing west. The first has a stone statue of Jizō; the next, the Shakadō, houses an image of Shakyamuni, the historical Buddha; the third, which is recessed, contains many small stone images of Jizō collected in the Kiyomizu area. The fourth, an Amida Hall, houses an image of Amida Nyorai. This Jōdo temple is called Ryūzanji or Takiyamadera, both readings meaning "Temple of the Mountain Waterfall." It is one of the six temples on the Amida pilgrimage in Kyoto. (The others are at Shinnyodō, Eikandō, Anshōji, Anyōji, and Seiganji. Each temple is supposed to represent one of the syllables in the chant *Nam'Amida Butsu,* the mantra of the Pure Land Sect.)

The fifth and largest building is the **Okunoin**. From its pillar-supported veranda one can get a better look at the magnificent structure of the Main Hall across the ravine. The gracefully curved cypress-shingled roof appears to float lightly above the extended veranda that runs the length of the building. Behind the Okunoin, a petite image of the Nurete-Kannon, the "Wet" Bodhisattva of Mercy, stands in a pool of water enclosed by a stone fence. Dippers are provided so that visitors may pour water over the figure, which constitutes an act of purification.

Continue towards a three-tiered unpainted pagoda and **Taizanji**, the "Temple of Easy Childbirth." From the path up to the pagoda there is a sweeping view of Kiyomizudera's main precinct. The bright red Niōmon and pagoda at the entrance to the unpainted tile-roofed halls and the somber brown bark roof of the Main Hall provide a memorable vista framed by the boughs of nearby maple and cypress trees. The scale is so immense that only from this distance can one get a feel for Kiyomizudera's mountain setting and understand the special popularity this temple has enjoyed over the centuries, and its status as a World Heritage Site.

Return to the path and continue down to the open pavilion-like restaurants. Simple fare and beverages are available, and here many visitors stop to enjoy a last look at the temple. Just beyond the three restaurants is **Otowa no Taki**, the "Sound of Feathers Waterfall," from which water is channeled into three spouts that pour down from above. Long-handled dippers are available for visitors to sample the clear, delicious water that inspired Enchin to build his hermitage here, and which is the source of the temple's popular name, which means "Temple of Pure Water."

Although many of the downtown streets of Kyoto were realigned in the late 1500s by Hideyoshi and widened after World War II, the streets that wind over and around the foothills of Higashiyama remain unstraightened and narrow—as charming as they have been for centuries.

NANZENJI 南禅寺

Murin'an 無隣庵
International Community House 国際交流会館
Lake Biwa Aqueduct Museum 琵琶湖疎水記念館
Himukai Daijingū 日向大神宮
Nanzenji 南禅寺
Eikandō 永観堂

The area of Kyoto known as Nanzenji has the honor of being home to the famous Zen temple that gives it its name, as well as to the graceful brick aqueducts that carry water from Lake Biwa into the city. Before it was designated a temple in 1291, Nanzenji had been the site of the villa of the retired emperor Kameyama (1249–1304). Nestled in the shade of Higashiyama (the Eastern Hills), the temple and its environs are lush with greenery, private estates, and several notable gardens, of which Murin'an is one—a place of politics past and gracious early twentieth-century living. And tucked into the hills behind the Nanzenji temple complex is one of Kyoto's most charming shrines, Himukai Daijingū.

South of Niōmon Dōri is **Murin'an** [Open 9 to 4:30. Admission ¥350. Tel: 752-0230]. Built at the end of the last century for the statesman and general Yamagata Aritomo (1838–1922), and landscaped by Yamagata himself with the help of the famous gardener Ogawa Jihei, this villa contains a spacious, stroll-type garden that incorporates a view of Higashiyama. An azalea-lined stream flows through the grass-covered ground, an element that gives the garden a Western, exotic touch.

A two-story Meiji-era (1868–1912) building near the exit features an elegant Western interior. On the first floor are photographs of other famous gardens designed by Ogawa, while the second

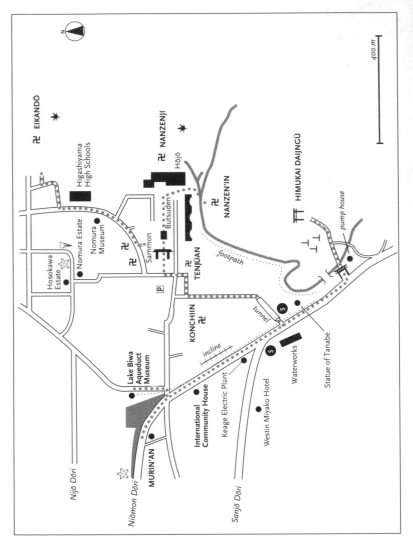

NANZENJI

floor is the site of the meeting room where the Russo-Japanese War (1904–5) was planned. With its vaulted ceilings, wood-paneled walls, and parquet floors, it seems a rather un-Japanese setting for talks concerning the fate of the empire. Unfortunately, it is a bit too dark for the visitor to fully appreciate the Kanō-school paintings that decorate the wall.

Around the corner is the **International Community House** [Kokusai Kōryū Kaikan. Open 9 to 9. Closed Mondays. Tel: 752-3010], a haven for students and visitors to Kyoto. Not only are beverages available from vending machines, but there is a reading library and a giant TV in the lobby, which broadcasts CNN all day long. Notices of events taking place in the city are posted on a bulletin board to the left of the entrance and are worth a glance. Volunteer teachers offer a variety of lessons in Japanese culture, such as language, calligraphy, tea ceremony, and brush painting.

The **Lake Biwa Aqueduct Museum** [Open 9 to 4:30. Free admission. Tel: 752-2530] is a new and attractive building designed by a team of local architects. There is a pamphlet in English, and the old photos and maps that comprise the exhibits are well displayed. On the lower level is a path and a sign which points to a section of railroad bed known as the Incline, where a wooden boat is mounted on a flatcar.

After Tokyo replaced Kyoto as the country's capital in 1869, the citizens of this city needed something to bolster their confidence in their future. In the early 1880s it was decided to construct a canal connecting the city to Lake Biwa. The project offered more than a balm to wounded pride: it provided a source of pure water more reliable than that of the Kamo River and the city's wells, for Lake Biwa, which lies just beyond the mountains east of the city, is the largest inland body of water in the country and is forty meters higher than the city. Allocating an amount equivalent to more than ten times the city's annual budget, the municipal government commissioned a twenty-one-year-old engineer named

Tanabe Sakurō to build the twenty-kilometer canal, much of it underground.

Japan had only recently emerged from three centuries of isolation, yet in a mere five years, Tanabe was able to overcome monumental problems of technology and bureaucracy to complete (in 1890) the country's first modern, large-scale public works project. In order to blast a hole through the mountain, dynamite was used for the first time in Japan. Barely recovered from the nerve-jangling skirmishes of the Meiji Restoration, the citizens thought that war had again broken out.

Besides water, the canal also brought rice, charcoal, ceramics, and other commodities into the city, at great benefit to the local economy and to that of Shiga Prefecture, where Lake Biwa lies. The barges used to transport these goods, however, could not navigate the tunnel section of the canal. To circumvent it, the Incline was built. The barges were eased onto flat railroad cars, transported down the Incline, and then were slid back into the canal. The old stones that you can see today are all that remain of the Incline. It was used for only twenty or thirty years, when a steam-powered railway built between Kyoto and Shiga rendered the canal obsolete as a mode of transportation.

A seven-minute walk east on Sanjō Dōri is a stone *torii* on the left, the entrance to the beautiful, little-known shrine of **Himukai Daijingū** (Hiyūga Daijingū). Walk under the *torii* and climb the steps. From this vantage point another Meiji-era building, a brick-and-stone electric pump house associated with the canal, can be seen below. Another minute up, and the path divides, the left branch leading to a cemetery. The sounds of flowing water and the luxurious shade of tall, leafy trees accompany the visitor.

The whole complex was burned to the ground during the Ōnin War (1467–77), but Himugai Daijingū was rebuilt with the approval of Tokugawa Ieyasu, founder of the Tokugawa shogunate, in the early seventeenth century. The deity enshrined in the in-

The moss-and-sand garden of Tenjūan, a subtemple of Nanzenji.

ner shrine is the sun goddess Amaterasu Ōmikami. The *kayabuki* (miscanthus) roof on the outer shrine was rethatched in 1980, and the inner one in 1988. The buildings are designated Important Cultural Properties. The path that leads uphill from the inner shrine brings you to a sacred cave dedicated to a Shintō deity, Amenotajikara Onomikoto, the god who pushed aside the boulder trapping the Sun Goddess in a cave and thereby restoring light to the world. It is said that following the circular route through this dark cave will purify one of all sins.

Retrace your steps until you reach a long, narrow brick arch on Sanjō Dōri that marks the entrance to a red brick tunnel. (There are trails leading to Nanzenji from this shrine, but they are not well marked.) The shady green refuge of **Nanzenji** [Open 9 to 5; 4:30 in winter. Tel: 771-0365] lies beyond it. Although there are a total of twelve temples in this Rinzai Zen complex, only three are open to the public year-round.

Konchiin [Admission ¥300. Tel: 771-3511] is one of Nanzenji's larger subtemples. A water-lily-covered pond lies just beyond the inner gate, and the path that weaves around it leads to Tōshōgū Shrine, a structure as resplendent as its namesake in Nikkō, and also dedicated to Tokugawa Ieyasu. The black-walled building features elaborate wood carvings and a painting of a dragon on its ceiling. The second building on the grounds contains a statue of the founder, the priest Ishin Sūden, whose political influence was so great that Ieyasu rewarded him with this temple. The garden attached to the Main Hall is one of the most beautiful in Nanzenji. One of the few gardens directly attributed to the famous commissioner of public works and gardener Kobori Enshū, it belongs to the "crane-and-tortoise" (*tsuru-kame*) category. The rounded rocks and rugged weather-beaten tree represent a turtle swimming in a "pond" of moss. The square, rough rocks at the foot of the large pine depict the crane swooping down towards the turtle. Every three years, the head priest redesigns the wave patterns in the gravel.

Back at the entrance to Nanzenji is the **Sammon**, or Main Gate [Admission ¥500], built in 1628 to console the souls of warriors who lost their lives in the Summer Siege of Osaka in 1615, the last great battle establishing the Tokugawa house as uncontested rulers of Japan. The second floor houses three Buddhist images, statues of the sixteen principal disciples of the Buddha, and wall paintings. Many Japanese are curious to enter because of the gate's associations with the notorious robber, Ishikawa Goemon, who hid here. After his capture, he was boiled to death in an iron cauldron; hence the popular name for an old-fashioned Japanese bathtub: *goemonburo*.

To the right, or south, of the Sammon is **Tenjūan** [Admission ¥400. Open from 9 to 4:30], the estate of the retired Emperor Kameyama, built in 1267. The extensive garden and ponds are unlike the contemplative Zen gardens found in other subtemples.

Farther back in the Nanzenji compound is a large brick aqueduct that carries water from Lake Biwa, part of Tanabe's canal project. This green and pleasant area is frequented by local residents,
who stroll along the narrow path that runs along the conduit.
Through the aqueduct's first archway is **Nanzen'in** [Admission
¥300], a subtemple that possesses a lovely stroll garden. Situated
back against the mountains is the **Nanzenji Hōjō**, or Abbot's Quarters [Open 8 to 4:30. Admission ¥500. Tel: 771-0365]. Its beautiful garden, poetically dubbed "Leaping Tiger," is of the *karesansui* ("dry landscape") type, composed of a large rectangle of white
sand with a narrow strip of rocks and plants against the enclosing
wall. The temple also owns many wonderful Kanō-school paintings, now carefully preserved behind glass panels. The covered
corridor that connects the buildings is a gift of Emperor Go-Yōzei
(1572–1617), an elegant reminder that the Daihōjō (Main Hall) and
the Shōhōjō (Small Hall) were once part of the imperial palace and
Fushimi Castle, respectively.

The area's long association with good water means that many
tofu restaurants congregate in the temple precinct. Most serve
yudōfu, a hotpot of bean curd and vegetables, a favorite of vegetarian monks.

The temple **Eikandō** is located northeast of Nanzenji. The
quiet, exclusive residential neighborhood that lies just north of the
Nomura Museum contains the estates of such well-known families as Sumitomo, Tatsumura, and Nomura. The Nomura estate,
by the way, is noted for its beautiful irises, which bloom in the
outside garden in late May and early June.

OKAZAKI 岡崎

Heian Shrine 平安神宮
Miyako Messe Exhibition Hall
　京都市勧業館みやこめっせ
Namikawa Cloisonné Museum
　並河靖之七宝記念館
Shōren'in 青蓮院
Chion'in 知恩院

岡崎

In a city renowned for its antiquity, it is a bit of a surprise to learn that Heian Jingū, one of the biggest and most popular shrines, is quite new—by Kyoto standards, anyway; in 1994, it turned one hundred years old. An even newer addition is the huge Miyako Messe Exhibition Hall, devoted to displays of traditional arts and crafts. The Okazaki district has an abundance of older sights as well. The former Awata Palace, now the temple Shōren'in, is a short walk away and the neighboring temple Chion'in is filled with wonders, including a marvelously large bell and gate.

In 1884, the city of Kyoto celebrated the 1,100 anniversary of its founding. To mark the occasion, the city fathers decided to build a shrine—Heian Jingū—in honor of Emperor Kammu (founder of Heiankyō, the "Capital of Peace and Tranquility" that evolved into the city of Kyoto), and Emperor Kōmei, father of then-reigning Emperor Meiji, the last emperor to rule with Kyoto as his capital. The main building of the shrine was conceived as a replica at two-thirds scale of the Chōdōin, The Great Hall of State of the Heian-period imperial palace.

When Emperor Meiji moved the capital to Tokyo in 1868, Kyoto's population declined by one-seventh, and land within the city's boundaries fell into disuse or was returned to agriculture. When construction began for Heian Shrine, the surrounding area

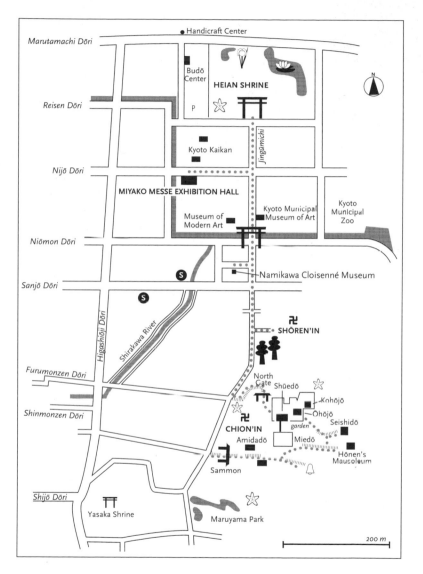

OKAZAKI

consisted mostly of vegetable and rice fields, but remains of six ancient temples, known collectively as the Rokushōji, were uncovered here. Records indicate that these temples covered a vast tract of land that stretched from the Shirakawa district to Sanjō. They were almost entirely destroyed by a great earthquake in 1185, and never rebuilt.

Entrance to the grounds of **Heian Shrine** [Open 8:30 to 4:30. Tel: 761-0221] is free, but there is a charge of ¥600 to enter the extensive and beautifully landscaped garden. Ogawa Jihei (1860–1933) designed it in the stroll-through style popular in Heian times, in keeping with the shrine's architectural style. Ogawa was one of Japan's great gardeners, and his work received national recognition almost as soon as it was finished. Today, its maintenance keeps ten gardeners busy year-round and requires a great deal of money, some of which comes from the admission fees. The garden is splendid in all seasons: April is especially beautiful because of the weeping cherry trees in the front garden; May with its two kinds of azaleas; June with its long-stemmed irises; and July with its pink, white, and yellow water lilies.

The steppingstones in the central garden are actually pillars from the Gojō and Sanjō bridges built by warlord Toyotomi Hideyoshi about four hundred years ago. Called the "Bridge of the Lying Dragon," the stones form the tail, while a small island forms the body. Many of the rocks came from Hideyoshi's castle in Fushimi.

When the garden was first constructed, the trees that form the north border were purposely kept short to allow a view of the mountains. Nowadays, they have been allowed to grow to block out all the high-rises that have gone up. Another recent development has been the proliferation of *ma-shijimi*, a tiny variety of freshwater clam. This little clam made its appearance in the garden's streams about 1985. Once found throughout Lake Biwa, it almost disappeared as pollution in the lake increased. A few must have made the journey via the aqueducts that carry water into the city and settled down here. The shrine is delighted to have them, thinking they are a good indication of the purity of the water.

Although Ogawa tried to create a garden using Heian-period garden conceits, the garden is modern in its use of space. Though essentially a stroll garden, it is also for viewing. Most visitors enjoy their last look from the seats that line the covered bridge, a structure that was moved here from the former imperial palace.

The **Miyako Messe Exhibition Hall** [Kyoto Dentō Sangyō Fureaikan. Open 9 to 5:30. Closed Mondays. Free admission. Tel: 762-2670] is a complex of halls that includes the Japanese Design Museum. The Museum of Traditional Crafts (Fureaikan) is located in the basement and houses displays and videos of Kyoto's crafts and craftsmen. The exhibits are well marked and beautifully presented. The top floor restaurant serves standard fare.

Walk south along Jingūmichi, cross the canal, and make a right at the noodle shop to **Namikawa Cloisonné Museum** [Namikawa Seino Kinenkan. Open 10 to 4:30. Open March 15 to July 27; September 15 to December 9. Admission ¥600. Tel: 752-3277]. It is the estate of the master cloisonné artist Namikawa Yasuyuki (1845–1927). His studio and home, built in 1894, are beautifully preserved, as is the garden by Ogawa Jihei.

Farther south of Heian Jingū along Jingūmichi is the Tendai temple **Shōren'in** [Open 9 to 5. Admission ¥400. Tel: 561-2345], also called the Awata Palace, once the residence of Empress Go-Sakuramachi. Built in the middle of the Muromachi period (1443–89), the temple was a *monzeki-dera*, or imperial temple, whose abbot was required to be chosen from the imperial family or high-court aristocracy. The massive eight-hundred-year-old camphor trees (*kusunoki*) that grip the moss-covered slope just outside its gate are a famous Kyoto landmark. Like Heian Jingū, it has an elegant stroll garden. Since it seems to be bypassed by most big tour groups, it is also one of Kyoto's better-kept secrets.

The entrance to the garden is through a low gate to the right of the ticket booth. The grounds are well tended, and visitors can wander along winding and hilly paths through shady woods and past a bamboo grove. The path circumambulates the temple grounds and brings you back to the main building, which, in addition to offering excellent views of the garden, also contains some splendid paintings on cedar sliding doors. At the very back of the grounds is another garden, a flat, open space of white gravel partly shaded by another huge camphor tree. The stone wall that backs it on the south is part of Chion'in, a temple complex that extends all the way to the huge public park, Maruyama Kōen.

Chion'in [Open 9 to 4:30. Tel: 531-2111] is headquarters of the Jōdo (Pure Land) sect of Buddhism (not to be confused with Jōdo Shinshū, the True Pure Land sect, a later offshoot, whose two main branches are headquartered at the Nishi and Higashi Honganji temples). Founded in 1175 by the monk Hōnen, this faith teaches that salvation is possible merely by repeating the name of Amida Buddha. Chion'in was also a *monzeki-dera*, and its immense grounds, a testament to the millions of followers that belong to the Jōdo sect, contain twenty-one subtemples. Many of the buildings and statues are National Treasures and Important Cultural Properties.

Chion'in is also known for various "wonders" on its premises. The first are represented by glass-enclosed sets of replicated paintings on sliding doors in the hallway of the Daihōjō and Kohōjō. On the original set of doors, the first images to fade and disappear from the painting were the sparrows. This gave rise to the belief that the birds were so realistic, they flew away. The next set of doors features a painting of a cat, whose eyes are said to follow the onlooker no matter where he or she views the painting from. Another "wonder" is revealed by an upturned portion of floor, showing iron stays under the planks that make a chirping sound when walked upon. The pleasant sound these "nightingale" floors

An eight-hundred-year-old camphor tree creates dappled shade at Shōren'in.

produce also alerted the building's inhabitants to the presence of intruders. Above, resting across several ceiling beams, is a giant rice-serving spatula said to have been made for Buddha's use.

The front garden of the Ōhōjō has Higashiyama as a backdrop. The side garden, composed of twenty-five rocks and azaleas, is named after the twenty-five deities who make up the retinue of Amida Buddha. The exit from the Ōhōjō and Kohōjō is through the front garden. Outside this exit to the left are stairs leading up to the mausoleum of the sect's founder, Hōnen. His tomb is located at the highest point on the grounds, to assure that the founder's spirit would always look out over his followers. Reconstructed in 1613, the heavily carved doors and transoms of the masoleum are beautiful examples of Momoyama-period architecture.

The largest building in the complex is the **Miedō**, or Founder's Hall, where an image of Hōnen is enshrined. Located behind massive raised lattice windows, the altar seems to float in a sea of gold ornamentation and brocade. Built in 1639 by the third Tokugawa shogun, Iemitsu, this building is a National Treasure. Open all year-round, its thousand-mat cathedral-like interior offers thousands of worshippers and visitors a quiet retreat. On the southeast corridor of the building there is a wooden plaque that reads, "The Forgotten Umbrella," pointing to another of the "wonders" of this temple. Legend says that to protect the newly completed building against fire, carpenters put a lacquered-paper umbrella under the eaves as a prayer for rain to douse any possible flames. It can still be seen today.

One night a year, on New Year's Eve, this temple appears on national television when its famous bell is rung 108 times by resident monks, an event ushering in the new year. Cast in 1636, at seventy tons, it is the largest temple bell in Japan, and possibly the best-known one as well. The bell tower in which it is housed is up a stairway beyond the pond with an arched stone bridge.

The Main Gate, or **Sammon**, is the largest wooden structure of its kind in the world and a National Treasure. Curiously it is not connected to the temple by a wall, and, as is the case with other gates throughout Japan, acts more as a symbolic entrance to the compound. Dotted with cherry and other shade trees, the area is surprisingly tranquil, considering its close proximity to downtown Kyoto—only a ten-minute walk away.

寺町

TERAMACHI 寺町

Kanga'an 関臥庵

Jōzenji 上善寺

Kami Goryō Shrine 上御霊神社

Shōkokuji 相国寺

Sainokami no Yashiro 幸神の社

Rōzanji 廬山寺

Nashinoki Shrine 梨の木神社

Kōdō 革堂

Honnōji 本能寺

Yata Jizō 矢田地蔵

Seiganji 西岸寺

Seishin'in 誠心院

Tako Yakushidō 蛸薬師堂

Nishiki Temmangū 錦天満宮

Somedono'in 染殿地蔵

In 1591, when warlord Toyotomi Hideyoshi reorganized the streets of Kyoto, he moved many of the temples to three streets: Teramachi, Shimo Teramachi, and Teranouchi. Today Teramachi is the best known of the three. Although many of the temples have been greatly reduced in size and influence, the street remains aptly named, for Teramachi means "Temple District," and religious establishments still give the area its character, from the large Zen temple complex of Shōkokuji to the many smaller shrines and temples along the way. A number of these have interesting tales involving animals associated with them: the guardian monkey of Sainokami Shrine, the deer whose hide inspired the name of the temple Kōdō, and the octopus who brought a young priest to the Buddha's attention at Tako Yakushidō. Others have more historical associations: the great warlord Oda Nobunaga lost his life at Honnōji, and the emperor Seiwa—thanks, it is said, to the intervention of the bodhisattva Jizō—was born at Somedono'in.

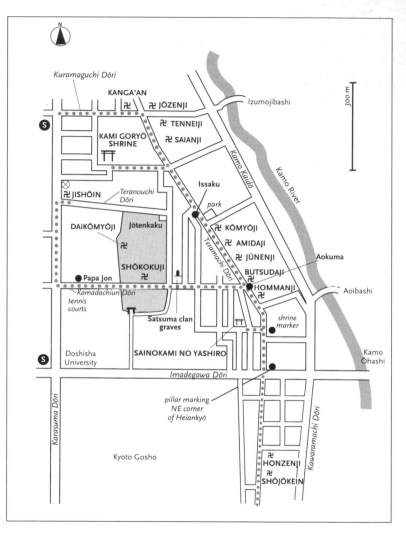

UPPER TERAMACHI

Natural calamities such as earthquakes, fires, and floods have always played a major role in Kyoto's history, altering the shape of the city and the size and numbers of its buildings. Besides natural forces, the relocation of the capital to Tokyo in 1868 and the official disestablishment of Buddhism during the early years of the Meiji era were responsible for a decrease in the size and number of the city's temples. With the removal of the capital, the temples lost many of their principal patrons among the court nobility and high-ranking samurai, many of whom moved family graves and had branch temples built in Tokyo to attend to their spiritual needs. Consequently, the temples on Teramachi are modest ones. Most house a priest and his family, who tend to parishioners' needs and maintain the cemeteries located in the temple compounds. Some have turned into businesses to survive, operating schools, dormitories, and restaurants, and others rent out parking space to local residents.

This walk starts at the north end of the district. Take the subway to Kuramaguchi Station and walk east on Kuramaguchi Dōri, an ancient road that existed before Kyoto became the capital. It led to the northern village of Kurama, from which it took its name. **Kanga'an** ["Restful Retreat." Open 11 to 3 and 5 to 8. Tel: 256-2480] is a small temple identifiable by its distinctive red Chinese-style gate. It belongs to the Ōbaku school of Zen Buddhism, the last Buddhist sect to come to Japan from China. With its upturned eaves and elaborate finials, it offers a glimpse of Ming-dynasty Chinese architecture common to Ōbaku temples. Kanga'an also is called Akebonodera (Temple of the Dawn) because Emperor Go-Mizunoo (1596–1680) planted a tree known as the "dawn cherry" in front of the Main Hall. Today azalea bushes grow where the cherry once stood. The Ōbaku school is known for a type of cuisine called *fucha ryōri*. This Buddhist banquet food, consisting of many deep-fried items, is served on trays in *tatami* rooms. Reservations are necessary, and parties must include at least four persons. Prices start at ¥5,500 per person.

Jōzenji is a temple complex belonging to the Jōdo sect that, in the Edo period (1600–1868), housed ten subtemples. Now only a few buildings remain. Enshrined here is an image of the bodhisattva Jizō supposedly carved from a single piece of wood by the Heian noble Ono no Takamura *after* he died; the legend goes that he returned to life specifically to complete this task. This image, and the location of the temple, are the reasons why Jōzenji is also known as Kuramaguchi Jizō, and is visited each year by pilgrims undertaking the Roku Jizō (Six Jizō) pilgrimage on August 22–23, the only time the image is shown to the public. (The other five temples are Tokiwa Genkoji, Yamashina Tokurin-an, Fushimi Daizenji, Toba Jōzenji, Katsura Jizō.) Originally built near Sembon-Imadegawa in 863, Jōzenji was moved here in 1594 as a part of Hideyoshi's restructuring of Kyoto.

The street that leads south from this temple is **Teramachi Dōri**. A sturdy *kaya* (*Torreya nucifera*) tree just north of the temple gate marks **Tenneiji**, a Sōtō Zen temple. This 16.2-meter tree still bears the scars of the great Temmei Fire of 1788, which destroyed most of central Kyoto. The entrance to Tenneiji frames a fine view of Mt. Hiei. **Saianji**, south of Tenneiji, was founded in 1224 in the northwest hills of the city. The present Main Hall dates from 1788, as do many of the temple buildings on this street, a consequence of the Temmei Fire. Inside the gate to the left is a small Jizō Hall. Push a button, and a light reveals walls painted with explicit scenes of heaven and hell. The painting, done at the end of the Edo period, was used for teaching Buddhist beliefs in the afterlife.

At the four-way intersection, walk west about two minutes to **Kami Goryō Shrine** [Tel: 441-2260]. Its counterpart, Shimo Goryō, is now much farther south on Teramachi, but in antiquity both were located here. Predating the capital of Heiankyō, they were originally Buddhist temples of the Izumo clan who occupied this area, known as Kami Izumodera and Shimo Izumodera. After the founding of the capital, Emperor Kammu reconsecrated them as Shintō shrines. Back on Teramachi a brief walk south is **Issaku** [Open 11 to 9. Closed Wednesdays. Tel: 231-5407], a noodle shop identifiable by the large lantern hanging in front. Congenial atmosphere and friendly service accompany the reasonably priced dishes.

South of a playground are the temples Jifukuji, Kōmyōji, and Amidaji. The first two are not open to the public, and the front gate of **Amidaji** is often closed, but the entrance to its parking lot provides access to its Main Hall, a raked-sand garden, and the cemetery, which has the distinction of being the site of Oda Nobunaga's grave. Historians believe the two-meter-tall pale green stone marker with three Buddhist images and scrolling lotus is the original gravestone, but others believe the original is the large stone-fence-enclosed grave nearby. Probably the most contemporary-looking temple on Teramachi is the Jōdo temple, **Jūnenji**, an innovative piece of futuristic temple architecture completed in 1993. The tile-work resembles that of ancient temples, but the straight dovetailed eaves are strictly modern. The Main Hall is of circular design, reminiscent of Chinese temples. **Butsudaji** is a Jōdo temple that was moved here in 1587 from its original location east of Ōmiya-Imadegawa near the former imperial palace. Enclosed in a small building in front of the gate is a wooden image of a seated Jizō. A Kamakura-period (1185–1333) statue of Amida, an Important Cultural Property, is housed inside the Main Hall.

The next east-west street leads west to **Shōkokuji** (Also pronounced Sōkokuji), once one of the major Zen monasteries of Kyoto [Open 9 to 4:30. Tel: 231-0301]. The layout of the complex is typical of Zen temple architecture: a courtyard with the main buildings on the north-south axis, surrounded by subtemples. It was founded in 1392 by Ashikaga Yoshimitsu, who also established a painting academy here where the renowned artists Sesshū and Kanō Masanobu studied. Shōkokuji's chief priests were politically astute men who acted as counselors to the Ashikaga shogunate, and the temple was closely associated with that clan. At one time, forty-six buildings stood within the complex. Fires, one of which occurred a mere three years after the complex was completed, destroyed many of the buildings, and it was not until 1596 that it was restored by Toyotomi Hideyoshi. Over the next fifty years, many magnificent buildings were added, but again were decimated by the Temmei Fire of 1788. The Hattō [Open 9 to 4:30. Open from March 24 to May 6, and September 15 to December 6. Admission ¥800], rebuilt in 1610, is one of the oldest examples of Zen architecture. Built on a raised stone base it measures thirty-three meters in height with no central support pillar and a three-hundred-square-meter ceiling painting of clouds swirling around a dragon by Kanō Mitsunobu. Clapping one's hands in a designated spot will make the sound reverberate through the building. The large north garden resembles a deep, rich moss-covered gulley of rocks and trees. Admission to the Hattō also allows one to view the Senmyo or bathhouse, recently renovated.

Jōtenkaku [Open 10 to 4:30. Admission ¥600. Tel: 241-0423] is located in the northeast corner of the complex. This museum houses numerous art objects from the Muromachi period (1333–1568) and Ming-dynasty China. **Daikōmyōji**, a subtemple in the northwest part of the complex, is open to the public free of charge. Its Main Hall, moved here in 1615 from Fushimi, was built as a memorial to Emperor Go-Fushimi (1288–1336) by his consort Kogimon'in (1292–1357). On the grounds are the graves of the princes of the Fushimi clan and the sixth Ashikaga shogun, Yoshinori (1394–1441). Another subtemple, **Jishōin** [Admission ¥600. Open 10 to 4. Tel: 441-6060], located outside the complex to the northwest close to Karasuma Dōri, is also open to the public. A small treasure house contains scrolls, tea utensils, and lacquered items. Graves of several Ashikaga shogun are found on its grounds.

The coffee shop **Papa Jon**, located near the west exit of Shōkoku-ji [Open 11 to 10. Tel: 415-2655], specializes in espresso and cheesecake. Quiche, sandwiches, and bagels are also available.

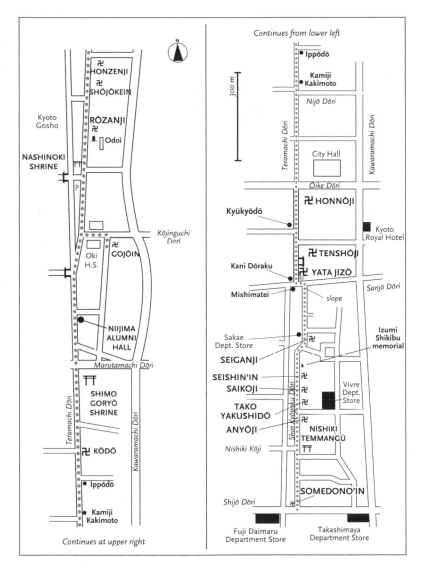

Continues from lower left

Ippōdō

Kamiji
Kakimoto

Nijō Dōri

Teramachi Dōri

Kawaramachi Dōri

City Hall

300 m

N

HONZENJI

SHŌJŌKEIN

Kyoto
Gosho

RŌZANJI

Odoi

NASHINOKI
SHRINE

P

Kōjinguchi
Dōri

Oki
H.S.

GOJŌIN

NIIJIMA
ALUMNI
HALL

Marutamachi Dōri

Teramachi Dōri

SHIMO
GORYŌ
SHRINE

Kawaramachi Dōri

KŌDŌ

Ippōdō

Kamiji
Kakimoto

Oike Dōri

HONNŌJI

Kyoto
Royal Hotel

Kyūkyōdō

TENSHŌJI

Kani Dōraku

YATA JIZŌ

Sanjō Dōri

Mishimatei

slope

Izumi
Shikibu
memorial

Sakae
Dept. Store

SEIGANJI

SEISHIN'IN

SAIKOJI

Vivre
Dept.
Store

Shin Kyōgoku Dōri

TAKO
YAKUSHIDŌ

ANYŌJI

NISHIKI
TEMMANGŪ

Nishiki Kōji

SOMEDONO'IN

Shijō Dōri

Fuji Daimaru
Department Store

Takashimaya
Department Store

Continues at upper right

LOWER TERAMACHI

Two blocks east of Shōkokuji, on the north side of the street, is the cemetery containing the graves of seventy-two members of the Satsuma domain (the old name for Kagoshima Prefecture). At the end of the Edo period, this domain played a leading role in the pro-imperial forces that overthrew the Tokugawa shogunate. The mortally wounded from the clashes that occurred at Hamaguri-mon and on the streets of Fushimi in the late 1860s are buried here.

Back on Teramachi is the sushi shop **Aokuma** [Open 11:30 to 9. Closed Mondays. Tel: 231-2877], which offers a reasonable selection of dishes starting at ¥1,500.

Hommanji is a Nichiren temple built in the Momoyama period (1568–1600). A two-minute walk south will bring you to a stone pillar standing on the east side of Teramachi that indicates the direction of **Sainokami no Yashiro**, or the Sainokami Shrine. When Kyoto was made the capital, this shrine was established to offer protection against the evil spirits that were believed to emanate from the northeast. As monkeys were considered lucky animals, long ago, one was kept in the old imperial palace to chase away mischievous spirits. Today, a wooden monkey, wearing a Shintō priest's hat and carrying a Shintō wand, is caged high within the northeast corner of Kyoto Gosho, the former imperial palace. An identical one is enclosed behind the latticework in the northeast corner of the main building of this shrine.

On the northeast corner of the Imadegawa-Teramachi intersection, a large stone post marks what was once the northeast corner of the ancient Heian capital. Continuing south on Teramachi, you come to **Honzenji**, a temple whose grounds have largely been converted into a parking lot. A lone white concrete building with cusped windows stands among the cars.

The gold chrysanthemum crests on the wooden gate of **Shōjōke'in** identify this as an imperial temple. Apartment housing for the elderly now stands on some of its land. The main temple buildings are closed to the public, but the grounds are not. Several members of the imperial family are buried in its cemetery.

Identifiable by a cylindrical stone pillar that stands outside the huge wooden gate, the temple **Rōzanji** [Open 9 to 12 and 1 to 4. Admission ¥400. Tel: 231-0355] occupies the site of the residence of the father of the famous Heian-period writer, Murasaki Shikibu, author of *The Tale of Genji*. Inside is a document that notes this was the site of Lady Murasaki's family home, as well as a roof tile from the original structure. Another room

The stately main hall of Tenneiji temple.

contains reproductions of a chapter from *The Tale of Genji*, part of which may have been written here. The unshaded moss-and-white-gravel garden planted with bellflowers was designed thirty years ago by an archeologist attempting to reproduce the original Heian-period garden.

The temple's cemetery is south and east of the main building. It is of special interest as it preserves a part of the large earthen embankment, called the **Odoi**, built to fortify the city in 1591. A stone pillar stands among the tall trees firmly rooted along the top of the remaining embankment.

Opposite Rōzanji is **Nashinoki Shrine**, founded in 1888. The spirits of Sanjō Sanetsuma and his son, Sanetomi, noblemen who fought valiantly for the emperor against the pro-shogunal forces in the struggles leading up to the Meiji Restoration of 1868, are enshrined here. As high-ranking court nobles, the Sanjō family possessed an estate here, close by the former imperial palace, and it is fitting that it became the site of their memorial. Famous for its bush clover, the shrine holds a festival dedicated to this flower on the third Sunday of September.

The east-west street that runs into Teramachi at Ōki High School is called Kōjin Dōri, a reference to Kōjin, a deity that protects the hearth. One block east of Teramachi, beyond the high school, is a small Tendai temple, **Gojōin** [Open 9 to 6. Tel: 231-3683], also called Kiyoshi Kōjin. Old-fashioned fire tongs, offerings to this deity, hang in a small building to the east of the Main Hall. The twenty-eighth of each month a large bonfire consumes the wooden prayer plaques written with wishes of supplicants, sending the ashes of the petitions heavenward (the largest event is in November).

Just north of Marutamachi Dōri is the Niijima Alumni Hall of Dōshisha University [Admission ¥200 when open. Tel: 251-3033]. The building to the north of this hall is the former residence of Niijima Jō (1843–90). As a young man, Niijima left Japan, an act then punishable by death. He studied at Amherst College in the United States, returning to Japan in 1874 as a Protestant minister to establish the school that would grow into Dōshisha University. This two-story house incorporates elements of Western architecture considered novel at the time of its construction in 1878. If you step into the parking area of the Niijima Alumni Hall, you can get a glimpse of the house. South of Marutamachi on the east side of Teramachi is **Shimo Goryō Shrine**, which was relocated here in 1590. The main gate was the former Kenrei-mon from the imperial palace that was moved here in 1791.

Gyōganji, beter known as **Kōdō** [Open 8 to 5. Tel: 211-2770], or "Hide Hall," is a Tendai temple founded in 1005 by the monk Gyoen Shōnin. When he was young, Gyoen killed a doe while hunting. Discovering an unborn fawn inside the animal, he was filled with remorse. He cured the deer's hide and wrote a sutra on it, gave up hunting, and traveled the countryside wearing the hide on his back and preaching Buddhism. The principal image in the Main Hall is a thousand-armed Kannon, a wooden statue said to have been found near the Kamo Shrine in 1004. To its right is an extremely well-preserved 225-centimeter image of Jizō, its head draped with a white silk scarf. Carved in the thirteenth century, much of the exquisite detail is still visible. The beautiful coffered ceiling, completed in 1815, has different flowers and birds carved in relief, not painted on inset panels as is usually the case. Gyōganji is temple nineteen on the thirty-three-temple Kannon pilgrimage in this region, and it is common to see pilgrims unrolling scrolls or unwrapping large paper cards on which they ask the nun to inscribe her beautiful calligraphy as a memento of their visit.

Another of Gyōganji's interesting objects, pictured on the postcards sold here, is the "Ghost Plaque," which depicts a young girl reaching for a bronze mirror. A legend says that in the 1800s, while caring for the baby of a pawnshop owner, a young maid was caught saying a prayer for the baby that infuriated the father, a follower of a different faith. In a rage, he killed her, but her innocent spirit returned as a ghost. Her parents, in an attempt to appease her restless spirit, had a wooden votive plaque, or *ema*, painted and attached one of her favorite possessions, a mirror, to it.

The neon silhouette of a tea canister identifies the tea shop **Ippōdō** [Open 9 to 6. Tel: 211-3421; www.ippodo-tea.co.jp]. Established in 1846, the shop sells fine tea from Uji, one of the most famous tea-growing districts in the country. The Kaboku tearoom on its premises allows one to sit and enjoy some of Ippōdō's renowned products. [Open 11 to 5. English menu available.] Although very modern in appearance, **Kamiji Kakimoto** [Open 9 to

6. Closed Sundays and holidays. Tel: 231-1544] is actually as old as Ippōdō. It sells a fine selection of handmade mulberry paper, as well as sets of stationery.

Honnōji [Open 6 to 5. Tel: 231-5338], a Nichiren temple, is just south of Ōike Dōri. This is where the warlord Oda Nobunaga was assassinated in 1582 at the age of forty-eight by one of his generals, Akechi Mitsuhide. Mortally wounded, Nobunaga retreated to an inner room, where he committed suicide as the temple burned. A monument to him, shaded by a towering 380-year-old gingko tree, stands south of the Main Hall.

The attractive Japanese-style building south and west of Honnōji is the incense shop **Kyūkyōdō** [Open 10 to 6. Closed Sundays. Tel: 231-0510], that has been in business for 320 years. Fine paper products, sachet bags, stationery, brushes for calligraphy, and utensils for the incense ceremony are available here. (Japanese especially prize aloeswood incense, the refined scent of which fills the shop. The aged, water-submerged aloeswood tree is very rare and valuable.)

Tenshōji is very easy to miss because the gate to this Jōdo temple is recessed and its grounds filled with cars. Built in 1577, an image of Amida is enshrined in the Main Hall. The grave of Tozaemon, the first Japanese to make brass in Japan, is here.

Next to the police box at the corner of Sanjō and Teramachi is Yatadera, known affectionately as **Yata Jizō**. Jizō is a bodhisattva known for rescuing sinners from hell, as the temple's votive plaques (*ema*) make graphically plain. In addition to the plaques, tiny stuffed images of Jizō are sold to devotees of this deity, who write their request on the stuffed images and leave them hanging in the temple, in hopes that Jizō will grant their wishes. Also at this corner is the crab restaurant **Kani Dōraku** [Open 11:30 to 11. Tel: 211-0671], identifiable by a huge automated crab on the front of the building. Diagonally across from it is the meat shop and restaurant **Mishimatei** [Open 11 to 9. Closed Wednesdays. Tel: 221-

0003], where a sign on the wall in English gives a brief history of Teramachi. Prices start from ¥5,000 per person.

Between Sanjō and Shijō Dōri, Teramachi becomes a covered shopping arcade; one block east on Sanjō Dōri, another covered street, Shin Kyōgoku, runs parallel to Teramachi, and the remaining temples on the walk are located along this street. The avenue forming the eastern border of the original Heian capital, Higashi Kyōgoku Ōji, was near here. But first, note that whereas the street is level at Sanjō-Teramachi, it slopes downward to Shin Kyōgoku. Several hundred years ago, when the Sanjō Bridge was under construction, huge mounds of earth were piled to raise the ground near the bridge. One mound extended to what is now Shin Kyōgoku. The entrance to Tenshōji was obstructed by the mounds of dirt, so huge stone slabs were placed there to allow access to the temple. The heavy stones sank and created this slope, which is now preserved for posterity in a shopping arcade. The street widens in front of the Sakae supermarket and department store. Directly east of this is the large concrete temple, **Seiganji**. Moved to this site during Hideyoshi's reign, the present building was completed in 1964. Petitioners are welcome to step inside to view the image of Amada Nyorai, which was first made in Nara 1,300 years ago. Candles for ¥500 and ¥200 are available for those who wish to write their name and prayer upon one and leave it for the priests to bless and use in their services. The temple has many followers of *gekidō*, the way of the performing arts, especially Rakugo performers (oral storytellers).

On the east, a half block beyond the triangular plaza, past a small temple gate, is a cemetery and a large stone **memorial to Izumi Shikibu**, a Heian-period poet. A few meters away, a larger gate leads back to **Seishin'in**, a temple moved here during the Kamakura period. The cemetery with Izumi's memorial is a part of this temple. Izumi Shikibu was fond of plum trees, and in her honor a tiny plum tree stands in front of the Main Hall, with one of her poems carved in stone beside it. A raised stone platform of twenty-five bodhisattvas now stands on the north side of the Main Hall. With all the cemeteries along this street, it is still surprising how much of downtown Kyoto remains sacred ground.

Myōshinji, better known as **Tako Yakushidō** ("Octopus Yakushi Hall") exhibits many objects in the shape of the creature. The story behind the temple's nickname is that long ago, a young monk went to buy an octopus in order to feed his sick mother. While carrying the live octopus, the monk was chided by others for preparing to kill a living creature. (It is against the Buddhist precepts to kill any living thing.) Yakushi Nyorai, the Healing Buddha, knew the monk's intentions were pure, and appeared to him, saying that his mother would be cured by her son's thoughtful act. The monk made a statue of this Buddha in gratitude and enshrined it here. Another image, a glass-enclosed image of Jizō on the left, is said to grant one's wishes and bring good luck. The temple was moved here five hundred years ago from Shijō-Muromachi, but the present building is one hundred years old. Follow the ancient stone path to the right of the Main Hall back to Amida Hall to view the image made in 1461. White boards line the passageway, filled with messages from visitors. On the left, or east side, of the street is the modern concrete exterior of **Anyōji**, a Jōdo sect temple founded in 1110 and relocated here in 1580. Its main image stands on eight upside-down lotus petals within a glass-encased area. Fudō Myōō and Benzaiten stand on either side of the main figure. Unable to complete an image with upright petals, the sculptors reversed the flower and succeeded.

Nishiki Temmangū [Open until 6. Tel: 231-5732] is the lantern-bedecked shrine on Shin Kyōgoku at the east end of the Nishiki Kōji market street. Although fires and battles claimed most of the temples and shrines in Kyoto, this one was reduced to a tenth of its original size when the streets were straightened about a century ago. All Temmangū or Tenjin shrines honor Sugawara no Michizane (845–930), a Heian scholar and nobleman who was falsely accused of plotting against the emperor, and banished from the capital. One sign that a shrine is a Temmangū is if it has a statue of a cow. Here, a handsome bronze image of one sits to the right of the entrance, its metal surface lustrous from where supplicants have rubbed it, hoping to be relieved of aches and pains or other troubles. In the Main Hall are two splendid guardian dogs sculpted in the Kamakura period (1185–1333). Glimmerings of gold foil can still be seen on these beautiful wooden images.

Somedono'in is located at the corner of Shin Kyōgoku and Shijō Dōri (just behind the roasted-chestnut shop on Shijō, behind the glass doors). This Jishu temple houses an image of Jizō who is said to grant pregnant women safe delivery. Legend has it that when Empress Akiko (829–900) was pregnant with Emperor Seiwa (858–76), she prayed to this Jizō and was blessed with an easy birth. To show her gratitude, she had this temple built. The offerings of lengths of cotton cloth, used as an abdominal support by pregnant women, can be seen piled on the side of the altar, and new ones on the tray cost ¥1,000.

South of Shijō Dōri, Teramachi is lined with electric-appliance stores. These have almost completely edged out the street's original inhabitants: the shrines, temples, and shops selling religious accessories, though some shops still sell altar candles, prayer bells, prayer beads, and incense. Although the religious element has waned, Teramachi is a reminder of the powerful presence of Buddhism in Kyoto.

DOWNTOWN 市内

Takase River 高瀬川
Kiyamachi Dōri 木屋町道り
Pontochō 先斗町
Minamiza 南座
Meyami Jizō 目病み地蔵
Shirakawa 白川
Shimbashi Dōri 新橋道り
Tatsumi Daimyōjin Shrine 辰巳大明神
Shinmonzen Dōri 新門前道り
Furumonzen Dōri 古門前道り
Ichiriki-chaya 一力茶屋
Gion 祇園
Yasui Kompiragū 安井金比羅宮
Kenninji 建仁寺
Nishiki Kōji 錦小路

Over the centuries, Kyoto has largely retained its ancient plan, based on that of the Tang-dynasty Chinese capital of Chang'an, now the city of Xi'an in western China. East–west streets follow almost the same course they have for over a thousand years, although many of the north–south streets were realigned and renamed as huge swaths of the city were destroyed by fires and subsequently rebuilt. The present downtown area, at least as far as its topography and layout is concerned, appears much the same as it did three hundred years ago, when warlord Toyotomi Hideyoshi rebuilt the city and reconstructed many of its major temples.

In recent years, the frantic, unchecked pace of commercial construction at the sacrifice of Kyoto's historic landmarks has produced a city that seems at odds with itself. As proud as the residents are of their city and its aristocratic beginnings, they seem

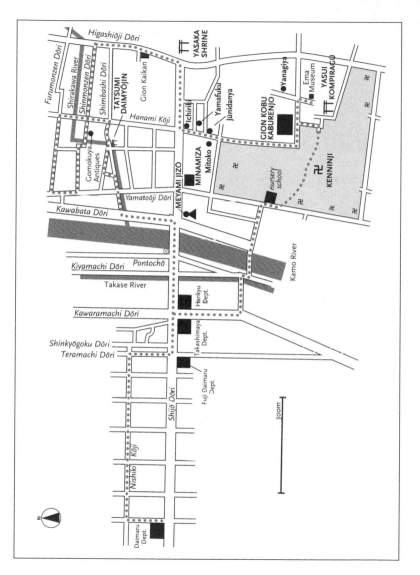

DOWNTOWN

equally determined to hide any reminder of their elegant past under jumbled bric-a-brac. The narrow sidewalks, made more narrow and unsightly by bikes and shop signs, make the city seem oppressively crowded with pedestrian traffic. Stripped of much of its history and greenery, downtown Kyoto could be interchangeable with any number of other Japanese cities. Even so, vestiges of the past poke their heads through the tangle of shops and restaurants, and a small detour through the back streets rewards the visitor with unexpected glimpses into a forgotten Japan.

The hub of activity is at the Shijō-Kawaramachi intersection where the Hankyō and Takashimaya department stores are located. One block east of this intersection, Shijō Dōri crosses the cherry-and-willow-lined **Takase River**. In 1615, this river was channeled into a canal, and flat-bottomed dories carrying rice, *sake*, timber products, and other goods were pulled and poled along the waterway south to Jūjō Dōri where the Takase joins the Kamo River. As a reminder of the river's busy past, slender boats stacked with rice bales are anchored a few blocks north at Nijō Dōri.

Kiyamachi Dōri, literally "Street of the Wood-Shop District," runs parallel to the Takase River on its east side. The timber and charcoal shops once located here had easy access to the canal and markets farther south. Much of the timber transshipped here was destined for the pottery kilns that once dotted the area from Gojō to Shijō along the foothills of Higashiyama. Charcoal was used then (and even today in some country homes) as the main fuel for cooking and heating. Today, all traces of the shops that supplied this fuel are gone, replaced by bars and restaurants that keep their customers warm in other ways.

One block east is a very narrow pedestrian alleyway called **Pontochō**. Lined with coffee shops, restaurants, and bars, it offers refreshments and amusement as it did four hundred years ago. Pontochō is an area where geisha (the preferred term in Kyoto is *geiko*) entertain, one of four such districts in Kyoto, the other three being Gion-Shimbashi, Miyagawa, and Kamishichiken. The name Pontochō comes either from the Portuguese word for "point" (at one time this strip of land extended out into the Kamo River) or for "bridge" (of which there are many in this vicinity, spanning the Kamo and Takase Rivers).

The vocation of a geisha or *geiko* is implied within the word itself. *Gei* means artistry, and *sha* or *ko*, person. About three hundred years ago, geisha were strictly forbidden to engage in prostitution; their job then, as now, was to entertain—to play the *shamisen*, sing, dance, and to talk with guests at social gatherings. Although confusion about their role exists in the minds of some foreigners, make no mistake: geisha are women who have chosen to be professional entertainers and are free to leave the profession if they so decide. Each of Kyoto's *geiko* quarters has a theater offering spring and autumn performances of song and dance for the general public by *geiko* and their apprentices (*maiko*). Otherwise, *geiko* entertain at private parties in exclusive *chaya*, or "tea houses," some of which are the most beautiful buildings in these districts. The theater for this district is the Pontochō Kaburenjo [Tel: 221-2025], located just southwest of the Sanjō Bridge.

Many of the restaurants along the east side of Pontochō abut the banks of the Kamo River, and during the summer months, outdoor platforms called *yuka* are erected so that patrons can enjoy their meals in the cool night air. The graceful plover, which inhabits the shallows of the Kamo River, has been adopted by the geisha of Pontochō as their symbol. In spring and fall, when the Kamogawa Odori dances are in session, the restaurants and *chaya* of Pontochō hang red lanterns, decorated with a plover motif, outside their doors.

Crossing the Kamo River at the Shijō-Kawabata intersection you will find the **Minamiza** kabuki theater on the southeast side of Shijō Dōri. Originally constructed in 1929, it was renovated in 1991. Although in use year-round, it is busiest in December, when it hosts the ever-popular *kaomise kabuki*. *Kaomise* literally means "to show one's face," a reference to the Edo-period custom whereby actors who had signed a yearly contract were presented to the public on the December playbill.

A little farther east on the same side of the street is **Meyami Jizō**, a bodhisattva to whom Kyotoites prayed to stop rain (*ameyami*) from flooding the area. An official placed the Jizō in this temple because of its proximity to the river. Over time, *ameyami* resembled the expression *meyami*, which means "diseased eyes" and attracted those with failing sight. Its reputation as a healer of damaged and tired eyes grew. A thousand-armed Goddess of Mercy and one of the seven lucky gods, Daitokuten, are in the Buddha Hall.

A few blocks north running into Kawabata Dōri is the river **Shirakawa**. Originating in the northeast of the city, the "White River" is so named because it carries fine white sand from Mt. Hiei into the river. Carp and ducks live along this section, which is now a canal, illuminating the shallow waters with their brilliant colors, and every June the locals eagerly await the coming of the fireflies that congregate over the clear flowing water, adding delicate traces of light to an already romantic part of town.

Walk east along the river, crossing Yamatooji Dōri to take a short detour along **Shimbashi Dōri,** a street lined with the exclusive teahouses for which geisha districts are known. The short street boasts many handsome examples of traditional architecture, some with recent innovative additions like the roof-tile wall and arched entrance of one building, keeping the aesthetic traditions of Kyoto alive. Although the shadeless street with its dark lattice-front houses may appear lifeless, that is an illusion. Inside, skylights and paper sliding doors let soft light filter into each room, while inner gardens allow the inhabitants to enjoy the four seasons. At night, the light radiating through the latticed woodwork of the houses creates a warm, welcoming atmosphere. Further along Shimbashi is **Tatsumi Daimyōjin Shrine**, a tiny neighborhood shrine patronized by the proprietresses of the nearby *chaya* and by *geiko* and *maiko* of Shimbashi on their way to lessons or appointments.

A block to the north on Hanami Kōji is **Shinmonzen Dōri** and a block north of that is **Furumonzen Dōri**. Most of Kyoto's antique shops are congregated on these streets, of which the names mean "New Street in Front of the Gate" and "Old Street in Front of the Gate," respectively, referring to the gate of Chion'in on the east side of Higashiōji Dōri. No appointments are necessary

Pickles on sale at the Nishiki Kōji market invite shoppers to stop for samples.

in the shops in this district; if a shop is open, step in and browse. Furniture, pottery, old kimono, miniature ivory *netsuke*, prints, and scrolls are sold here. Museum-quality items are available (for a price) and a visit to some of these shops is almost equivalent to going to an exhibition of fine Japanese art. The antique shops on Furumonzen are concentrated between Yamatoōji Dōri and Hanami Kōji, but those on Shinmonzen extend as far as Higashiōji Dōri. This district is also the center of Kyoto's nightlife, with thousands of tiny bars (some for members only) and restaurants with their specials, customers, and hostesses. (A word of caution to bar-hoppers: unless there is an English menu and set prices, let the buyer beware.)

Walk south on Higashiōji Dōri until you return to Shijō Dōri, where many shops sell traditional goods. At the southeast corner of Shijō Dōri and Hanami Kōji stands **Ichiriki-chaya**, one of Kyoto's landmarks. At one time, most of the *chaya* in this area, known as Gion, had the same red clay walls and dark-stained wood exteriors as this 130-year-old establishment. Part of Ichiriki's fame stems from the role it played in the story of the Forty-Seven Samurai. Their leader, Ōishi Kuranosuke, whiled away years pretending to party in this *chaya* in order to trick his enemies into thinking that he had no intention of avenging his lord's death. The ruse worked, and the many stories, plays, and songs that have been written about this vendetta often mention this *chaya*.

More than an area, **Gion** is a legend—one both romantic and tragic, like the many love stories set here. Originally, the area took its name from Gion-san, now known as Yasaka Shrine. Long ago, the *chaya* were just what their name implies: merely tea shops that offered beverages and a bite to eat to the hundreds of pilgrims who poured into the city to visit the great temples of Chion'in and Kiyomizudera. Centuries later, when the theater-goers attending kabuki mingled with the pilgrims, some *chaya* started to offer more substantial fare, as well as a little entertainment. A fire destroyed the area in 1670, but it was soon rebuilt. In an attempt to control the burgeoning nightlife, the government licensed Gion as an entertainment district in 1713. Together with Shimabara, Miyagawachō, Kamishichiku, Pontochō, and Shimbashi, Gion began to attract a clientele, and the number of its entertainers grew. The government then attempted to restrict prostitution to only one of these areas and officially sanctioned the walled gay district of Shimabara in the southwest part of the city as a brothel quarter.

The famous ninety-year-old restaurant near the corner of the next block, **Jūnidanya** [Open 12 to 2 and 5 to 9. Closed Thursdays.

Tel: 561-1655], serves *shabu shabu*, thin slices of beef cooked by swirling them in a vegetable broth. The interior is beautifully decorated with works by well-known artists, including pottery by Kawai Kanjirō and screens and prints by Munakata Shikō.

The **Gion Kobu Kaburenjo** [Tel: 541-3391] theater, designated by a sign that reads "Gion Corner," specializes in traditional music and dance performances. Built in 1913, it is busiest in April and October, when the *maiko* and *geiko* of Gion appear in the Miyako Odori dance performance. During this period, red lanterns, decorated with a motif of five skewered rice dumplings, are hung throughout the area.

One block to the east, on the street that runs along the east side of the Gion Kobu Kaburenjo compound, is a *chaya* known as **Yanagiya**. It occupies the site of the residence of Awa no Naishi, the favorite concubine of Emperor Sutoku (1119–64). The classic-looking *chaya*, built in 1922, took its name from the former building, which was called Yanagi no Gosho (Willow Palace).

On the right, or south, is a stone *torii* that marks the entrance to a shrine called **Yasui Kompiragū**, home of the Kompira Ema Museum and Glass Gallery [Open 10 to 4. Admission ¥500. Closed Mondays, except national holidays. Tel: 561-5127]. Just to the right of the entrance, hanging on the fences of the inner shrine, are hundreds of small wooden prayer tables called *ema*. A supplicant purchases an *ema*, writes a prayer on the blank side, and then leaves it at the shrine so that the resident deity may read it and grant the wish. The word *ema* means "horse picture," and horses, highly prized possessions, are the most frequently depicted motif, although other animals of the zodiac or event connected with the shrine are also popular.

Usually small, *ema* kept by large shrines can sometimes be huge slabs of wood as large as a door, depicting mythological or historical figures. The two-story museum on the grounds of this shrine is the only one of its kind in Japan devoted to this folk art.

The first floor houses many examples of boldly drawn *ema*, while the *tatami*-floored upstairs displays new ones, some rather cartoonlike. After showing the *ema,* the curator will guide you to a specially built room which houses the shrine's glass collection, the prize of which is an installation of sea-like forms created by Seattle artist Dale Chihuly.

Yasui Kompiragū also boasts another unusual property: a large rock with a hole in its center, covered with strips of paper known as *en musubi*, or "ties that bind." If you would like to form a relationship with someone, write your name and your prospective partner's name on a slip of paper which is sold at the counter for ¥100. Dab a little paste on it, crawl through the hole in the rock (though most supplicants seem to settle for passing it through by hand), and paste it to the rock. Apparently, this rock has the power to unbind you, too, if you reverse the process.

Retrace your steps out of the shrine and wind your way back to the north gate of **Kenninji**. This temple was founded by Eisai (1141–1241), a monk who traveled to China to study and brought Zen Buddhism back with him to Japan. After his return, he spent ten years in Fukuoka in northern Kyushu, where, in 1191, he founded a Rinzai Zen monastery. In 1202, he was invited by the shogun to build Kenninji, Kyoto's first Zen temple. Destroyed by fire, the temple was restored in 1596. As is the case with other Zen complexes in the city, the style of architecture is Chinese: the central buildings are aligned on a north–south axis, and the interiors have slate floors instead of *tatami*, as well as latticework doors and window shutters that swing up to open instead of sliding. The subtemples located along the perimeter of the grounds, however, are Japanese-style. Generally, except during the occasional exhibition of flower arrangements, calligraphy, tea ceremony, or special openings, the subtemples are not open to the public, but visitors are welcome to walk through the temple grounds.

From the northwest exit near the nursery school, turn right, then turn left and cross the Kamo River. Jog right, cross the Takase River, and you will have come full circle to the Shijō-Kawaramachi intersection. The Hankyū and Takashimaya department stores at the south corners of the intersection are typical Japanese department stores, which all have a similar floor plan: foodstuffs in the basement, sale items and restaurants on the upper floors. Department stores also have art galleries and hold exhibitions on a regular basis. Restaurants in both stores offer a fairly wide selection of reasonably priced dishes.

For an additional look at a seemingly endless array of Japanese delicacies, the stretch of **Nishiki Kōji** between Teramachi and Takakura streets, one block north of and parallel to Shijō Dōri, is a covered shopping arcade with plenty to offer.

Nishiki means silk brocade, but that is not what is sold here, and the street's name has a surprisingly indelicate history. When the capital was new, the street was twelve meters wide and called Gusoku Kōji, one reading of which is Armor Street. Gusoku Kōji, through generations of lazy tongues, was eventually corrupted to Kuso Kōji, meaning Excrement Street. A curious story then evolved to explain the name. One day, it is said, a hermit appeared, accompanied by hordes of beasts and hungry ghosts (two classes of beings from the six realms of rebirth). The people living along this street gave large amounts of rice to him and his companions, who quickly ate it, then proceeded to defecate as they strolled down the street. In 1054, deeming the popular name unbecoming a street in the capital, Emperor Go-Reizei renamed it Nishiki Kōji to complement a street two blocks south called Aya no Kōji (Twill-Weave Street). About three centuries ago, at the beginning of the Edo period, several popular fish shops were set up here. These attracted other food merchants, and the street began to prosper as a market area with the same types of businesses you see today. Most shops are open from around 8:30 to 7 and closed on Sundays and national holidays when the central food market is closed.

SHŪGAKUIN 修学院
and ICHIJŌJI 一乗寺

Shūgakuin Rikyū 修学院離宮
Sekizan Zen'in 赤山禅院
Manshuin 曼殊院
Saginomori Shrine 鷺森神社
Kirara-chaya きらら茶屋
Enkōji 円光寺
Shisendō 詩仙堂
Hachidai Shrine 八大神社
Tanukidani Fudōin 狸谷不動院
Honganji Kitayama Betsuin 本願寺北山別院
Kompukuji 金福寺
Ichijōji Sagari Matsu 一乗寺下がり松

Shūgakuin and Ichijōji are areas of northeastern Kyoto nestled among the foothills of Higashiyama (the Eastern Hills). Graced with many temples, shrines, and former residences of the literati, this part of the city retains a rustic residential quality, though trendy boutiques and restaurants have also made their mark here. Spring and autumn are especially popular seasons to visit because of the cherry and maple trees that flourish on the mountainsides and adorn home and temple gardens, providing a romantic blend of the wild and cultivated. One of Kyoto's three imperial villas, Shūgakuin Rikyū, is located here, in a setting famous for its beauty and tranquility. Another jewel of the area is Shisendō, the retreat of the Edo-period scholar-poet Ishikawa Jōzan, with one of the city's most celebrated gardens. Complementing the area's beauty are the temples Manshuin, Enkōji, and Kompukuji, and the secluded Saginomori shrine, while the lively Tanukidani Fudōin adds some zest and sparkle to its sedate mountain setting.

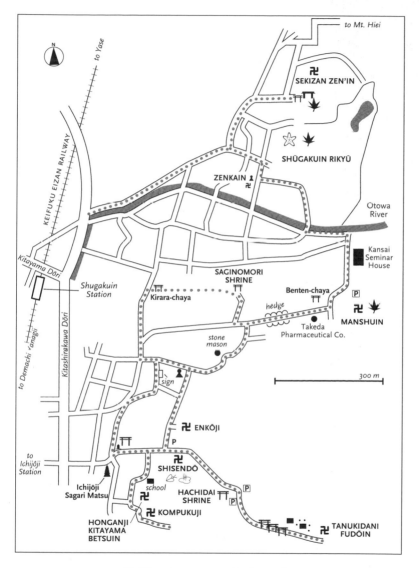

SHŪGAKUIN and ICHIJŌJI

The spacious villa and grounds of **Shūgakuin Rikyū** [Free admission but permission to enter is needed. Closed national holidays and December 25 to January 5. Tel: 211-1215] were designed by Emperor Go-Mizunoo (1596–1680). When he came to the throne, the Tokugawa shogunate was consolidating its hold on the newly unified country. The power of the shogunate, which greatly surpassed that of the emperor, made Go-Mizunoo's life a difficult one; he was even forced to marry the shogun's daughter. Unhappy with this and other shogunal interference in his affairs, Go-Mizunoo abdicated at the age of thirty-three, placing his five-year-old daughter on the throne as the Empress Meishō. For the next half century he occupied himself with various pursuits, among them the writing of verse and the construction of Shūgakuin Rikyū. After falling into disuse several times in its history, Shūgakuin Rikyū was restored to its present condition in the Meiji era (1868–1912), when it was used as a place for entertaining state guests.

Today, the villa is shown by appointment only. Applications should be made several days in advance at the Imperial Household Agency [Kunaichō; http://sankan.kunaicho.go.jp] located in the northwest corner of the park that surrounds the Kyoto Gosho. Applicants must be over the age of twenty and show identification, preferably their passports. Groups are limited to four or less. Written information in English is provided free, so it is not necessary to be able to understand Japanese in order to enjoy the tour. As the guide told the Japanese visitors gathered there one day, "You can try to remember all the names of the mountains, or who painted what, but it is all right to just sit and gaze at it all." That's probably the best way to visit the villa—just relax and enjoy the day and the beautiful scenery.

Take City Bus Kita 5 from Kitaōji Bus Terminal (¥220) or City Bus 5 from Kyoto Station via Keihan Sanjō Station (¥220) to the Shūgakuin Rikyū Michi stop, or take the Eizan Railway from the Demachi Yanagi to Shūgakuin Station (¥200). Near the traffic signal at the corner of Shūgakuin Rikyū Michi and Shirakawa Dōri, a sign in both Japanese and English points the way uphill to the villa. Visitors are requested to arrive ten minutes before the tour starts, so keep in mind that it is about a fifteen-minute walk east from the traffic signal.

Signs near the imperial villa point the way to several nearby temples. The closest one, **Sekizan Zen'in** [Open 9 to 5. Tel: 701-5181], is a very eclectic temple just a few minutes north of the villa; if you arrive early at Shūgakuin Rikyū, you can visit this temple first. About fifty meters west of Shūgakuin's entrance, the road forks to the north and passes Sekizan Zen'in. This junction is marked with an upright stone with the carved characters for Sekizan Zen'in in red and a small stone Buddhist image. A two-minute walk north brings you to a stone *torii*, the entrance to the temple. Beyond is a wooden and tile-roofed temple gate and a gravel road that leads back to the temple buildings, canopied by a dense growth of maple trees making this approach a beautiful place to view the autumn colors.

Sekizan Zen'in is a place for dreams and offers several means to achieve them. You may purchase a set of three sheets of paper with a picture of the treasure ship (*takarabune*) in which the Seven Gods of Good Fortune ride. The sheets of paper (one wish per sheet) are to be inscribed with your wish, placed under your pillow for several nights, then returned to the temple to be blessed. After that, it should be only a matter of time until your prayer is granted. Another means of petitioning the Buddha is a votive candle on which the person's name is written and the candle left for use by the temple. Also for sale are small sticks of wood (*goma*) to be inscribed with prayers and burned in a fire ritual on the twenty-fifth of every month.

This Tendai temple was founded in 868 by the followers of the eminent scholar-priest Ennin (794–864) of Enryakuji, who spent nine years in China studying Buddhism. Twice on leaving

China, his ship failed to reach Japan. Before his third attempt to return, he went to a place sacred to the deity Sekizan Myōjin to pray for a safe journey, and his prayer was granted. Many years later, just before he died, he requested that a temple named Sekizan be established to thank the god for his safe return. The temple is still associated with Enryakuji and between the seven-hundredth and eight-hundredth days of the thousand-day circumambulation of Mt. Hiei, monks embarking on this religious austerity include Sekizan in their walk. One of the main paths up the mountain begins just outside the temple. It takes about two and a half hours to reach Enryakuji from here. (See Mt. Hiei walk, page 164.)

Upon entering the grounds, the first large building is the Haiden, a Shintō structure. Sekizan Zen'in is unusual in that buildings of both Shintō and Buddhist styles of architecture are found together, a reminder of the syncretic faith that existed in Japan before the Meiji Restoration of 1868, at which time Shintō was declared the state religion and separated from non-indigenous Buddhism. The Haiden has a ceramic monkey on its roof—the monkey being the totemic animal of the indigenous "landlord" god of Hieizan. Located directly northeast of the former imperial palace, this monkey and one placed in the northeast corner of the wall of the inner palace face each other across the city rooftops and guard against evil forces that might penetrate Kyoto from the northeast. Monkey is pronounced *saru* in Japanese, and a homophone means "Go away," making this wily creature an appropriate talisman for warding off evil. Another newer monkey, fashioned from gray roof-tile clay, is perched on the roof of the water trough.

Beyond the Haiden to the left is a lovely Jizō Hall, in which the enshrined image of Jizō has colorful decorated robes. The Hondō (Main Hall) is directly north of the Haiden, and mounted under its eaves are three large circular plaques with a Sanskrit character for the bodhisattva Jizō carved into them. Why this is so is unclear. Over the ages, the buildings probably served different purposes.

Behind and to the left of the Main Hall is a small hall dedicated to Benten, a goddess among the Seven Gods of Good Fortune.

The path leads on to the Fukurokuju Hall, named after another of the gods of fortune. He has a distinctive elongated forehead and is associated with longevity, and is Sekizan Zen'in's representative deity in the Gods of Good Fortune pilgrimage. All the shrines and temples on this pilgrimage are in the Kyoto area: Ebisu Shrine, Matsugasaki Daikokuten, Tōji, Rokuharumitsuji, Mampukuji, Kōdō, and Sekizan Zen'in, and each represents one of the seven deities. It is considered especially propitious to dream of their treasure ship on the first three nights of January, and for that reason many people make this pilgrimage at the start of the New Year, but it can be done any time. A scroll or an accordion-folded book may be purchased here and will be inscribed with beautiful calligraphy by the priests and nuns at each of the temples or shrines on this pilgrimage. At Sekizan Zen'in, wooden figures of Fukurokuji containing paper fortunes are also on sale.

A path runs uphill to two small Shintō shrines: Konjinsha, at the northeast corner of the temple precincts, the unlucky direction known as the *omote-kimon* ("outer demon corner"); and Aioisha, a shrine dedicated to binding couples in matrimony. At the foot of the steps is Otakidō, a building open in the back, facing a double waterfall under which people practicing religious austerities sit and meditate. A Fudō Hall is on the left: the main image of Fudō Myōō, which is not open for viewing, is in a shrine within the hall.

Back at the entrance to Shūgakuin Rikyū is a sign in Japanese characters with a large red arrow at the bottom which points south to the temple Manshuin, a twenty-minute walk away. A minute's walk south along this route is **Zenkain**, a small temple with a charming bell tower topping the upper part of the entrance gate. The garden supposedly was designed by the famous Edo-period architect and garden designer Kobori Enshū (1579–1647). If the gate is open, visitors are welcome to enter and view the impressive Kamakura-period (1185–1333) stone images of Amida Nyorai and the bodhisattvas Jizō and Kannon that stand in the northeast corner of the garden.

The road continues south through a residential area, past rice fields, and crosses a river. Turn left, and after six or seven minutes you will come to a T-junction. Turn right. This road leads up to the Kansai Seminar House; a minute's walk south is Manshuin [Open 9 to 4:30. Admission ¥500. Tel: 781-5919], a temple originally founded in the eighth century on Mt. Hiei but moved here in 1656.

Manshuin is known for its *shoin*-style rooms. *Shoin* means a writing room or study, and in a temple, the *shoin* was the abbot's private audience room. This elegant example of Edo-period architecture became popular with the upper classes, and came to include such elements as staggered shelves set in a decorative alcove, ornate painted sliding doors (*fusuma*), and elaborate wood latticework on the lighter paper-covered sliding doors known as *shoji*. In fact, the elegant rooms of this Tendai temple seem more suited to a private villa of the nobility, which is not surprising since it was a *monzeki* temple whose reconstruction on the present site was supervised by an abbot, Ryōshō (1622–93), who was an imperial prince and son of Hachijō no Miya Toshihito, the man who began construction of Katsura Rikyū. Manshuin's main garden is a quiet space of raked sand, informal and restful, with the mountains as its backdrop. The beautiful maple and cherry trees attract crowds of tourists in April, and again in November.

Nestled in the grounds of the small shrine across from Manshuin is the noodle shop **Benten-chaya** [Open 9:30 to 5:30. Tel: 711-5661]. There is seating outside under red umbrellas or inside on *tatami* mats. Prices range from about ¥700 to ¥1,500 for the various noodle dishes served. Beer and other beverages also are available, as are bowls of powdered green tea (*matcha*) with a sweet.

Small, rustic, unpretentious temples and shrines are scat-

The monkey talisman perched on the roof of Sekizan Zen'in fends off evil spirits.

tered through this section of the city. Two such are Enkōji and **Saginomori Shrine**, which may take time to find because their sites are not as well marked as Manshuin. The road that passes Benten-chaya turns downhill toward the city. After passing the hedge that lines the Takeda Pharmaceutical Company grounds, a large up-right carved stone signpost displays the characters for Saginomori Shrine. There is a switchback path that cuts in front of a private home, then veers left through a forest to a small stone bridge, dat-ing from Go-Mizunoo's time, which was moved to span this slim branch of the Otowa River in 1967.

Saginomori Shrine is much older than this bridge, having supposedly been founded between 859 and 877. The main shrine building is elevated, with a stone stairway leading to a mounted gleaming mirror, symbol of the sun goddess, Amaterasu. Leg-end has it that this goddess fled deep into a cave, incensed by the shocking actions of her headstrong brother, Susanoo. When she entered the cave, the world was plunged into a terrible darkness. To entice his sister to leave the cave and restore light to the world, he performed a suggestive dance, having placed a mirror near the cave entrance. When Amaterasu rolled back the rock opening and saw her reflection in the mirror, light was restored to the world, and ever since then, a treasured silver or bronze mirror rests in the inner sanctum of shrines across this land.

Sagi means egret, a slender, elegant fish-eating bird of elongated form often seen in rice paddies, streams, or high in trees, and *mori* means woods. From long ago, flocks of egrets lived in this patch of forest and since birds are considered messengers of the gods, the shrine became known as the shrine-in-the-egrets'-woods. Walking west from here, down the wide stone stairway, will bring one to the main entrance. Turn left, and on your right you will see the old *chaya*, or teahouse, the **Kirara-chaya** [Open 9 to 5. Tel: 781-5023]. For centuries, this teahouse has provided simple refreshment for pilgrims and priests on their journey back to Enryakuji on the top of Mt. Hiei. Other travelers stopping here for a cup of tea and a taste of their famous eggplant pickles (Kirara-zuke) include those crossing Mt. Hiei via the Shiratori or Imaji passes, on their way to the former port of Sakamoto, which lies beside Lake Biwa in Shiga Prefecture. These delicious pickles are still sold, and samples are offered to all visitors. The interior and garden of the present building is about 250 years old. South of the Kirara-chaya is an intersection with a signboard on the left, a stone marker, and a stone lantern. Turn left and go east toward the mountain and Manshuin. Follow the sign and take the narrow paved road to the right that leads to Enkōji.

The wide and rather formal entrance to **Enkōji** [Open 9 to 4:30. Admission ¥400. Tel: 781-8025], a former nunnery, is flanked by pine trees. The temple claims to have the oldest landscaped pond in this area, and indeed, it appears ancient because of the way time has rounded and softened it. Slender maple trees shade the moss-covered ground. Beyond is the inner tearoom and a small garden of azaleas and moss. Until the introduction of public education in the Meiji era, most schooling was conducted at Buddhist temples. Enkōji, built in 1601, served this purpose. It also functioned as a printing house for the Confucian classics. One of its most prized possessions in its treasure house is a set of wooden type consisting of fifty-two-thousand characters. Hand carved four hundred years ago, it is the oldest such set in Japan.

Exit Enkōji, turn left, and left again at the junction. On the left is a small parking lot. The bamboo front fence of **Shisendō** [Open 9 to 5. Admission ¥500. Tel: 781-2954] is just across from it. The entrance is so narrow and unobtrusive that many people miss it. The buildings and gardens reflect the sinicized tastes of the samurai and literatus Ishikawa Jōzan (1583–1672), who retired here after falling out of favor with shogun Tokugawa Ieyasu. Ishikawa named his villa Shisendō (Hall of Poet Immortals), dedicating it to thirty-six renowned classic Chinese poets whose portraits, by the famous painter Kanō Tan'yū, line the upper wall of his former study. This rustic hermitage is the original structure built in 1641. Although officially listed as a Sōtō Zen temple, its atmosphere is still very like the beloved residence of its original owner.

As in Manshuin, Shinsendō's garden is of the *kare sansui* (dry landscape) type. An expanse of raked white sand is bordered by round, clipped azaleas and maples and shaded by an ancient, massive sasanqua-camellia tree. In spring, the contrast of the color of blooming azaleas against the white sand is stunning. Out of sight, in the shrubbery, a length of bamboo slowly fills with water. When full, it tips over, clacking on impact, then empties, and flips upright to fill again. Originally, this was a farmer's device used to frighten away deer, but it has become a popular garden conceit that allow listeners to imagine a time when the woods were full of wildlife. The newer lower garden provides an interesting foil to the upper one. When reentering the villa from the garden, the Tower for Whistling at the Moon (Shogetsudō), which juts out of the roof, can be seen. This small chamber was used for moon viewing and writing poetry.

Just beyond Shisendō are the tall, slender red banners that mark the entrance to **Hachidai Shrine**, believed to have been founded in 1294. The male Shintō deity Susanoo no Mikoto, his wife Kushiinada Hime, and their eight children, the Hachiōji, are enshrined in this quiet wooded setting. The shrine also honors swordsman Miyamoto Musashi and his adventures in this vicinity by preserving a section of the pine tree that once marked the site of his most famous duel. This memento is to the left of the Main Hall, encircled by a sacred straw rope.

The next temple, **Tanukidani Fudōin** [Open 9 to 4:30. Free Admission. Tel: 781-5664], resembles a shrine with its brightly colored banners, red *torii*, and hand-clapping supplicants. Ceremonies for traffic safety and good health are conducted every thirty minutes, making a visit to this temple a rewarding experience for those who enjoy rituals.

As isolated as it appears on the map, the road leading to the temple is heavily traveled, for this is where Kyoto residents come to have their cars blessed, which explains why the first things you see are parking areas and an office selling amulets for traffic safety. After applying for a charm (prices from ¥5,000), drivers gather in front of the altar and wait to be blessed. Mountain priests, called *yamabushi*, dressed in unbleached hemp robes festooned with pompons, small pillbox hats, white cotton leggings, and deerskin aprons, conduct the ceremonies. Tanukidan Fudōin now belongs to the Shingon set, whose many esoteric rituals and meditation practices show the influence of Tantric Buddhism. It is also associated with Shūgendō, a cult in which members seek superhuman powers by doing austere practices in the mountains.

A tunnel of red *torii* ending in a Chinese-style gate leads to an image of the Hakuryū Benzaiten, the White Dragon Goddess of

Fortune. Many visitors pause to say a prayer here and some even leave eggs, a favorite food of dragons. The next building houses an image of Kōbō Daishi, who founded the Shingon sect in Japan in the ninth century. A pilgrimage to eighty-eight temples associated with him was established on the island of Shikoku. Here, at Tanukidani, eighty-eight steppingstones have been laid around the hall, making it possible to do the eighty-eight temple pilgrimage in a mere two minutes, rather than the usual two-month walk!

A very large stone statue of Kōbō Daishi, draped with tiny straw sandals, stands before the stairs leading to the Main Hall. Long ago, pilgrims wore roughly woven sandals of straw, the common footwear of travelers. When worn out, the sandals were left at the nearest temple. The miniatures left here represent spiritual adversities faced and surmounted. At the top of the steps, the wide, open courtyard has a small shrine on the right surrounded by an assortment of mischievous-looking ceramic *tanuki*, or badgers (the Tanukidani of the temple's name literally means "Badger Valley"). Although there might be badgers in this area, this name probably originated from a reading of the Chinese characters for "Angry Demon."

The Main Hall, set into the mountainside and supported by pillars, looms over it all. The veranda provides a view of the city, and the interior offers a glimpse into the world of esoteric Buddhism. Fierce-looking, multi-limbed images drift in clouds of heavily scented incense in the flickering candlelight. The atmosphere is one of mystery and magic and centuries-old traditions. There are two approaches: the forty-two stairs on the left are for men; the thirty-three on the right for women. The number of steps represents the ages for each sex that are thought to present special hazards.

A new adjoining building houses several counters that sell amulets and also have the applications for the blessings ceremonies, the cost of which starts at ¥5,000. On busy days and weekends, these ceremonies are held every thirty minutes. After applying, petitioners are summoned by a loudspeaker to assemble in front of the main altar. Visitors can watch from inside the Main Hall behind the raised *tatami* area. The ceremony takes about ten minutes. It is one you are unlikely to encounter elsewhere and worth the wait. Those who have requested a blessing have had their prayers written on thin sheets of wood by the priests, who then wave them over the fire burning in front of the main image of Fudō Myōō and add them to the flames. Bells are rung, a drum is beaten, prayer beads are rubbed together, and incantations are chanted as the fire sends its flames higher. This is Buddhism in one of its most exotic and visually exciting forms.

On the mountainside behind the Main Hall, there is another pilgrimage: visiting the thirty-six attendants of Fudō Myōō. The walk begins at the stairs beyond the foot of the red *torii*. The entire walk takes about twenty minutes, but appropriate shoes are necessary as the ground is sometimes slippery and loose.

Retrace your steps, taking the first left after Shisendō. A Japanese sign points to the temple Kompukuji. The street to this temple zigzags through a residential neighborhood, making Kompukuji a little hard to find, but there are signs along the way. Another temple, **Honganji Kitayama Betsuin**, is on the north side of the street, its grounds occupied by a Main Hall, bell tower, and kindergarten.

Around another corner is an upright ovoid stone engraved with the characters for **Kompukuji.** Founded in the ninth century as a Tendai temple, Kompukuji [Open 9 to 5. Admission ¥300. Tel: 791-1666] later changed its affiliation to the Rinzai school of Zen. The temple is famous for its association with Bashō (1644–94) and Buson (1716–84), Japan's most famous haiku poets. More than three centuries ago, Bashō stayed in a thatched-roof cottage on its grounds during his travels around Japan. The cottage, later named after him, is called Bashō-an. A hundred years later, when

Buson visited the temple, he was dismayed to find the cottage in a state of collapse and arranged to have it restored. Although the roof is rethatched every fifteen or so years, the cottage's basic architecture has not changed in more than 250 years. Buson's grave, on the hillside behind the temple, is surrounded by those of many of his disciples and later poets. (Buson was also an accomplished painter, and one of his paintings is displayed inside the temple.) It is easy to imagine why both poets found this area inspiring. The main garden, which incorporates a view of the thatched Bashō-an, is fronted by a steep slope of planted azalea bushes that rise in waves on the hillside. Within the grounds are three kinds of azaleas: *dodan tsutsuji*, *mitsuba tsutsuji*, and *tsutsuji*, which bloom from March to early June.

Return to the road that runs past Shinsendō. Turn left, and walk downhill to where several roads intersect. On the south side of the intersection stands a pine tree known as **Ichijōji Sagari Matsu**, the Pine of Lower Ichijōji. The area takes its name from Ichijōji, a Tendai temple founded in 981 that no longer exists. From ancient times the pine tree here was a landmark for travelers bound for Shiga Prefecture by the Shiratori or Imaji passes through the mountains east of here. It also marks the spot where the swordsman Miyamoto Musashi (1584–1645), author of the *Book of Five Rings*, dueled with Yoshioka Ichimon, a famous martial arts instructor. Musashi won. A portion of the tree that stood here when Musashi fought Ichimon is preserved in the nearby Hachidai Shrine. The present pine is the fourth generation.

Continue downhill (west) to Shirakawa Dōri, where City Bus 5 runs, or cross at the traffic light and continue due west on that street to Ichijōji Station on the Eizan Railway.

ENRYAKUJI 延暦寺

Hieizan 比叡山

Enryakuji 延暦寺

Tōdō 東塔

Kokuhōden 国宝殿

Daikōdō 大講堂

Kaidan'in 戒壇院

Amidadō 阿弥陀堂

Daikokudō 大黒堂

Kompon Chūdō 根本中堂

Saitō 西塔

Sannōin 山王院

Jōdoin 浄土院

Jōgyōdō 常行堂

Hokkedō 法華堂

Shakadō 釈迦堂

Yokawa 横川

Yokawa Chūdō 横川中堂

Eshindō 恵心堂

Ganzan Daishidō 元三大師堂

Jōkōin 常光院

Nyohōtō 如法塔

Mudōjidani 無動寺谷

At 848 meters (2,780 feet), Hieizan is one of the highest mountains surrounding Kyoto. Its unspoiled forests provide a luxurious alternative to the skimpy greenery along the city's sidewalks. But the principal reason to visit this scenic mountain is Enryakuji, the imposing temple complex that graces its summit and is now a World Heritage Site. This mountain temple has had a long, intimate, and sometimes stormy relationship with the city it overlooks.

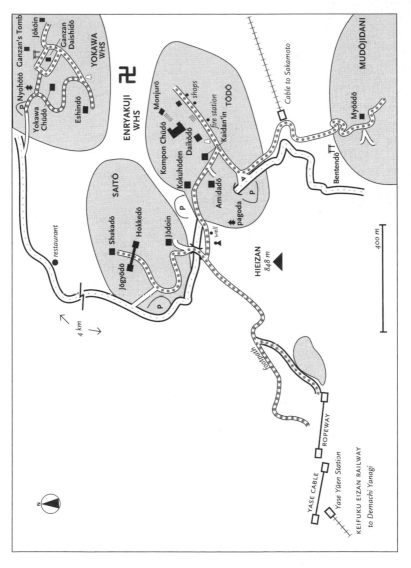

ENRYAKUJI

More than a thousand years ago, a priest named Saichō was given imperial permission to build a temple to protect the newly founded capital from the spirits of misfortune believed to come from the northeast. Enryakuji, as this Tendai temple came to be called, grew into one of Japan's main centers of Buddhism. The immense power it accrued also brought it into intermittent conflict over the centuries with other Buddhist sects and with the imperial court. So pervasive was its influence that even the powerful eleventh-century emperor Shirakawa once lamented that the only things that he could not control were "The roll of the dice, the Kamo River, and the monks of Enryakuji."

Enryakuji's days of glory came to an end in 1571, when politics pitted the temple against the famous warlord, Oda Nobunaga, whose aim was nothing less than the total destruction of the vast complex of temples and associated structures (which numbered some three thousand at the beginning of the sixteenth century). Nobunaga was the victor, and Enryakuji was razed and its inhabitants slaughtered—leaving only smoldering remains where one of Japan's most majestic temple complexes had stood. But further power struggles led to Nobunaga's assassination in 1582, and Toyotomi Hideyoshi, the warlord who succeeded him, permitted Enryakuji to be rebuilt.

Several buses run daily to Enryakuji: the Keihan Bus leaves from Stop No. 3 at the Central Post Office in front of Kyoto Station (eighty minutes to Enryakuji, ¥750), stopping along the way at Sanjō Keihan Railway Station (fifty-five minutes to Enryakuji), at the northeast corner of the Imadegawa-Kawabata intersection, and at the northwest corner of Imadegawa-Shirakawa (¥580). Another option is to catch a Yase-bound train (¥260) from Eizan Railway's Demachi Yanagi Station and get off at Yase Yūen Station. It's a one-minute walk to the cable-car station, which connects with a ropeway. The trip takes about twenty-five minutes altogether; a round-trip fare of ¥1,640 includes both cable-car and ropeway trips.

The cable car departs every half hour, ascending the steep slope with a great clanging of bells and horns. It is hardly the way one would expect to approach a sacred mountain, but Hieizan also accommodates more secular establishments: a hotel and the "Flower Museum," a European-style garden. Getting off the cable car, follow the other passengers to the ropeway station. Seating is on a first-come-first-serve basis, so do not dawdle. After leaving the ropeway, follow the other passengers along a road that winds slightly to the left and downhill.

Enryakuji [Open 8:30 to 4:30 in summer; 9 to 4 in winter. Tel: 012-033-0044 or 077-578-0001], a sprawling temple complex, is divided into three main areas: the Tōdō (East Precinct), the Saitō (West Precinct), and Yokawa. The shuttle bus makes a circuit of all three, and even makes a stop at a large restaurant located between the Saitō and Yokawa that has a good view of Lake Biwa. An all-day pass may be purchased at the concession in the parking lot or from a machine at the front of the bus for ¥800. Bus-pass holders get a ¥100 discount on temple admissions, so keep it handy. (Single fares are indicated on the display at the front of the bus.)

Beyond the parking area is the entrance to the main compound of the **Tōdō** (combined admission to the Tōdō and Enryakuji as a whole is ¥550, or ¥1,000 with admission to the museum). The **Kokuhōden** [Open 8:30 to 4:30. Admission ¥500] houses many of Enryakuji's treasured statues, scrolls, and manuscripts. Beautifully preserved, these artifacts will be of interest to lovers of Buddhist art. The first temple building you will see is the **Daikōdō** (Great Lecture Hall), which is filled with oil paintings depicting all the prominent priests who studied at Enryakuji, with life-size wooden statues of the most famous: Hōnen, founder of the Jōdo sect; Shinran, founder of the Jōdo Shin sect; Eisai, propagator of the Rinzai school of Zen: Dōgen, propagator of Sōtō Zen; and Nichiren, founder of the Nichiren sect. The adjacent bell tower is one structure that survived Nobunaga's fires and visitors are welcome to strike the bell. (Bells are not struck while still resonating, so still the clapper after striking.)

To the right on a separate raised area is the Ordination Hall, **Kaidan'in**. When it was established in the Heian period, this was the only such center for the ordination of Buddhist priests in the Kyoto area. The present structure dates to 1604, and the lovely gabled roof, cusped windows, and decorated hinged doors are typical architectural features of the era in which it was built. Beyond the Kaidan'in is the bright red three-tiered pagoda, completed in 1980 after a hiatus of four hundred years, and the nearby **Amidadō**, also painted a bright cinnabar, which holds daily services and is always open.

Huge cryptomeria trees line the path and add to the magnificence and allure of the temple's mountain setting, perfectly complementing the approach to the **Kompon Chūdō**, the Central Hall of the entire Enryakuji complex. Actually, there are two approaches to the Central Hall: the wide stairway on the left, and a more dramatic one beyond the **Daikokudō**. Renovated in 1996, this small temple is dedicated to Daikokuten, one of the Seven Gods of Good Fortune, who brings riches to his supplicants. The stone pillar in front of it is a prayer wheel. Supplicants say a prayer and turn it. Across from the Daikokudō is a fire station, a souvenir stand, and a resthouse, the first floor of which is a Japanese-style restaurant serving simple fare from about ¥500. Beyond the Daikokudō on the left, stone steps lead up to the **Monjurō**. This gate, a mixture of native and Chinese architecture, was originally located at the foot of Hieizan near Lake Biwa, and marked the main entrance to the Enryakuji complex. It was moved to this spot in 1642. The handsome wooden figures on the altar of the bodhisattva Monju astride a lion accompanied by four guardian kings were carved in 1700.

Exit the gate, and from the top of steep steps the distinguished Kompon Chūdō comes into view. The present structure was rebuilt in 1642, and its impressive dimensions and majestic

An ancient lantern-lined stairway descends to Saitō, or the Western Precinct.

natural setting call to mind the temple's long history and past glories. In the Heian and medieval periods, the temples of Nara and Kyoto attracted many men who took minor vows, not so much out of religious conviction as out of a desire for economic and political security. For hundreds of years, Enryakuji could thus muster larger troops of warrior-monks who periodically stormed the capital below, demanding that the monastery's rights and privileges be guaranteed by the imperial court. One can easily imagine hundreds of these fierce monks assembling here before setting out for the city below to act in the temple's interest.

Two stone-enclosed thickets of bamboo planted on either side of the main entrance follow a Chinese custom, and the bamboo itself is said to have been brought from Mt. Tientai in China, home of the Tientai (Tendai) sect, more than a thousand years ago, symbolizing the hope that Tendai Buddhism might take root and flourish in its new home. Inside, panels of painted flowers cover the coffered ceiling—reputedly offerings from the different provinces of Japan in the seventeenth century. The three huge lanterns in front of the main altar are said to have been lit by the founder and not to have been extinguished for more than a thousand years. Enshrined within the altar is an image of Yakushi Nyorai, the Buddha of spiritual and physical healing, carved by the temple's founder, Saichō. Exquisite winged creatures with female heads, some holding ancient instruments, can be seen in the carved panels that form the upper part of the wall that divides the secular from the sacred. Beyond is a cavernous sunken area with a Chinese-style inset stone floor and altars that seem to float in the blackness of the dark interior. The flickering light of the candles and the drifting scent of incense, lit by followers, enhances the holiness of this hall.

After leaving the Kompon Chūdō, you might go down the wide, shallow stone stairs on the right and retrace your steps to the parking lot to board the shuttle to the **Saitō**, or the Western Precinct. But a better way to sustain the mood inspired by the Kompon Chūdō is to walk to the Saitō along an elegant stone-lantern-lined path that will take you there in twenty minutes. After passing the Kaidan'in, the path divides. Keep to the right. On the left is a black wooden structure that encloses a sacred water source and a stone Jizō. Again the path divides. Turn right and cross the bridge that spans the highway. The small temple across the bridge is known as Sannō'in, Hall of the Mountain King. In early spring, this densely wooded area resounds with the song of bush warblers, and later, tits, grosbeaks, and pygmy woodpeckers add their notes, which in summer are drowned out by the whirring of the cicada. Midway is **Jōdoin**, a lovely temple that houses the tomb of Saichō, founder of Enryakuji. Its courtyard consists of white gravel edged with moss, and is tended by the monks as part of their training.

Where the path forks, the right path leads to two symmetrically balanced, perfectly square wooden buildings, the **Jōgyōdō** and **Hokkedō,** both dating from 1595. These buildings represent active and passive religious practice. In the Jōgyōdō (Continuous Walking Hall) monks practice circumambulating the altar for three months while reciting the *nembutsu*, while the Hokkedō (Lotus Hall) is devoted to reading and meditation upon the Lotus Sutra. These finely crafted buildings appear to be weightlessly poised on a rich carpet of star moss, and the brilliant green ground cover presents a stunning contrast to the buildings' cinnabar paint.

Walk under the passageway joining them to the **Shakadō** (Shakyamuni Hall), the Main Hall of the Saitō. Its vast, barren courtyard was once the scene of many esoteric rituals. Originally, this building was the Main Hall of Onjōji on the south side of Hieizan. Escaping destruction by Nobunaga, it was moved here in the late 1500s. Today, the Shakadō is the oldest main building on the mountain. Before the enshrined image of Shakyamuni stand two huge incense burners in which powdered incense smolders in symbolic grid patterns. The attending monk said that it takes about three days for one pattern to burn completely.

The bus stops in the Saitō parking lot so check for departure times before entering the complex.

Because **Yokawa Chūdō**, the Central Hall of the **Yokawa** precinct, is made of concrete and only fifty years old, most tourists skip it. Regardless, the atmosphere inside is deeply religious. Fragrant swirls of incense fill the darkened interior, in which an image of Shō Kannon (one of the manifestations of the bodhisattva of mercy) is enshrined. At the back of the hall, row upon row of smaller versions of this image and plaques bearing the names of petitioners are assembled. Offerings of vegetables and fruit piled on large dishes add a rustic touch. Here, as at the Kompon Chūdō, hand-painted billboards line the path near the hall. These depict the lives of important religious figures who studied at Enryakuji and played an important role in the development of Japanese Buddhism. There are also explicit renderings of the Buddhist hells.

Leave the Central Hall and walk uphill toward the bright red bell tower. Take a right and continue on to the **Eshindō**, a tiny hall where the priest Eshin studied and wrote. The modest setting of the small square building sets the tone for most of the halls in this precinct. Yokawa feels like the home of a religion with austere practices, unlike the other two precincts with their opulent buildings.

Retrace your steps to the bell and continue on to the **Ganzan Daishidō** (also known as the Shikidō). This countrified hall exudes the kind of charm one expects of a mountaintop temple. A pair of handsome *ōtsu-e* pictures on wooden panels hang under the eaves, one of a warrior, the other of a maiden. (*Ōtsu-e* are folk-art paintings from the city of Ōtsu that were sold to travelers as souvenirs at the way station on the Tokaidō Road.) In addition, two gaudily painted panels mounted high up in the interior depict Buddhist tales. One is of the demon priest known as Oni Daishi (*oni* means demon and *daishi*, teacher). Long ago, in the Heian period, there lived a very handsome priest. A favorite of the court ladies, he was invited to join a cherry blossom viewing party. When he wanted to go home, the ladies implored him to stay. Since he knew it was his handsome exterior to which they were attracted, he changed into an ugly demon and took his leave. The second picture portrays a legend about a statue of Ganzan (912–85), the temple's founder, which cast a permanent shadow on the wall of the temple. A young monk decided to paint this image, and as he applied brush to paper, the image began to disappear, stroke by stroke. At this, he and all the attendant monks attained enlightenment.

Continue past a concrete dormitory built to house monks and occasional visitors who are making a retreat. The path forking slightly to the right leads to **Jōkōin**, a small temple in a woodland setting where Nichiren studied. The path to the left leads through a heavily wooded section of varied growth along which are two large stone lanterns and a Shintō *torii* that marks the grave of Ganzan.

The last major structure is the **Nyohōtō**, a two-tiered pagoda that houses a copy of the Lotus Sutra transcribed by the great teacher Ennin (794–864) who founded the Yokawa Chūdō. Along the circular pathway are thirty-three stone images of Shō Kannon, an incarnation of the bodhisattva of mercy. Many of the faithful come to Yokawa to make this mini-pilgrimage, praying at each image and occasionally offering a coin. The first image is near the front of the Yokawa Chūdō; the second is near the pagoda. The thirty-third stone image is near the billboards with the paintings of hell. Return buses leave Yokawa on the hour and half hour.

The Tōdō, Saitō, and Yokawa are the three main precincts and the most visited. However, there is another area known as **Mudōjidani** where several more temple buildings are located. It is a fifteen- to twenty-minute walk south of the cable-car station for Sakamoto. The most important image housed at Mudōjidani is the Fudō Myōō in the **Myōōdō**. It is said to be over a thousand years old and the work of one of Enryakuji's respected priests, Soō (831–918). Wide and easy to follow, the path continues on to the bottom of the mountain at Sakamoto, but the descent is a bit steep in places. Mudōjidani is the site of one of the most austere practices undertaken by the monks who participate in Sennichi-mairi. As part of it, the practitioner, rising at two in the morning, must walk to all of the main temples in Enryakuji, stopping to pray at each, and return by six in the evening. This must be repeated one thousand times, after which the monk meditates in a sitting position for seven days and nights without water or food.

There is much to explore on this mountain. How much you can see will depend on the time you have available. Remember that rather than trying to see everything, it is better to come away with a sense of the vastness and majesty of this centuries-old monastery, once a religious city unto itself.

It is about five degrees cooler at this elevation than it is in the city below, so taking a jacket or sweater in summer and dressing warmly in other seasons is advisable. The last bus to Kyoto Station leaves at 4:30.

MT. HIEI 比叡山

Hieizan 比叡山
Kirarazaka きらら坂
Ruridō 瑠璃堂
Kurodani Seiryūji 黒谷青竜寺
Bentendō 弁天堂

For centuries, the only access to the mountain temple complex of Enryakuji was via footpaths that wound up Hieizan (Mt. Hiei) from Kyoto or the lowlands around Lake Biwa. Some men climbed these trails to renounce the world, study the Buddhist teachings, and enter the priesthood. Others—the infamous warrior-monks of Enryakuji—stormed back down the same trails into the capital, causing Emperor Shirakawa (1053–1129), for one, to lament his lack of control over these marauding forces. Today, a scenic drive sweeps up the mountain and through the temple grounds, making it accessible to the casual visitor, but the well-trodden, thousand-year-old paths remain.

Several well-known trails begin in the vicinity of Shūgakuin Rikyū. Two can be reached from the Shūgakuin Station on the Keifuku Railway or the Shūgakuin-mae bus stop north of Kitayama Dōri on Shirakawa Dōri. The climb takes approximately two hours to reach the top of Mt. Hiei (Hieizan) and at least two hours to return, depending on your choice of trails. The Kirarazaka Trail is steep, but easier going up than coming down. The trail from the temple Sekizan Zen'in is slightly wider and the more popular of the two. Shoes suitable for hiking are recommended, as is bringing something to drink, especially in hot weather. This hike can be done year round, but during the winter months patches of snow and ice may make the path slippery. An excellent reason to stay

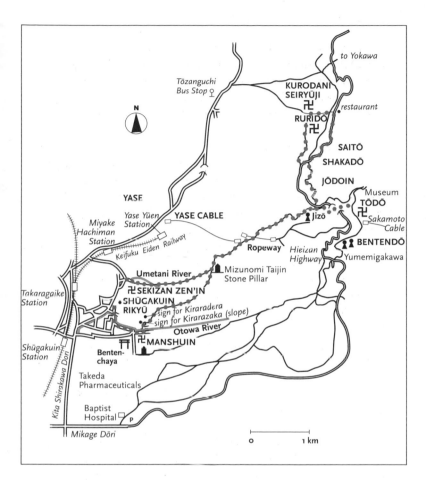

MT. HIEI

on the trails is to avoid meeting two poisonous vipers (the *mamu-shi* and the *yamakagashi*; stamping the ground should drive them away). Another reason to keep to the trail is the poison sumac plant (*urushi*), which grows in abundance, and the painful sting of the centipede (*mukade*) that clings to the undersides of leaves in the summer.

To reach **Kirarazaka** (Sparkling Slope), walk south from Shūgakuin Rikyū along the road that skirts the rice fields adjacent to the imperial villa. Cross the Otowa River, a narrow stream with steep concrete banks, and turn left toward the mountain. After a few minutes, the path crosses the river again, at which junction stands a low wooden sign pointing to Kirarazaka and a wooden plaque about the temple, Kiraradera. (The paved path on the right leads to a rest area in the mountains.)

Kirara actually refers to mica, a shiny mineral that gives rocks or sand a sparkling appearance, and from which the slope takes its name. Now badly eroded, the path has been worn to a deep groove that is just narrow enough for one person to pass through. The wooden plaque tells of **Kiraradera** (also known as Unmoji), a Tendai temple that was founded here in the late ninth century. A two-and-a-half-meter statue of Fudō Myōō was housed in this temple, and the slope was also known as Fudōzaka. Kiraradera occupied vast precincts here for nearly a thousand years until 1885, when it was dismantled during the upsurge of anti-Buddhist sentiment in the years following the Meiji Restoration. Most of its buildings were incorporated into Enryakuji. The Fudō Hall was transfered to Sekizan Zen'in, and a stone image inscribed with the date 1126 is now housed in Zenge'in. Follow the Kirarazaka sign to a narrow, dirt trail that winds upward past stone posts strung with barbed wire. This fence encloses Shūgakuin Rikyū.

The other trail starts in front of Sekizan Zen'in. Pass through the temple's stone *torii* and walk toward the wooden temple gate. The path to the left of the gate runs along the perimeter of the temple, which is enclosed with stone posts strung with barbed wire. When the trail emerges into a residential area, stay next to the barbed wire fence. After a few minutes, the fence ends and the slender Umetani River appears on the left. On its lower reaches, this path is wide enough for two, and occasional clearings provide sunny patches on an otherwise shady trek. The woods are varied and excellent for bird watching. (Besides the usual tits, pygmy woodpeckers, and sparrows, Hieizan is home to the warbler, gray-faced buzzard eagle, common cuckoo, and red-rumped swallow.) Wildflowers grow along the path, scenting the air and adding touches of color to the green mountainside.

After forty-five minutes, both trails merge at a large stone pillar on which are the engraved words *Mizunomi taijin no ato.* This stone serves as a memorial to Chigusa Tadaaki, who died on this spot in 1336 as he returned to Kyoto from battle. Chigusa was the deeply trusted councilor of Emperor Go-Daigo (1288–1339) who fought the army of Ashikaga Tadayoshi (1306–52) at Mizunomi in present-day Shiga Prefecture.

At the *Mizunomi taijin* junction, take the uphill trail. It is another thirty minutes or so to the cable-car station. Midway is a section of forest planted with *hinoki*, or cypress trees, and beyond this, about a hundred meters off the trail, is a large tombstone marking the grave of Chigusa Tadaaki, a warrior who lived in the fourteenth century. The trail circles around the abandoned ski slope and buildings, and another worn trail crosses the grassy slope.

Ten minutes beyond it are a stone lantern and boulder engraved with images of a Buddha and two bodhisattvas, which mark an entrance to Enryakuji. The trail continues until it reaches the pedestrian bridge that spans the Hieizan Driveway. To the right is the Tōdō, or Eastern Precinct of Enryakuji. Across the bridge is a small temple building, the residence of the mountain deity. Farther on is a stone-lantern-lined stairway that descends to Jōdoin in Saitō, or the Western Precinct.

Hikers can descend via the same trail or take another route, one that passes the temple west of the oldest extant structure on Mt. Hiei, **Rurido** (Lapis Lazuli Hall), the only building to escape the destruction wrought by Oda Nobunaga in 1571.

The trail beyond Rurido is closed and to reach **Kurodani Seiryuji**, a Tendai temple where Honen (1133–1212) first studied Buddhism, one must continue to walk along the highway toward Yokawa. A new path to the left will lead you to Seiryuji.

At the age of forty-three, Honen established the Jodo sect, which maintains that salvation can be obtained by repeating the name of Amida Buddha. Four-hundred-year-old paintings of paradise and divine beings cover the walls and ceiling of Seiryuji's Main Hall. A gold-leaf image of Amida sits on the main altar under a glittering canopy. Several images stand along the back wall, among them a gilded image of an eleven-headed bodhisattva of mercy, Juichimen Kannon. Visitors are welcome to view the images and to partake of the tea set out on the low table.

The path to Rurido and Seiryuji starts behind the Shakado in the Western Precinct of Enryakuji. From there, cross the Hieizan Driveway and take the unpaved road marked by a Japanese sign. This leads to Rurido. To reach Seiryuji, visitors are requested to return to the highway, turn left and walk until they reach the sign on the left for the temple, and approach it that way. Traveling down the mountain from Seiryuji requires care since half of the trail resembles a gully of sharp, loose rock; allow about forty-five minutes for a safe descent. Packing a pair of gloves might prove beneficial.

From Seiryuji a trail leads straight down to the Tozanguchi bus stop in Yase. Kyoto buses depart here for Kyoto Station, Sanjo Keihan Station, and Shijo-Kawaramachi approximately every fifteen minutes. City Bus No. 6 goes to the Kitaoji Bus Terminal and subway.

The other descent starts at the Sakamoto Cable Station, in the Todo precincts.

After emerging from the "ski" area, instead of crossing the

Shintōism and Buddhism are both present at Bentendō.

bridge and Hieizan highway, veer right and walk toward a stone statue of Jizō and a black-fenced enclosed sacred spring. Just beyond is a ticket gate to Tōdō where pamphlets about Enryakuji and a map come with the ¥550 entrance fee. On the grounds are restrooms and restaurants located near the Main Hall, Kompon Chūdō, and at the bus terminal. At the ticket booths, if you have no intention of visiting Enryakuji, please tell the ticket taker: "Hiking *dake desukara haikan shimasen. Tōri nukete ikimasu.*" ("I'm only hiking through and will not enter Enryakuji.") Or, you can show this to the attendant: ハイキングだけですから拝観しません。通り抜けて行きます。

Large signs point the way to the Sakamoto Cable Station, a large square yellow building down past the No. 3 car parking lot. A ten-minute walk past the cable leads to a stone *torii* on the right. Go through the *torii* and down the stairs to the **Bentendō** (the path continues on to the left to the Myōōdō temple), a shrine dedicated to the Goddess of Wealth and Good Fortune. Benten is also referred to as Benzaiten, a deity which is often associated with a dragon or snake because the figure of the deity Uga-jin, who is half man and half snake, rests atop her head. For this reason, two snakes are engraved in the flower receptacles in front of the Main Hall. (In Japan, snakes are associated with money, and finding a snakeskin or even a live specimen in one's house is considered lucky. Women born in the year of the snake are considered to be great beauties, and the men handsome.) Benten also is one of the Seven Gods of Good Fortune, often pictured holding a lute.

This particular shrine has a number of devotees who make monthly visits via cable car or car. The walk down takes approximately two hours, and except for a few stretches near the beginning and end of the trail, is relatively easy.

The path on the left of Bentendō has a stone post that reads, "The approach to the waterfall," and, after two minutes, descends to a constructed waterfall pouring forth from a dragon's mouth, a place where monks performed the religious practice of standing under the chilling stream.

Continue past the two small stone images of Fudō Myōō on the left wayside. The path is worn in places as it winds up and down; attempts to widen it and prevent landslides are underway. Most of the signs warn to watch one's footing or head where jagged boulders jut out of the mountainside. Pass another stone *torii* and cross the flat wooden bridge. After thirty minutes, the next stone *torii*, erected during the Meiji era, comes into view. There are several other stone *torii* on this route, all inscribed with Meiji-era dates (1852–1912), a time when nationalist tendencies determined that Shintō was the state religion and Buddhist practices were considered alien. Soon after, the path divides: one to the left goes to Yumemigaoka, an amusement park for children; the other goes under the road and eventually splits again, with one trail heading to Kitashirakawa and the other to Shūgakuin.

At several places along the way, the Higashiyama trail markers indicate the two main destinations: Kitashirakawa, which ends near the Baptist Hospital northeast of Kitashirakawa Dōri and Mikage Dōri; and Shūgakuin. A word about these markers: the solid line indicates the path to be taken, and the dotted line, an alternate path. Try to stay with the trail markers because there are many, many small paths that meander through these foothills, mostly used by woodsmen. It is easy to lose one's way. From trail marker No. 60, it is about twenty minutes down the Kitashirakawa trail to the shrine near the Baptist Hospital parking lot. The trail has small streams on both sides in turn, and the bamboo grass- and fern-lined path is quite beautiful, a small throwback to what Japan's forests must have looked like before the timber industry replanted its mountains. The water pouring forth at this shrine is potable and delicious.

The alternate route, the Shūgakuin path, comes out just south of Manshuin and the Takeda Pharmaceutical Company. It is here that the stone *torii* marking the approach to Bentendō is located. Across from Manshuin is the Benten-chaya noodle shop and small shrine, also called Bentendō. In the past, people walked up the mountain to the main shrine, but those who could no longer make the trek prayed at this smaller Bentendō.

Either path is a satisfying walk, however on the lower reaches, a land reclamation project is underway to reforest spots along the Otowa and Shirakawa rivers. Concrete dams attempt to slow the loss of hillside from heavy rains, and trees have been cut to widen the paths, which present a jarring sight until the project is complete and the greenery reasserts itself.

Beautiful in all seasons, the mountain is well trod by student groups, middle-aged hikers, and those trekking as a religious practice.

ŌHARA 大原

Raigōin 来迎院
Sanzen'in 三千院
Jikkōin 実光院
Shōrin'in 勝林院
Hōsen'in 宝線院
Jakkōin 寂光院
Amidaji 阿弥陀寺

Crossing the mountains that surround Kyoto was once a perilous undertaking. Until the nineteenth century, only a few steep and narrow roads led out of the city to the west, north, and east. One of these roads, Saba Kaidō (Mackerel Highway), even older than the capital, winds its way to the Japan Sea, along which seafood made its way to Kyoto markets. This highway passes through Yase and Ōhara, once self-contained villages, now northeastern suburbs of the Kyoto metropolis. Ōhara lies in the shadow of Hieizan, and the Ro and Ritsu Rivers flow through the valley. The beauty of Kyoto's seasons is very much in evidence in this farming community, and visitors come to enjoy the cherry and maple trees. Many of Ōhara's farmhouses still have thatched roofs, the distinctive shapes of which have sometimes been covered with tin to prevent fire. Visitors should allow a whole day to explore this district. Among the sights are a number of famous temples, including Sanzen'in, founded by the monk Saichō in 788; Raigōin, Shōrin'in, and Hōsen'in, which housed students of Buddhist liturgical music; Jakkōin, famous in literature as the refuge of an emperor's mother; and the remote and secluded Amidaji, a Pure Land temple.

There are a number of buses going to Ōhara. City Bus Kita 6 leaves from the Kitaōji Bus Terminal, while Kyoto Buses 16 and 17 depart from Kyoto Station (¥580) and reach their terminus at Ōhara

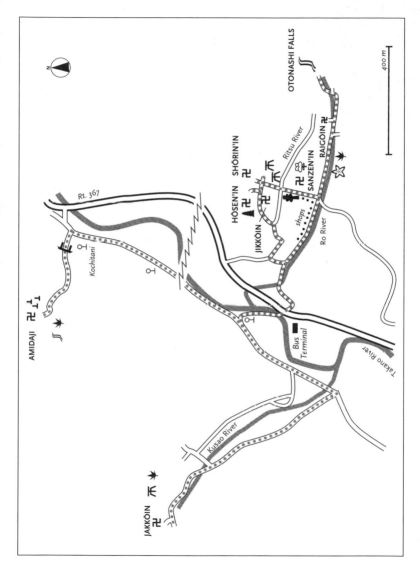

ŌHARA

via Shijō-Kawaramachi (¥510), Keihan Sanjō Station (¥470), and Demachi Yanagi Station (¥410). Kyoto buses from the Kokusai subway station (¥340) also go to Ōhara and may be the fastest way to get there. (These buses often have a ticket-dispensing machine at the back of the bus where one boards. The fare changes according to the distance traveled and amounts are shown on a screen at the front of the bus. The number on the ticket indicates the fare to be paid when disembarking.) A few steps from the bus terminal in Ōhara is the beginning of a footpath that leads up to Sanzen'in. Some of the signs on the path are in English, and all arrows point in the direction of the temple. While he was overseeing the construction of the vast Tendai temple complex of Enryakuji, Saichō founded Sanzen'in to house an image of Yakushi Nyorai, the Buddha of Healing. Originally located on the other side of Hieizan, in Sakamoto, the temple was moved to its present site centuries later.

A stream rushing down the mountain on the right of the sloping path to the temple accompanies you, as do the cries of the *Ōharame* women in traditional farming costumes, inviting visitors to try their home-grown products. The left side of the path is lined with tiny stalls selling rice cakes filled with sweet bean paste, rice dumplings on sticks, and cups of delicious *shisocha*, or beefsteak-plant tea, as well as restaurants, many of which serve simple country-style meals.

At the top of the slope, the path widens. Several large, handsomely painted signboards depict the Ōhara area and its temples. A left here will take you directly to Sanzen'in, but continue straight ahead to **Raigōin** [Open 9 to 5. Admission ¥300. Tel: 744-2161], which is a ten-minute walk up a quiet gravel path leading toward the mountain. This temple was the center of musical training for Enryakuji. The monk Ennin (744–864) brought back a form of chanting from China called *shōmyō*, which became the basis for all Buddhist chants and even influenced secular music. Another monk, Ryōnin (1072–1132), is renowned for consolidating seven styles of chanting. He founded Raigōin to train monks in liturgical music, and as part of that legacy, a cassette tape of *shōmyō* chants by modern-day monks is on sale at the ticket booth for ¥2,000.

At one time, there were as many as forty-nine buildings in this complex. The main building of today's small temple faces a garden of azalea and moss that is a sunny respite from the shady cryptomeria trees that cover the mountain. Inside are three gilded Buddhist images that have been designated Important Cultural Properties, as well as two standing figures of Fudō Myōō and Bishamonten, carved in the latter part of the Heian period (794–1185). A photo in the Main Hall shows a New Year's ceremony in which monks chant to the beat of wooden sticks against the floor (an event which takes place on the afternoon of January 2).

The Ro River flows past Raigōin to the south. At one point, a simple bridge crosses the river and small wooden signs mark the way to **Otonashi no Taki** (Soundless Falls). Surrounded by wisteria, cryptomeria, and maple trees, this waterfall is better described as a cascade, as the river tumbles over a large jutting boulder. Legend says that the monk Ennin silenced the waterfall. Supposedly, monks came here to compete with the sound of the falls as part of their vocal training. One version of the story says that no matter how loudly Ennin sang, he couldn't hear himself over the falls, so he put a spell on it. Another version relates that he rearranged the shape of the boulder to soften the sound.

Retrace your steps to the signboards, and turn right to **Sanzen'in** [Open 8:30 to 4; 5 in summer. Admission ¥550. Tel: 744-2531], readily recognized by its fortress-like wall. After passing through the Reception Hall of the Abbot's Quarters, the first garden that comes into view is the Shuhekien. A spreading maple tree shelters the azalea-bordered carp pond. Rhododendron, a miniature pine, bush clover, and Solomon's seal have been carefully arranged to delight viewers in all seasons. Although the second building, the Shinden, is new, it houses statues designated as Important Cultural Properties: a central figure of Amida, flanked on the left by a thousand-year-old image of Fudō Myōō backed by flames, and on the right by Kannon. The last rooms to the east were for the use of recent emperors. Painted at the time of the building's construction in 1926, the sliding doors are the absolute in minimalist art. The soft outline of a rainbow testifies to the Japanese love of simplicity.

The lush green Yuseien garden that spreads outward from the porch of the Shinden has the hall known as the Ōjō Gokurakuin as its focal point. A canopy of tall cryptomerias filters the sunlight reaching the rich moss ground covering, creating a cushion-like setting for the hall. Constructed in 985 and rebuilt in 1143, the Ōjō Gokurakuin is the oldest temple hall in Ōhara. Its convex ceiling, which resembles an overturned boat, was once completely covered with scenes of Amida's paradise, as were the walls and beams. Now, darkened by age, only vestiges of the colorful scenes are visible. The impressive seated Amida was sculpted in 986, and the two kneeling attendant bodhisattvas, Seishi and Kannon (with the lotus) were completed later. All three were constructed by fitting together carved blocks of cedar, covering them with cloth, then lacquering them—a technique practiced in the late tenth and the eleventh centuries. The exceptional beauty of their forms and the splendor of the setting are unforgettable. All three images have been designated Important Cultural Properties.

Sanzen'in is filled with visitors during the spring when the cherry trees are in bloom, and in autumn, when the maples turn red. Now, thanks to the rather recently landscaped hydrangea garden to the north of Yuseien, Sanzen'in has several beautiful varieties of *ajisai*, or hydrangea, including one delicate variety, called the *gaku ajisai* (lace-cap hydrangea) which produces a flower with peripheral blossoms. Because of the acidity of the soil at Sanzen'in, almost all of the hydrangeas are a rich blue. Besides the two indig-

A small pond catches the sunlight at the little-visited garden at Jikkōin.

enous varieties growing here, one native to Portugal was presented
to the temple fifty years ago by the Portuguese consul in Kobe. Its
stems are spindly, and the leaves sharp and narrow. The blossoms
have a delicate star-shape, hence its name: *hoshi ajisai,* or star hydrangea. The garden was the pet project of Kambara Gen'yū, a former abbot of Sanzen'in. Years ago, he decided to re-landscape the
hilly back portion of the temple grounds. Today, there are about
three thousand bushes of five varieties that have been naturalized
among the tall cedars.

One path through the hillside garden leads to a two-meter
stone image of Amida. A poem in the Japanese brochure describes
thin wisps of smoke from charcoal makers' kilns cloaking the valley of Ōhara. At one time, many of Ōhara's residents made their
living from making charcoal, and the woodcutters venerated this
stone image, which is said to have been carved for them in the
Kamakura period (1185–1333) by the monk Ryōzen. A rest area in

the front part of the hydrangea garden, across from the Gomagidō, offers free samples of a local tea made from the leaves of the *shiso* (beefsteak plant). The brew has a slightly salty taste and contains flecks of gold, added for medicinal efficacy. Packets of it are on sale.

Often overlooked by large guided tour groups, the three temples just north of Sanzen'in generally are quiet and uncrowded. Although the center of chanting was Raigōin, these temples also housed and taught students of sacred music. From Sanzen'in walk north, passing a towering three-hundred-year-old tree on the left, and cross the Ritsu River. On the right are the tombs of the exiled emperors Go-Toba and Juntoku. On the left, a humble wooden tile-roofed gate leads to Jikkōin [Open 9 to 5. Tel: 744-2537]. Steps down to the main building lead to a delicate little garden and a new stroll garden. The ¥800 cost of admission includes a sweet and a bowl of green tea.

At the end of the same road is the stately **Shōrin'in**. As there seldom is anyone in attendance, just leave ¥300 in the container at the gate and enter. The Edo-period building with its cedar bark roof seems to stand aloof from its treeless, sunny front garden. The main image enshrined is Amida, which like the Amida trinity in the Ōjō Gorakuin of Sanzen'in, faces south. Fudō Myōō is the attendant on the left. Bishamonten, guardian general of the north, is on the right.

To the west of Shōrin'in is **Hōsen'in** [Open 9 to 5. Admission ¥800. Tel: 744-2409]. Admission includes a sweet and a bowl of tea and a view of the valley, which makes this a perfect place to relax and enjoy some refreshments. The building beyond the front garden is the temple proper where a huge, many-limbed white pine has made its home for seven hundred years. Surrounded by wooden supports, its dome-like upper branches completely shade the moss below, reminiscent of a king whose voluminous robes are carried by many attendants. The west-facing garden on the side is bordered by a hedge, and beyond, a leafy bamboo grove allows a glimpse of mountains across the valley between the smooth green bamboo trunks. The ceiling of the outer corridor is constructed of wooden planks taken from a building at Fushimi Castle in which hundreds of retainers of the first Tokugawa shogun, Ieyasu, committed ritual suicide (*seppuku*) rather than surrender during battle. The blood-stained floor was broken up and incorporated as ceilings in several of Kyoto's temples so that prayers would be said in perpetuity for the warriors' souls. A reminder of Hōsen'in's musical heritage, a primitive xylophone, is displayed in one alcove. A tiny mallet is set beside it for visitors who wish to test the timbre of the granite-like rock.

Retrace your steps after leaving Hōsen'in, or follow a winding passageway down to the right until it rejoins the shop-lined path. From the traffic light at the bottom of the path, it is a twenty-minute walk across the valley to **Jakkōin** [Open 9 to 5. Admission ¥600. Tel: 744-2545], a nunnery since 1186. Here, the empress Kenreimon'in retired from the world to pray for the soul of her son, the infant emperor Antoku, and those of her clansmen who drowned during the battle of Dannoura in 1185. Kenreimon'in was the daughter of the head of the Taira clan, a warrior family of Kyoto. Their position was challenged by their rivals, the Minamoto, who drove them from the capital. In the straits of Dannoura, when the Taira realized that they were about to lose the decisive battle, Kenreimon'in's mother jumped into the sea, holding her infant grandson, the emperor Antoku. Kenreimon'in followed, but was pulled out by a member of the Minamoto army and returned to Kyoto. She first went to Chōrakuji in Higashiyama where she cut her hair and became a nun, a practice encouraged for aristocratic widows. She then retired to remote Jakkōin, where she spent the rest of her life in prayer. Time passed without contact with the capital until Go-Shirakawa, a retired emperor, decided to make her a visit. Upon seeing her humble hermitage, he was so moved by the cruel fate that this former empress had to endure that he composed a poem about the stillness of the temple embodied by the cherry tree that stood in the garden. Today, the dead gnarled root of that cherry tree is respectfully enclosed by a rope, as a reminder of the imperial nun and visitor. This temple is much humbler than Sanzen'in; its appeal is intertwined with the very tragic figure of Kenreimon'in. The image in the Main Hall is of Jizō, the bodhisattva particularly revered as the guardian of children. A steep stone stairway east of the temple leads up to Kenreimon'in's tomb. Now enclosed with a stone fence and landscaped with pines, the tomb resembles the many other imperial tombs found throughout Kyoto. Erected in the Meiji era, many centuries after her death in 1213, it looks like a modern monument, one that does not adequately reflect the antiquity of the site.

In Ōhara, several routes lead to Sanzen'in and Jakkōin, and even the visitor who strays from the main path is assured of many delightful discoveries in the form of handsome thatch-roofed houses and thick-walled storehouses. The walls of many houses are rust-red. Called *bengara*, this color is found on typical Japanese farmhouses; you are unlikely to encounter it in central Kyoto unless the homeowner tries to affect a country look.

Another of Ōhara's temples, **Amidaji** [Open 9 to 4:30. Admission ¥300. Tel: 744-2048], is just enough out of the way that few people take the time to visit it. At the bottom of the slope leading to Sanzen'in is a traffic signal. North of that traffic signal, across the bridge on the left, a road leads to Amidaji in Kochitani, the Valley of Ancient Knowledge. The walk takes forty minutes. Buses that travel this route leave the terminal in Ōhara approximately on the hour and the ¥160 ride takes ten minutes. (If you are unsure of which bus to take, ask a passenger or the driver, "*Kochitani desu ka?*" and you will either be motioned aboard or pointed to another bus or boarding place.) Kochitani is the third stop from the Ōhara terminal.

A distinctive Chinese-style gate provides an exotic entrance to the narrow valley in which the temple is located. The contribution of a believer, the gate is only sixty years old. The walk to the temple takes twenty minutes and goes through a thick and varied forest in which the stillness is punctuated by the splashing stream on the left, the calls of birds, and the wind in the trees. This valley is renowned for a variety of maples called *Takao kaede*, four hundred of which are found here. Within sight of the temple, near a short two-step waterfall, there is a massive ancient maple believed to be almost eight hundred years old. This tree may also be the largest of its kind in Kyoto. A sloping walk leads up to the temple.

In the Main Hall, the central figure is a seated image of Amida Nyorai, designated an Important Cultural Property. The slim, hirsute standing image on the right is that of the founder with strands of his hair attached. The mummified remains of the founder are entombed in a cave-like shelter within the precincts. (By his own wish, he fasted until death, often in a seated position of meditation, and then was buried for several years before an image of him was placed as a Buddha figure within the temple.) Little has been done to remodel or extend the present buildings, which are old and almost devoid of color. Someday they will be rebuilt, but now the creaking floors and bareness are part of the temple's charm and mystery. Further testimony to the temple's age are three old palanquins that hang from the eaves on the east side of the Main Hall. Also on the grounds are a bell tower and six stone statues of Jizō, representing that bodhisattva's vow to save those suffering in all six realms of rebirth: heavenly beings, humans, warring spirits, animals, hungry ghosts, and hell.

Amidaji is in a very quiet area. There are no shops along the way, nor restaurants. To accommodate visitors, tea is set out in the temple's front room. The long walk up through the forest deepens the feeling of antiquity and remoteness that imbue the valley, a sense that must have been present at Ōhara's other temples not so long ago.

貴

舟

鞍

馬

KIBUNE 貴舟
and KURAMA 鞍馬

Kibune River 貴船川
Kibune Shrine 貴舟神社
Kuramadera 鞍馬寺
Yuki Shrine 由岐神社
Kurama Onsen 鞍馬温泉

Kibune Shrine and the temple Kuramadera are locat-
ed in the northern part of Kyoto, only fifteen minutes
by train from the city center, yet in surprisingly rural
settings. Kurama is a small village and Kibune home
only to a few restaurant owners whose establishments
line a strip of road beside the sparkling Kibune River.

Kurama-bound Eizan Railway trains depart from Demachi Yanagi Station approximately twice an hour. Kibuneguchi, the station at the road leading to Kibune Shrine, is one stop before the terminus at Kurama; the fare is ¥410. The shrine is a thirty-minute walk from the station up the gently sloping valley. There is also a bus for the shrine (¥160) that leaves from a stop just outside the station. A return bus leaves from a stop near the shrine in time to meet the Demachi-bound train. A one-way train fare is ¥210.

A variety of old forest growth and wildflowers fill this beautiful ravine and line the pristine **Kibune River**. Only the cleanest rivers attract the brown dipper (*kawagarasu*), which can be seen here. This plump bird, the color of dark chocolate, dives into the water and while submerged, strolls along the stream bottom searching for food. Another testimony to the purity of the water is seen in June when hundreds of fireflies hover and dart over the river. Large fence-enclosed boulders along the road on the riverside near

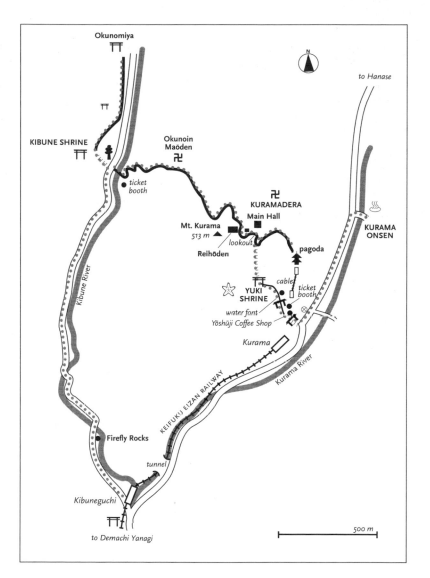

KIBUNE and KURAMA

the station are known as the **Firefly Rocks**. The name refers to a poem written by the Heian-period poetess, Izumi Shikibu. One evening while waiting in vain for her lover to meet her in this area, she felt as though her spirit turned into a firefly to announce its presence. Tiny firefly replicas are among the amulets available at Kibune Shrine, an appropriate choice for those awaiting love.

The approach to **Kibune Shrine** [Tel: 741-2016] is marked by a huge red *torii* that sits at the bottom of a lantern-lined stone stairway shaded by towering trees. Next to the *torii* is a magnificent six-hundred-year-old zelkova tree with a tiny unpainted shrine at its base. At the top of the stairs is another gate, beside which stands a three-hundred-year-old Judas tree encircled with sacred rope. Behind the tree is an interesting garden in the shape of a boat, in deference to the legend that claims Takaokami no Kami, the god of rain, and the deity enshrined in the Main Hall, descended to this valley in a boat. Festivals held on March 9, June 1, July 17, and November 7 all give thanks to this spirit. Shintō is deeply concerned with purification and cleansing, and shrine visitors regularly rinse their mouths and wash their hands before offering prayers. The water here is particularly delicious, but take it from the spout, not the trough. The shrine's Main Hall looks fresh and clean, as befits the home of the rain god.

The archives of Kibune Shrine record that it was founded about fifteen hundred years ago at a site eight hundred meters up the road where the god descended to earth in his yellow boat (*kibune*). Later *ki* was given the reading "divine," the meaning it has today. In 1045, a great flood made it necessary to reconstruct the shrine on its present site, but the original shrine, Okunomiya, remains. Along the way to Okunomiya is a red *torii* which marks the way to **Musubisha,** a subsidiary shrine visited by couples wishing to "tie the knot" (a metaphor common to both Japanese and English). Oblong green strips of paper sold at the main shrine for ¥200 are tied and left on the picket fence with a prayer that the god may grant the union of the two inscribed names. A simpler gesture is to knot the leaves of a local wild orchid or vine, say a prayer, and tie it to the fence. The area behind the shrine has been landscaped with paths and hydrangea bushes. A large red *torii* marks the beginning of the path leading to **Okunomiya**, near which is a forty-three-ton boulder formed of volcanic ash. Farther up the valley, on the grounds of Okunomiya, is an ancient mound of stones in the shape of a boat to the left of an open stage. The area's slightly higher elevation and dense vegetation moistened by the river makes Kibune a favorite summer spot for Kyotoites.

To offer relief from the enervating heat of Kyoto's summer, many of the restaurants in Kibune—located along the river near the shrine—set up platforms in the river so that diners may be cooled by the water flowing beneath them. Meals served on these platforms are quite expensive and specialize in seasonal delicacies. Lunch ranges from ¥2,500 to ¥10,000. Besides the exclusive restaurants, there is a fair selection of reasonably priced rustic eateries and newer coffee shops to chose from.

The trail that leads over the spine of Kuramayama from Kibune to **Kuramadera** [Open 9 to 4:30; 5 in summer. Tel: 741-2003] begins at the red bridge that crosses the river a little below the main shrine. This entrance to the mountain is known as the Nishinomon (West Gate), and the sign says that it is a 588-meter walk to Okunoin, the Inner Hall of the temple. When the admission booth is closed, the climb is free; otherwise visitors are asked to contribute ¥200 to the mountain's upkeep. The stone steps near the bottom are wide and easy to climb, but after a few minutes the roots of trees form the natural stairway under a canopy of towering trees. Only when packed with snow or slippery after a heavy rain would this walk be difficult, although it is steep in places. Drinking water is not available on the mountain, so you should take some, especially on hot days.

Ancient cypress, cedar, pine, wild camellia, mountain cherry, and maples make this one of Kyoto's most inviting mountain hikes. A number of small, low signs near the trail give explanation of the limestone outcroppings that appear along the way. This limestone, the signs explain, consists of compacted piles of shells of creatures similar to modern oysters and snails, as well as plants which flourished on the ocean floor a billion years ago. Until about eighty years ago, this stone was one of the souvenirs sought by tourists to the area: it contains deposits of flint that were valued for firemaking.

After twenty minutes or so, you will reach **Okunoin**, the innermost hall of the mountain, a place imbued with one of the most exotic myths in the realm. Shaded by a luxurious and varied forest, the hall sits atop an ancient volcano that formed the mountain. According to legend, 6.5 million years ago, Maō-son, conqueror of evil and spirit of the earth, descended here from the planet Venus to help humankind overcome wickedness. Local people claim that in ancient times this spirit was called Kurama, and the mountain was named after it. The deity is enshrined in the smaller building behind the Main Hall. Before it lies a collection of limestone rocks, representative of those thrown to the surface millions of years ago when the volcano erupted and broke through what was then the floor of the sea.

Nearby are large rocks that appear to have been cleanly sliced in half. Legend attributes this to a young boy who secretly met here with a master swordsman to learn the art of warfare. This young boy was Ushiwakamaru, later known as Yoshitsune, one of Japan's most famous heroes. The members of his clan, the Minamoto, had been killed by rivals when he was a small child, but his life was spared on the condition that he enter the priesthood at Kuramadera. People came to believe that the split stones were the result of Yoshitsune's skill with the sword. Actually, limestone is soft enough for rainwater to penetrate, and if water collects near the center of a boulder and weakens it, the rock will split cleanly apart.

A five-minute walk brings you to the Fudōdō (not open for viewing), which houses the Buddhist guardian deity Fudō Myōō. Tall, straight cedar trees encircled with sacred straw rope stand in the clearing near this hall, gigantic reminders of the age of the forest. A small shrine dedicated to Yoshitsune is located on the upper edge of the clearing and the sign relates the history of his clan and his heroic deeds. After another ten minutes, there is a small unpainted shrine tucked against the roots of a massive cedar tree. This marks another spot

Rows of lanterns beckon the way to Kibune Shrine.

where Yoshitsune, after slipping away from the watchful eyes of his teachers, came to practice his skills as a warrior. This cedar tree is reputed to be so tall that no sunlight penetrates to the forest floor, making it the perfect place for a stealthy swordsman to practice unseen. The flat, raised ground opposite this sacred tree is crisscrossed by interwoven tree roots, evidence of the erosion Kuramayama is undergoing. This area also is considered a sacred place, one to which the monk Gantei, a pupil of the founder of Tōshōdaiji in Nara, was led in 770 by a vision of a white horse.

The path continues until it reaches a wooden fence that marks the end of the forest trail and emerges into a large, open sunny area where the temple museum, the **Reihōden** [Open 9 to 4. Closed Mondays and holidays, and mid-December through February. Admission ¥200. Tel: 741-2368], is located. The first floor exhibit is dedicated to the natural history of the mountain; the second to scrolls and artifacts related to the history of the temple; the third, a collection of Buddhist images from the late Heian and Kamakura periods, some Important Cultural Properties, one a National Treasure. Among the precious images is one curious item, the remains of an ancient cryptomeria that stood near the place where Maō-son descended to earth. An early believer claimed that when a cloud hovered near this tree, the image of the spirit was reflected on the tree. It was then regarded as sacred and was given this honored place.

The main temple buildings of Kuramadera were destroyed by fires over the ages, and the modern ones are brilliant red ferroconcrete structures. The central image in the **Main Hall** is a statue of Bishamonten, the guardian deity of the north, brought from Nara when the temple was founded in 770 by Gantei. (The two images flanking the central one, Maō-son and a thousand-armed Kannon, are not on view.) Although the building is concrete, the atmosphere of the interior is ancient and spiritual, and its setting beautiful. One of Kyoto's most beautiful festivals takes place here the night of the full moon in May.

Directly in front of the Main Hall a red fence and straw rope enclose a large low rock surrounded by a halo of moss; the rock upon which Maō-son descended to earth. A short walk from the main precinct of the temple, the path divides. To the left is the two-tiered pagoda and the cable-car station. The three-minute cable-car ride to the bottom of the mountain costs ¥100, but this means missing several sights along the winding descent, the most interesting of which is **Yuki Shrine**. Moved from the imperial palace grounds in 940, this shrine was placed here to protect the city from the evil forces thought to emanate from the north. Reconstructed by Toyotomi Hideyori (Hideyoshi's son) in 1610, the wooden pavilion-like building is noted for its elegant cypress roof and its divided hall. The shrine precincts have several immense trees known as *tamasugi* (ball cryptomeria), as the ends of the branches seem to form fists or balls.

Between the main temple gate and stairs is the coffee shop and restaurant **Yōshūji** [Open 10 to 6. Closed Tuesdays. Tel: 741-2848], which, besides the usual simple fare, serves temple vegetarian meals from ¥2,100. An English menu is available.

Kurama Onsen, one of Kyoto's loveliest outdoor baths, is a fifteen-minute walk away through the little community of Kurama. The homes built along the sloping road are in a distinctive architectural style. Kurama Onsen [Open 10 to 9. Tel: 741-2131] charges ¥1,100 for use of the outdoor bath and ¥1,600 for both the indoor and outdoor baths, the spring water of which has been heated. Tickets may be purchased from the machine at the entrance to the main building or at the foot of the steps leading up to the outdoor bath. Shampoo, rinse, and soap are available free in the baths. Remember as a courtesy to other bathers, Japanese wash themselves or rinse well before they enter the tub. Washcloths are not put in the water, but often bathers put them on their heads while they sit and soak. There is also a restaurant offering reasonably priced dishes from ¥1,000 to ¥3,000. The free shuttle bus takes bathers back to the station to meet departing trains, but it is a good idea to check departure times before entering the bath to make sure that you will have enough time to relax and enjoy soaking beneath the treetop-framed sky.

KAMIGAMO 上賀茂

Kamigamo Shrine 上賀茂神社
Nishimura House 西村屋
Ōta Shrine 太田神社
Kyoto Botanical Gardens 京都府立植物園

Along the upper reaches of the Kamo River, to the east of Misonobashi, is Kamigamo Shrine. Founded in 678, it is one of the city's oldest Shintō shrines. After Kyoto became the capital, the shrine was headed by an imperial priestess in the same manner as the Grand Shrine of Ise. And like the Ise shrine, it was rebuilt every twenty-one years until the 1860s, when the capital was transferred to Tokyo. The shrine's main building dates from 1863. Nearby is the smaller Ōta Shrine, famous for the thousands of rabbit-eared iris (kakitsubata) that bloom in its shallow pond. Despite the fame, historical significance, and age of the shrines, the surrounding area is still pleasantly rural and undeveloped, not clogged with charter buses and tourists. A brief walk to the south will take you to the Kyoto Botanical Gardens, with its extensive grounds and conservatory for exotic plants.

Kamigamo Shrine is the northern terminus for City Buses 9, 37, 46, 54, 67 and Kyoto Buses 25, 26, 27, 32, and 37. Bus passengers disembark at the shrine's main gate, a large cinnabar-red *torii*. To the left of the *torii*, a sign admonishes visitors not to ride horses, catch birds or fish, uproot bamboo, or disturb the raked-sand pattern within the shrine precincts. To the right of the *torii*, a large sign bears black and red numbers indicating the ages considered unlucky for men and women. Other ages can be unlucky as well, but forty-two for men and thirty-three for women are thought to be the absolute worst years in a person's life, perhaps because these are the times when caring for growing children and aging parents

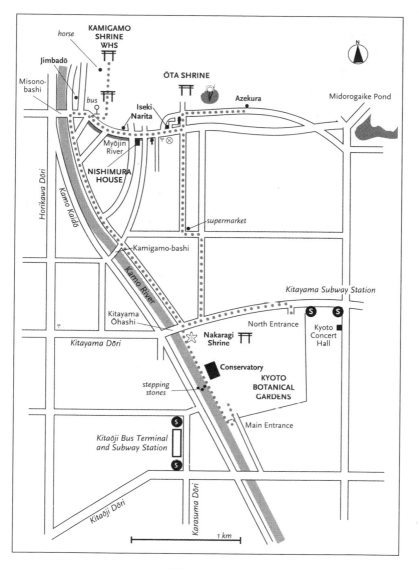

KAMIGAMO

cause the most difficulties. Please note these ages are calculated according to the Japanese system, in which a person is considered a year old at birth and two years old the following New Year.

Passing through the *torii*, you will see two expanses of grass on either side of the path, favorite picnic places for couples with young children. In May, one of these becomes a course for horse racing and displays of equestrian skill. On special days and occasionally on weekends, a white horse may be seen tethered in a wooden hut to the left of the second *torii*, the entrance to the inner shrine. Traditionally, the emperor rode a white horse, and this one serves as a kind of mascot to the god of the shrine. If you place a few yen in the tray before the horse, the attendant will give you a tiny plate of sliced carrots. Place a slice on the palm of your hand and offer it that way; otherwise, you may contribute more than you expected.

Inside the courtyard are two cone-shaped piles of sand. They honor the mountain behind the shrine, upon which a god allegedly descended, designating this place as sacred. The shrine is a beautiful example of Shintō shrine architecture, making it a popular place for weddings. Kamigamo Shrine maintains close ties with all the descendants of the priests of the shrine, a fact that accounts for the neighborhood's distinctive quality. Such shrine-affiliated families are known as *shake*, and the area boasts many of their long-established homes.

One of Kyoto's traditional sweets shops, **Jimbadō** [Open 9 to 4. Closed Tuesday afternoon and Wednesdays. Tel: 721-0090], is on the street west of the *torii*, housed in a building that dates to 1872. The shop specializes in hot grilled rice cakes filled with bean paste, sold for ¥120 each. Retrace your steps to the shrine and walk east to a famous pickle shop called **Narita** [Open 10 to 6. Closed Wednesdays. Tel: 721-1567]. The shop has large, exposed rafters supporting the high ceiling, a feature of country-style architecture. This particular building is 280 years old, although the business only dates back 220 years. There are seasonal specialties and many others among the forty or so varieties of pickles beautifully displayed in massive barrels in the center of the shop. Even if you are not planning to buy, the management does not mind visitors who drop in to see the store.

A picturesque waterway flows by on the south side of the street, passing some of the area's older residences. This district values its rural appearance, and tall clumps of pampas grass and willowy flowers such as cosmos have been left to grow on the bridges which span the waterway, adding to the beauty of the old homes. One of these, the **Nishimura House** [Open 9:30 to 4:30. Closed December through mid-March. Admission ¥500. Tel: 781-0666], has been designated a historic structure and is open to the public. Ring the bell at the gate and then walk back to the main building where the entrance fee will be collected. Visitors are shown into a *tatami* room facing the front garden. A recording of the history of the area and house (in Japanese) plays in the background.

A little farther east, on the northeast corner, is a long sand-colored clay wall encompassing the house and shop **Iseki** [Open 10 to 5. Tel: 781-8417]. A beautifully preserved example of a *shake* house is this 250-year-old residence, the thirty-third owner of which is a descendant of the head priest of Kamigamo Shrine. The sign outside the door states that this structure is a Historic Property. One part of the house has been converted into a tiny shop of whimsical fabric items: some are sachet bags, other bags are for carrying the ivory finger plectrums used by *koto* players, and still others are for ornamental use.

The features that make this a distinctly *shake* house are the beams that form the entrance in the shape of a *torii*, the stone step up to the house, the three-*shaku* (a term of measurement approximately one foot long), shallow, divided *tokonoma*, and the rounded beam edges. The well in the front garden is constructed of stone brought from the Kurama district.

Originally comprised of only one story, second and third floors were added about 150 years ago. If you request to see the top floor, the owner will guide you up the narrow wooden spiral staircase to the room used for moon viewing and watching Daimonji alit on August 16.

Continue east until you come to a towering sacred camphor tree surrounded by a red picket fence. The waterway on your right veers south here and disappears. At the next traffic light, turn left and walk one block to **Ōta Shrine**. This shrine and its ancient iris garden first appeared in Japanese literature about a thousand years ago, and the garden is said to have provided the model for the famous pair of folding screens by the artist Ogata Kōrin (1658–1716) featuring irises and a rustic footbridge. The irises blossom twice, so anytime from May to early June, visitors are likely to see several hundred of them in bloom. The iris pond is so old it is almost decrepit, but is an excellent example of the style of garden popular centuries ago. Adrift in a sea of soft purple flowers, the island in the center of the pond is known as "the floating isle," an allusion to the isle of eternal youth of the Chinese immortals.

Fifty meters east of the iris pond, marked by long brown banners, is a three-hundred-year-old *sake* storehouse called **Azekura** [Open 9 to 5. Closed Mondays. Tel: 701-0161]. Enter the complex through the gatehouse. The large storehouse (*kura*) is a few meters to the right. Beyond the sliding door is a cavernous entryway, to the left of which is an Italian restaurant. The building itself was transported all the way from Nara Prefecture, and reconstructed beam by beam with few nails. Upstairs is a display area that offers special exhibitions. On the grounds are a number of interesting buildings and stone statues which visitors are welcome to view.

Leaving Azekura, return to the bus terminal at Kamigamo Shrine, or wind through the old back streets. This area is famous for its pickles and more than a few homes still make them in the traditional way. A contraption of long poles weighted with stones

Conical mounds of white sand honor the sacred mountain behind Kamigamo Shrine.

keeps the lids of the barrels tightly closed. The vegetables (sometimes just the leaves of certain plants) are carefully washed and salted, then placed in these barrels for a few days or sometimes just overnight, depending on the season and vegetable. Strands of onions and radishes hang from eaves and red peppers are spread out on straw mats to dry in the sun, giving the area a distinctly rural atmosphere.

The **Kyoto Botanical Gardens** [Kyoto Furitsu Shokubutsuen. Open 9 to 4:30; 6:30 in summer. Admission ¥200. Tel: 701-0141] is a fifteen-minute walk south of this district. Walk either along the cherry-tree-lined Kamo River or straight south from Ōta Shrine until you reach Kitayama Dōri. A few minutes' walk east is the north entrance to the gardens. Designed by Terasaki Ryosaku, the gardens were complete in 1923 to commemorate the enthronement of Emperor Taisho. They were among the many public gardens created during this emperor's reign—one of the ways in which the country sought to emulate the West. Construction was funded by the Mitsui family, owners of the powerful Mitsui business consortium. Since Kyoto was home to that clan, they were asked to contribute to Kyoto's future by sponsoring the gardens. From 1949 to 1957, the gardens were put to a different use, as temporary quarters for the American Occupation forces. They were opened again to the Japanese public in 1960, and today the gardens are maintained by the Kyoto prefectural government.

A photograph taken in 1911 of the site shows the Kamo River before it was embanked: a massive copse stands in the middle of the landscape with few distinguishing features, since this area of the city was still very undeveloped. Legend has it that a thicket of trees "floated" down from Kamigamo Shrine, and hence it was named Nagaregi no Mori ("The Floating Woods"). In fact the thicket still exits, and the Botanical Gardens were laid out around it. Another name for the woods is Nakaragi no Mori ("Halfway Woods"), probably because it lies midway between the Kamigamo and Shimogamo shrines. In its midst is the **Nakaragi Shrine**, and Nakaragi no Michi is also the name given to the footpath which runs along the Kamo River at the western edge of the Botanical Gardens, a stretch of the river embankment renowned for its beautiful hanging cherry trees.

The northeastern part of the Botanical Gardens is formed by a Japanese-style garden called Nihon no Mori, deliberately tended to resemble natural woodland, with lotus ponds, streams lined with irises, and groves of plums and cherry trees. Rose arbors and sculpted shrubbery are among the flora found within the European-style gardens in the southeast. An exhibition hall near the south entrance offers year-round displays of seasonal flowers and plants that have been cultivated by private citizens.

In 1993, the Botanical Gardens opened the largest **Conservatory** [Open 10 to 4] in Japan, an impressive piece of architecture featuring undulating arcs of glass that echo the shapes of the mountains to the city's north. At its base is a pool fashioned after the pond at the Kinkakuji (Golden Pavilion) in northwestern Kyoto, while a weathervane-like object is an abstract version of the phoenix that sits atop that temple.

The first hall of the Conservatory contains water plants on the left of the walk and insect-eating plants to the right. The second is a jungle zone, and of all the rooms houses possibly the largest collection of plants. The third contains useful plants: edible ones, medicinal ones, some used in dyeing and weaving, and others for roofing. In the fourth hall are summer plants found in alpine regions. The fifth contains desert and savannah plants. The sixth houses plants of the temperate forest and their fruit, while the seventh room is devoted entirely to bromeliads, of which there are over a hundred varieties. The eighth room is devoted to orchids, including an example of the largest species in the world. It was brought from Malaysia for this exhibit. The ninth room is reserved for special exhibits and video viewing. The entire Conservatory complex covers 4,612 square meters and the path through it is wide enough to allow a leisurely look at all these beautifully maintained plants. Sloping round and gently upward, the path leads to a pavilion that affords a delightful view of the treetops. There are two eateries on the grounds, which serve simple fare.

The Kitayama subway station is at the north exit of the Botanical Gardens. A five-minute walk south from the main exit along the Kamo River leads to Kitaōji Dōri, and another five-minute walk west is the Kitaōji subway station and bus terminal.

NISHIGAMO 西賀茂

西賀茂

Daitokuji 大徳寺
Ryūgen'in 龍源院
Daisen'in 大仙院
Zuihōin 瑞峰院
Kōtōin 高桐院
Imamiya Shrine 今宮神社
Saihōji 西方寺
Shōdenji 正伝寺
Funagatayama 船形山
Jinkōin 神光院

North of busy Kitaōji Dōri, an older, slower-paced Kyoto can be found. The reverberations of temple bells blend with the clatter of looms, while the aroma of freshly tilled fields reveals a part of the city known as Nishigamo that is simultaneously rural and refined. This northwest sector of Kyoto is home to the Rinzai Zen temple complex of Daitokuji, one of the largest in the city. On the grounds of its subtemples are some of the country's most beautiful Zen gardens as well as many fine teahouses. Nearby is Imamiya Shrine, dedicated to ridding the capital of pestilence. Farther north, amidst the fields, are the little-known temples Saihōji and Jinkōin, while Shōdenji is nestled among the foothills of Mt. Funagata.

Daitokuji [Tel: 491-0019] can be easily reached by City Buses 1, 12, 61, 204, 205, and 206. It is also a fifteen-minute walk west from the Kitaōji subway station and bus terminal. A small temple founded in 1309 by the Zen priest Sōhō Myōchō (1282–1337; posthumously known as Daitō Kokushi) originally stood here. Emperor Go-Daigo, an admirer of the priest, decreed that a grand temple should be built under Myōchō's supervision. The courtyard was

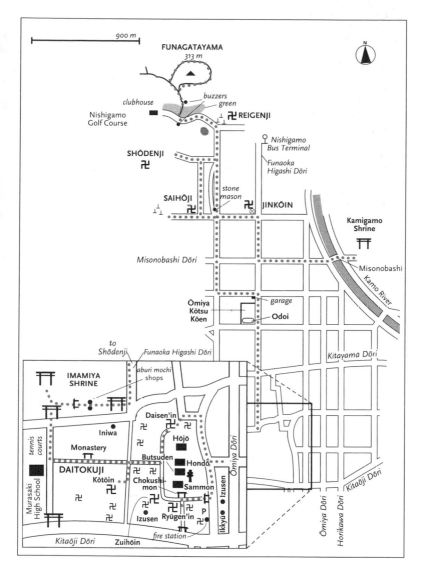

NISHIGAMO

complete in 1326. In the decades that followed, the complex was destroyed by fire and war, but it was rebuilt by one of its abbots, the famous Zen master Ikkyū Sōjun (1394–1481). It is he who is credited with encouraging the head of the various subtemples to pursue the arts of calligraphy, gardening, and tea, thus transforming these temples into repositories of art.

The main buildings are aligned facing south and the subtemples are located along the perimeter of the courtyard. The southernmost structure in the courtyard is the unpainted **Chokushimon** ("Imperial Messenger's Gate"), a gift of the Empress Meishō (1624–96). The vermilion gate to its north is the **Sammon**, which was restored in 1526 and the upper story added sixty years later. It is also a reminder of the pride of two of Japan's most famous men, warlord Toyotomi Hideyoshi (1537–98) and tea master Sen no Rikyū (1511–91). Although these two men came from vastly different backgrounds, they greatly admired each other in the early years of their acquaintance. Both profoundly influenced the political and cultural life of their times. Hideyoshi was the first of three great unifiers of Japan (his successors being Oda Nobunaga and Tokugawa Ieyasu). He rebuilt much of the city of Kyoto. He was also an avid practitioner of the tea ceremony, which Sen no Rikyū was transforming into a ritual with deep philosophical and spiritual implications. In the teahouse, all who sit and share a cup of tea together become social equals—a revolutionary idea in a rigid, hierarchical society. As much as these two men respected each other, their pride clashed and distrust grew. Rikyū incurred Hideyoshi's wrath when he placed an image of himself among the Buddhist images in the upper story of the Sammon, knowing that Hideyoshi would pass under the gate. When Hideyoshi found out that Rikyū had "elevated" himself in this manner, Hideyoshi commanded him to commit ritual suicide.

The **Butsuden** (1665), or Buddha Hall, houses the central image, a large Shakyamuni, flanked by two attendants and seated on an immense lacquered altar. The dark slate floor is typical of build-ings in the Chinese style, as are the suspended window panels and doors that open out, rather than slide. An *ibuki* tree (a member of the cypress family) towers in front of the Butsuden. It is thought to have been planted around the time of this building's construction, which makes it more than three centuries old.

The **Hondō**, Main Hall, is located behind the Butsuden. North of it is the **Hōjō**, or Abbot's Quarters. Neither of these buildings is open to the public.

At present, four subtemples of Daitokuji are open to visitors and all of them offer an instructional look at Zen in its most physi-cal guise. The Zen temple endeavored to provide its students with an environment conducive to reaching enlightenment. As gar-dens fulfilled this requirement, their landscapes were constructed around abstract themes, such as light and dark, masculine and feminine, the Isle of the Immortals, or the universal vortex. There are as many themes as there are gardens. These four subtemples are so filled with exquisite artifacts, gardens, and teahouses that they may prove a little overpowering to see at one time. A visit to one or two of them might be more satisfying. All of them offer good English explanations of their histories and possessions.

Ryūgen'in [Open 9 to 4:30. Admission ¥350. Tel: 491-7635] is noted for having five distinct rock gardens, one of which claims to be the smallest of its kind in Japan. Constructed on a narrow strip of earth between two buildings, it is as compact and concise as the spiritual lesson it imparts.

Daisen'in [Open 9 to 5; 4:30 in winter. Admission ¥400; ¥600 with tea. Tel: 491-8346] is the best known and most visited of all Daitokuji's subtemples. Its gardens are dynamic; the East Garden of the Abbot's Quarters here is one of the most famous in Japan and often taken as the embodiment of the Zen garden aes-thetic. There is a tradition in the Rinzai school of Zen of sudden enlightenment via a shout, a blow, or sudden noise encountered while deep in meditation that jolts one out of the world of petty concerns and into another realm. The gardens of Daisen'in seem prepared to do that.

Zuihōin [Open 8 to 5. Admission ¥400. Tel: 491-1454] has a strong, attractive rock garden as its centerpiece. Founded in 1535, it is the funerary temple of Ōtomo Sōrin, a *daimyō* from Kyushu who had converted to Christianity. The tea garden is unusual in that it is completely lacking in any greenery; an arrangement of flat stones fans out from the cylindrical stone water basin. Flecks of straw accent the black earthen walls of the tearoom, transforming the rough, farmhouse-like walls into a masterpiece of plaster-work, embodying an aesthetic concept of rustic simplicity known as *wabi*.

Kōtōin [Open 9 to 4:30. Admission ¥300. Tel: 492-0068] has no rock garden but an expanse of moss shaded by graceful maples. Thus, it is perhaps the only one of these temples whose gardens reflect the changing seasons. Founded in 1601 by the powerful *daimyō*, Hosokawa Tadaoki (1563–1645), the temple houses memorials to this lord and his wife, Tomo (1563–1600), who took the name Gracia when she converted to Christianity. In 1619, Takaoki became a Buddhist monk, taking the name Sansai and retiring to this temple, where he became a student of tea under Sen no Rikyū. The tearoom on the grounds has the traditional low entrance known as *nijiriguchi*, which requires one to crawl through it to enter. Not only does this entry symbolize the passage from the secular world to the sacred, in practice it forced warriors to abandon their weapons, and to assume a humble attitude in keeping with the occasion. This tearoom can only be viewed from outside as the rope-bound rock placed before the entrance indicates.

The northwest corner of Daitokuji is occupied by the monastery, which is not open to the public except on special occasions.

Vegetarian restaurants may be found near all the major Zen complexes in Kyoto. **Izusen** operates two restaurants at Daito-

A bamboo grove grows beyond the monastery wall of Daitokuji.

kuji: one within the southwest part of the complex [Open 11 to 4. Closed Thursdays. Tel: 491-6665] with indoor and outdoor seating (weather permitting), and one outside the east gate [Open 11 to 5. Closed Wednesdays. Tel: 493-0889]. Courses start from ¥3,000 and are served in lustrous red lacquer bowls in a *tatami* room with views of a garden. An English menu is available. An older, more expensive vegetarian restaurant, **Ikkyū**, [Open daily, noon to 6. Tel: 493-0019], is also located outside of the east entrance of Daitokuji. This four-hundred-year-old restaurant specializes in sesame tofu. Courses start from ¥6,000, and reservations are necessary.

To the north of Daitokuji is the large red *torii* of **Imamiya Shrine**. Founded on Mt. Funaoka in 994, the shrine, like Yasaka Shrine, offers prayers to protect the population from pestilence and epidemics. It acquired its present name when it was moved to this spot. To the left of the beautiful Main Hall is a subshrine dedicated to the families of the weavers who live in the vicinity.

It is fronted with marble monuments shaped like the shuttles of looms. In a little structure near the center of the ground, a dense, black rock rests on a brocade pillow. Its age and provenance are unknown, but it is believed to cure illness. To benefit from its restorative powers, say a prayer and lift it gently three times, or rub the rock and then the places where you suffer from aches and pains.

Outside the East Gate of the shrine are two old shops that sell *aburi mochi* (rice dumplings charcoal-roasted on bamboo skewers and topped with sweet *miso* sauce). One serving (*ichinin mae*) consists of fifteen bite-size dumplings for ¥500 and is enough for two. A pot of tea is included. The rustic Edo-period buildings are as unpretentious as the fare, and the warmth of the proprietors and the charming setting are reminiscent of a bygone era.

This part of Kyoto is also known for its pickles. If you care to sample some, the restaurant/café and pickle shop **Iniwa** [Open 11 to 5. Closed Tuesdays. Tel 777-5322] is across the street. A reasonably priced menu with photos is provided.

For those in a mood to walk, the secluded temple of Shōdenji is thirty-five minutes north of here, and along the way is a surviving section of the earthen embankment, the Odoi, which used to surround Kyoto. Walk north along Funaoka Higashi Dōri. Cross Kitayama Dōri and continue north to the **Ōmiya Kōtsū Kōen** [Ōmiya Traffic Park. Open 9 to 4]. This little amusement center for toddlers and small children offers go-carts and lessons in traffic safety. The grounds are free and tickets for the rides can be purchased from machines at the entrance.

As you approach the park from the southeast a small shrine is visible through the park's fence. This is next to a section of the **Odoi**, built in the late 1590s by Toyotomi Hideyoshi. Before its defensive features could be tested, however, Hideyoshi decided that Fushimi, located in the southeast of Kyoto, was a better site strategically, and built his castle there. The Odoi stood for a little over a hundred years. With its disintegration, fields were planted and houses built, until most of the wall vanished.

Turn left on any street and walk two blocks to Shichiku Nishi Dōri. Walk north about ten minutes to a stonemason's shop. The road that runs west leads to **Saihōji**, a small, quiet temple with a large adjacent cemetery. This area is still so rural that water for use in the cemetery is drawn from two wells on its grounds. Saihōji (no relation to the famous Moss Temple) was founded in 874 as a Tendai temple, but was converted to the Jōdo sect in the fourteenth century. On the ground of Saihōji is a memorial to Richard Ponsonby-Fane (1878–1937), a British scholar and historian. North of the temple is Funagatayama (Mt. Funagata), one of the five mountains upon which fires are lit on August 16, at the conclusion of the Obon festival, to guide the spirits of the dead back to the netherworld. Eighteen of Saihōji's parishioners take part in the yearly ritual of climbing the mountain to light fires laid out in the shape of a boat, as the name of the mountain indicates (*funa* means boat, *gata* form, and *yama* mountain).

Return to the stonemason's shop and turn left. Continue north until you reach a corner house with an outer wall formed of massive stones. A sign for Shōdenji (in English) stands opposite it. The approach through the temple gate is a bamboo- and cryptomeria-lined stairway. After the second gate, the path divides: the cemetery to the left and the temple to the right. **Shōdenji** [Open 9 to 5. Admission ¥300. Tel: 491-3259] is a Rinzai Zen temple built in the Kamakura period (1185–1333). The three-room Main Hall boasts very fine ink paintings by Kanō Sanraku (1559–1635). You are permitted to enter the rooms adjacent to the altar. If a large hanging scroll depicting the death of Buddha is on display, look carefully. Every line of the figures, flowers, and animals is actually the minute script of a sutra.

Shōdenji is one of the five *chitenjōji*, literally, "temples with bloody ceilings." When warlord Toyatomi Hideyoshi died in 1598, his son, Hideyori, moved to Osaka the following year, leaving retainers of the Tokugawa clan in charge of Fushimi Castle. In 1600, the castle was attacked by troops loyal to Hideyori. Greatly outnumbered, the Tokugawa defenders fought valiantly but hopelessly. Rather than surrender when defeat became obvious, those still alive assembled in the corridors of the castle and committed ritual suicide. Legend says that 1,200 lost their lives that day—384 by their own hand. This struggle for power was eventually won by the Tokugawa house however, and the Tokugawa shoguns gave planks from the corridors of Fushimi Castle to five different temples—the *chitenjōji*—to place in their ceilings, honoring the spirits of the warriors by putting the boards where no one could ever tread upon them. This gristly remnant of Japan's past is offset by a beautiful rock garden that incorporates large azalea bushes and a view of Mt. Hiei in the background. The garden, called "Shishi no Ko Watashi," is said to represent a lioness and her cubs.

Those interested in climbing **Funagatayama** must be prepared for the harrowing possibility of having to dodge golf balls! Access to the mountain ("open" except during preparations for the Obon festival, August 15–16) is through the Nishigamo Golf Course. Walk north from Shōdenji, and take the paved road on the left that leads to the golf course and enter the grounds. The temple near the entrance is **Reigenji**, founded in 1671 with the patronage of the Iwakura family. Just before you reach the clubhouse, a paved strip cuts across the fairway to the right. Push the buzzer attached to the sign there and, when it starts to sound, take a few steps out onto the fairway (making sure the golfers teeing off notice you), and continue across. There is another buzzer on the opposite side. Cross the fairway until reaching the "entrance" to the mountain, marked by two stone posts. The steep climb takes only fifteen minutes. A small stone marker is at the peak (313 meters). Continue in the same direction until you reach a wider path. The path on the left returns to the golf course, the right path leads to the pass called Kyōmitoge. Again, before crossing the green, press the buzzer.

Retrace your steps to Shōdenji, and from there to the stonemason. The road running east from the stonemason's leads to a bus route, before which you will find the Shingon temple **Jinkōin** [Tel: 491-4375]. Founded in 1217 and rebuilt in 1914, the Main Hall has some very old images of Fudō Myōō, Yakushi Nyorai, and Jizō. However, the hall is only open on the twenty-first of each month, in honor of Kōbō Daishi, the great teacher who brought the Shingon sect to Japan. The modest grounds contain a carp pond.

City Buses 1 and 2, bound for the Kitaōji bus terminal and subway station, and City Bus 9, bound for Kyoto Station, stop along this street. The fare is ¥220. More buses leave from the bus terminal in front of Kamigamo Shrine, a ten-minute walk east along Misonobashi Dōri.

TAKAO 高雄

Kōzanji 高山寺
Saimyōji 西明寺
Jingoji 神護寺
Kin'unkei 錦雲渓

Famous for its magnificent scenery and glorious autumn foliage, the northwest corner of Kyoto is home to the ancient temples Kōzanji and Jingoji. A leafy canopy of bamboo, cherry, and maple trees covers Route 162 as it winds through a narrow mountain pass. The fragrance of freshly cut trees permeates the air, a by-product of the small lumber mills along the Shūzan Kaidō, the other name for this highway. The mountains in northwest Kyoto are covered with cultivated cryptomeria trees (Kitayama sugi). Some are raised as ornamentals for gardens, but most are raised to be made into attractive alcove posts for traditional homes. The wood is valued for its silky smooth sheen and for its textured surface, which is enhanced by binding plastic chopsticks to the tree trunk, constricting and contorting the surface until it causes indentations in the trunk. The resulting rippled surface creates a "natural" look favored by the Japanese.

Takao is served by blue-and-white JR buses departing from Kyoto Station or from Shijō-Ōmiya. The trip takes about an hour. After a steady climb, the road crests at Gokeizaka Pass and descends. Five minutes beyond, the highway widens at the Togano'o bus stop (the destination on the bus) to accommodate a parking lot on the left and a turnaround for the bus. The restaurant **Toganojaya** [Open 8 to 5. Tel: 841-4206] on the right is a collection of open-sided pavilions and *tatami*-mat rooms overlooking the Kiyotaki River. Prices are reasonable, the menu varied, and the setting inviting. Many of the restaurants in Takao feature the spectacular scenery known for its mountain peaks and brilliantly colored maples. Takao is

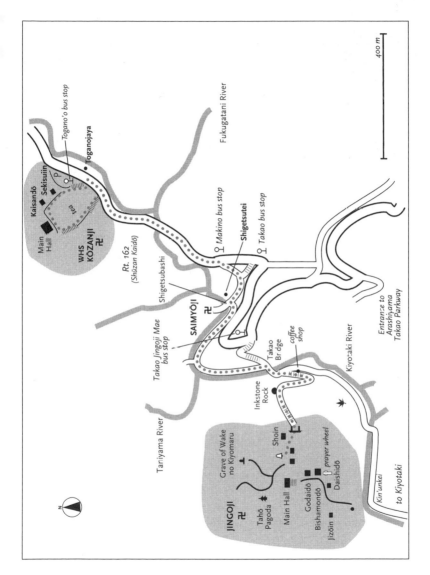

TAKAO

crowded in the fall, but the bright young leaves in the spring and the cool river water and dense shade of summer draw their share of visitors as well.

The entrance to **Kōzanji** [Open 9 to 4:30. Tel: 861-4204] is up the stone steps at the south end of the parking lot, where there is a large map of the area. During October and November, admission is ¥600; otherwise entrance is free. Kōzanji was originally a subtemple of the nearby Shingon temple Jingoji, but its founder is considered the priest Myōe (1173–1232). While Myōe was the abbot, the temple received the patronage of the emperor Go-Toba (1180–1239) who, in 1208, renamed it Kōzanji. Myōe was a friend of Eisai (1145–1215), the priest who introduced the Rinzai school of Zen Buddhism to Japan. Along with Zen, Eisai brought back the tea plant from his travels in China, and with seeds received from Eisai, Myōe created one of Japan's first tea plantations. Even today, a portion of the well-tended plantation remains on the grounds just diagonal to Sekisui'in.

A National Treasure, the elegant yet austere **Sekisui'in** [Open 9 to 4:30. Admission ¥600. Tel: 861-4201] is the only building that stands from Myōe's day. It is an excellent example of Kamakura architecture and the pragmatic nature of its founder. The building's sparse detail and undecorated surface contrast with its lush green setting among tree-covered peaks. Unfortunately, the low roar of traffic passing below the Main Hall intrudes enough to offer a contrast of another kind. The temple possesses a number of National Treasures and Important Cultural Properties among which are four handscrolls of frolicking birds and animals (known as the *Chōjū Giga*), which are presently housed in the Tokyo National Museum. Reproductions of these famous scrolls are on display, and packets of postcards are on sale. Tall cryptomeria trees provide a heavy canopy of shade over the complex. The path now passes by the tea plantation and the **Kaisandō** (Founder's Hall), the next oldest building after Sekisui'in. Its graceful, sloping cypress

roof and bell-shaped windows present an elegant example of thir-
teenth-century architecture.

Near the south exit, two large moss-covered stone lanterns
stand on either side of the walkway of diamond-shaped stones.
Beyond them is a long flight of stone steps that descends to Route
162. Walk south for several minutes and turn right at the Makino
bus stop, the last stop for City Bus 8. Several direction signs (in
Japanese and English) mark this junction. From here it is a seven-minute walk to Saimyōji and a twenty-minute walk to Jingoji
along the paved road.

In front of an arched red footbridge called Shigetsubashi
there is a large sign with Japanese characters reading **Saimyōji**.
The winding path beyond the bridge is lined with attractive stone
lanterns, and just inside the temple gate is a six-hundred-year-
old *maki* tree (a type of yew) which is considered the oldest of its
kind in Japan. Saimyōji, once a subtemple of Jingoji, is small and
its buildings are few, but the Main Hall has three fine statues.
Those who wish to enter are asked to leave a donation of ¥400
on the inside table or in the offering box and remove their shoes.
Two of the statues, the Shaka Nyorai (historical Buddha) and the
thousand-armed Kannon (bodhisattva of mercy) are Important
Cultural Properties. There is also a fine image of the bodhisattva
Fudō Myōō.

From Shigetsubashi, several small rooms of the picturesque
restaurant **Shigetsutei** [Open 10 to 5. During winter, open only on
weekends. Tel: 861-1801] can be seen perched on the cliff overhanging the Kiyotaki River. Prices are reasonable: the vegetable set
is ¥1,800, the bean-curd hot pot is ¥2,500, and sukiyaki is ¥3,800.
Outside tables tempt passersby to sit, have something to drink,
and enjoy the scenery.

The paved road continues to descend to another bridge, Takaobashi, an area crowded with restaurants and inns open only in the
fall. At other times of the year, visitors are few—the sounds of the

river, the birds, and the rustle of the wind in the trees are all that accompany you up the steep stairway to **Jingoji** [Open 9 to 4. Admission ¥500. Tel: 861-1769]. For centuries, access to this remote place was hampered by the steepness of the mountain setting and the lack of passable roads and bridges. Today's visitor only has to contend with the sharp final ascent, but is instantly rewarded by the beauty of the approach. The climb takes about five minutes, but there is a refreshment stand along the way that offers cool drinks and shaved ice in summer. Near the top, on the riverside, is a large light-colored stone known as the Inkstone Rock. This stone is associated with Kūkai (774–835), the founder of Shingon Buddhism in Japan. The story goes that one day Kūkai came to paint the name of the subtemple Kongōjōji on the plaque, but was prevented from entering the temple grounds by the rain-swollen river. Instead, Kūkai prepared his ink on this stone, dipped his brush and then threw it across the river, where it miraculously painted the temple's characters on its entrance plaque. However fanciful the legend, the rock is real and a solid reminder of Kūkai's connection to this temple, where he served as abbot after returning from his studies in Tang-dynasty China.

At the top of the steps is the Main Gate and admission booth. Beyond the gate lies an open and unlandscaped courtyard, a sunny contrast to the densely forested peaks that surround it. On the right is the **Shoin**, the Priest's Quarters, where the temple's treasures are aired in May. At other times, it can only be viewed from the courtyard through its elaborate, carved gate. The building, enclosed by a red fence, is a memorial to Wake no Kiyomaro (733–99), a courtier who prevented the scheming priest Dōkyō from ascending the imperial throne. To escape Dōkyō's wrath, the courtier retreated to the mountains of Takao, and in 781, founded Jingoji. Consequently, the temple served as a retreat and haven for those who were disillusioned with the increasingly political Nara sects of Buddhism. Jingoji is a Shingon temple and many of its treasures are related to this sect of esoteric Buddhism. On May 1–5, a magnificent pair of hanging scrolls called the Mandalas of the Two Realms, a National Treasure, is displayed in the **Kondō** (Main Hall).

The outside of the Main Hall is painted a bright red, as is the coffered ceiling of the interior. Visitors are welcome to enter and even to walk behind the altar to view the magnificent collection of images. The central figure is a Yakushi Nyorai carved from a single piece of wood. This is the Healing Buddha and both hands are raised: the right

The moss-covered stone lanterns of Saimyōji.

in a gesture meaning "Fear not," the left holding a medicine jar. Thought to have been brought here twelve hundred years ago by the founder, Wake no Kiyomaro, this image is a National Treasure and a masterpiece of Buddhist art. Thousand-year-old images of Nikkō and Gakkō, bodhisattvas representing sunlight and moonlight, stand on either side. Next to these are six-hundred-year-old images of the twelve Divine Generals; on the crown of each sits a zodiac animal. The four images at the end, equally old, are of the Shitennō, the heavenly kings who guard the four directions. The dark, cool interior offers a peaceful refuge in the mountain setting; others share this knowledge, for hikers and pilgrims alike often stop and rest here and on the stone steps outside the hall.

Paths behind the Main Hall lead to two gravesites, one of a former abbot, the other, reached by the lower path, that of Wake no Kiyomaro. The white plastic chopsticks bound to the cedar trees along the path are reminders of the local lumber business, and give the visitor a look at an unusual use of temple land.

The wide path at the bottom of the steps to the Main Hall on the right leads to the two-tiered pagoda while the other path slopes down toward a Jizōin (a hall dedicated to the bodhisattva Jizō). Along the way is a well that dates from 612. A narrow stone stairway leads down to a view of a valley and peaks beyond. The clay disks sold here, two for ¥100, are purchased by visitors who write their wishes on them before pitching them off the mountainside. This seems a more recreational activity than a spiritual one, especially among visiting schoolchildren and young couples.

Although closed, the Godaidō, Bishamondō, and Daishidō halls in the main courtyard are fine examples of sixteenth-century temple architecture. On the south side of the Bishamondō is a tall stone pillar, into which is mounted a rounded stone prayer wheel, smooth and shiny from the touch of faithful hands.

Both the winding road and stone stairway on the other side of Takaobashi (Takao Bridge) lead back to Route 162. Here, JR buses depart for Shijō-Ōmiya and Kyoto Station; City Bus 8 departs here for Keihan Sanjō Station via Shijō-Ōmiya.

For those in the mood to walk, the path at the bottom of the steps of Jingoji follows the river south through **Kin'unkei** (Brocade Gorge) where steep mountainsides are covered with a rich variety of trees and plants. The hour-and-a-half walk to the village of Kiyotaki offers some of the city's most beautiful scenery. The songs of birds and cicadas echo through the gorge; dragonflies sun themselves on boulders in the crystal clear river; and wildflowers growing from crevices in the rock outcroppings appear to be tumbling down the mountainsides. This is a lovely picnic area and a favorite swimming place, particularly closer to Kiyotaki where the river has been cleared of large rocks to allow small children to wade. Blessedly, there are no vending machines along the way, nor are there toilets. It is not until reaching the village that such amenities are available. The bus terminal is at the top of the road before the tunnel. From here, Kyoto Bus 62 departs for Keihan Sanjō Station and Bus 72 for Kyoto Station, both via Arashiyama; each runs about once an hour.

SAGANO 嵯峨野

嵯峨野

Saga Shakadō 嵯峨釈迦堂
Nison'in 二尊院
Chōjin no Mori 長人の社
Gioji 祇王寺
Toriimoto 鳥居本
Adashino Nembutsuji 化野念仏寺
Otagi Nembutsuji 愛宕念仏寺
Atagosan 愛宕山
Atago Shrine 愛宕神社
Tsukinowadera 月の輪寺

Justly acclaimed for its rural beauty, the Sagano district lies at the foot of the western hills of Kyoto. Here, within short walks of each other, are the beautiful temples Saga Shakadō (Seiryōji) and Nison'in; Gioji, the religious retreat of an ancient warlord's cast-off mistresses; and the intriguing stone Buddhist images at Adashino Nembutsuji and Atago Nembutsuji (Otagidera). Fine old thatched-roof houses and thick earthen-walled storehouses line the narrow winding road that leads to Ichi no Torii, the first gate on the approach to Atagosan (Mt. Atago). Bicycle rental is a popular way to tour, but walking is preferable because of the many small wayside images and the number of places to explore.

Seiryōji, popularly known as **Saga Shakadō** [Open 9 to 4. Tel: 861-0343], is a ten-minute walk from JR Saga Station and a fifteen-minute walk from the Saga Ekimae Station on the Keifuku Arashi-yama Line. The street passing in front of both stations leads north to Shin Marutamachi Dōri. Walk to the traffic signal at the intersection with Shin Marutamachi, turn west one block, then continue north through an old neighborhood until you come to the Main Gate of the temple, built in 1776.

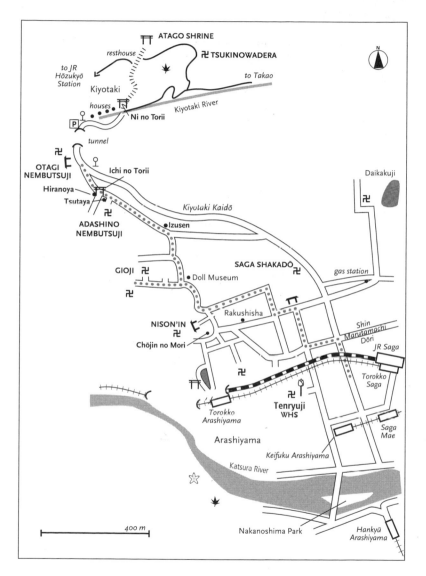

SAGANO

Founded in 986 by the priest Chōnen, Seiryōji has several National Treasures among the numerous works of art in its museum, the Reihōkan. Open only in April, May, October, and November, the museum houses a fine collection of Buddhist sculpture, hanging scrolls, and handscrolls. Admission to the Main Hall is ¥400; the museum is another ¥400. Tickets for both may be purchased for ¥700 in the Main Hall. The main image is of Shaka Nyorai (Shakyamuni, the historical Buddha). The soft folds of the robes are compact yet fluid, an extension of the grain of chinaberry wood from which it is carved. It is said to be a Chinese replica made a thousand years ago of a statue brought from India into China, the replica then making its way to Japan. A large painting at the back of the hall depicts the carvers and their advisors making the replica.

It was custom in ancient times to place sutras and various objects inside Buddhist statues. In 1954, Seiryōji's image of Shakyamuni was opened, and among the things found inside were pieces of dyed silk, some shaped like human organs, with Chinese and Sanskrit characters painted on them. It is believed that these were made by Chinese nuns and placed inside to ensure that the statue was a complete and faithful physical representation of the holy man—providing evidence of Chinese knowledge of human anatomy a millennium ago. Replicas of these artifacts are displayed in a cabinet left of the altar. To the right of the altar is a three-hundred-year-old set of paintings called "The Five Hundred Rakan." Rakan are disciples of the Buddha who have attained enlightenment but who are always depicted in very human guise, rather than in the idealized manner typical of Buddhist iconography.

Exiting the Main Gate, take two rights and then a left. The road narrows, but not enough to slow the young rickshaw drivers who ply their trade in this district. A thirty-minute ride costs ¥5,000 for an individual and ¥8,000 for a couple (a bit expensive, as one driver admitted), but even so, all sorts of people like to take a spin.

Until the capital was moved to Tokyo, **Nison'in** [Open 9 to

5. Admission ¥300. Tel: 861-0687] was one of four temples that administered Buddhist ceremonies for the imperial house, and its hillside cemetery is studded with the graves of emperors and aristocrats. The main building has two central images, a Shaka Nyorai and an Amida, and beautifully painted *fusuma* (sliding doors). The spacious grounds still provide a tranquil and dignified setting for the graves of the temple's aristocratic patrons.

Close by Nison'in is **Chōjin no Mori**, a small woodland park that offers quiet paths and a relaxing respite from all the tourist activity. [Open daily 10 to 5. Free admission.]

The road curves to the left and then left again to the retreat called **Gioji** [Open 9 to 5. Admission ¥300. Tel: 861-3574]. Gio and her sister Gin'yo were Heian-period dancers who performed *shirabyoshi* (traditional Japanese dance). According to the *Tale of the Heike*, Gio became the mistress of Taira no Kiyomori (1118–81), the famous warlord. When he became smitten with another dancer with the stage name of Hotoke Gozen (Lady Buddha), he banished Gio from his palace. Gio, her mother, and her sister became nuns and moved to a humble cottage. A year later, Hotoke Gozen, now also out of favor with Kiyomori and filled with remorse for the rejected mistress, joined her at this secluded retreat. Inside the thatched building, on either side of an image of Amida, are small figures of these women. There also is one of Kiyomori, but it is obstructed by a pillar—perhaps the ladies' last word on the subject.

Back at the main road, turn left and walk along the upward-sloping road. This area is known as **Toriimoto**, the Foot of the Gate, and the street is lined with typical Kyoto-style farmhouses and many shops, some selling pickles, others knickknacks, still others offering coffee and tea or the area's famous delicate *yudōfu* (bean curd hot-pot). Prices range from ¥500 to ¥1,000 for various courses. The slightly more expensive **Izusen** [Open 11 to 4. Closed Tuesdays. Tel: 881-7016] serves Japanese dishes in a traditional setting with courses starting at ¥3,150. The **Ogawa Coffee Shop** next door offers *yudōfu for* ¥1,900 and an attactive inner garden.

Adashino Nembutsuji [Open 9 to 4:30. Admission ¥500. Tel: 861-2221] is a temple with more than a thousand stone Buddhist images. Long ago, the dead were buried along the foothills of Atagoyama, then far beyond the city limits, and graves of commoners were marked with pieces of granite on which crude images of Buddhas or bodhisattvas were carved. About a century ago, as the city advanced westward, these gravestones were collected and arranged here as if attending a sermon. Often featured on posters of the area, this temple is familiar to tourists, especially from photos taken when the stones are lighted by hundreds of candles during the Obon festival in August. The large red **Ichi no Torii** marks the beginning of a three-hour climb up Mt. Atago. On either side of the gate are large, beautiful, four-hundred-year-old teahouses that have served pilgrims and visitors for centuries. The first is **Tsutaya** [Open 11 to 6. Tel: 871-3330], where a sweet and a bowl of green tea served in the gleaming smoke-darkened interior are ¥800. A similar set is available for ¥840 at **Hiranoya** [Open 11:30 to 9. Tel: 861-0359]. Meals are also served at both places, but these start at ¥5,000 and reservations are necessary.

Otagi Nembutsuji [Admission ¥300. English pamphlet available upon request. Tel: 882-5192] was originally located in the area of central Kyoto known as Otagi, and was moved here about ninety years ago. The Nio guardians at the gate and the Main Hall are Important Cultural Properties dating from the Kamakura period (1185–1333). The temple's Jizō image, known as the Hiyoke Jizō, is believed to protect against fire, as does the god inhabiting Mt. Atago. Perhaps it was for this reason that the temple was located here. This Tendai temple has a wonderful array of carved stone Rakan. Some of the fanciful figures clutch babies or children, and one even cradles a collie. All the carvings have amusing or contented expressions, a contrast to the severe mien of the more orthodox figures of Rakan found in other temples. Surprisingly,

Throngs of expressive stone Rakan are on display at Otagi Nembutsuji.

most of the sculptors are women, a fact supplied by the temple's priest, Nishimura Kōei. It was his idea to offer carving lessons for those who wished to acquire the skill while making a contribution to the temple. The idea became popular, as can be seen by all the present images. Besides attending to his spiritual duties, Kōei-san composes New Age Buddhist music. Three CDs, the most recent featuring music used as a soundtrack for a television series on Buddhist images, can be purchased. Ring the bell for assistance.

For those wishing to end their walk here, buses for Keihan Sanjō Station and JR Kyoto Station leave from a stop just across from Otagi Nembutsuji. They are infrequent, so times should be checked before entering the temple. On a fine day, in the refreshing mountain air, the walk back to Saga Station (which will take about forty-five minutes) would definitely be a better choice.

Atago Shrine, founded in 781, is dedicated to the fire god, the child of Izanami. (The climb up to the shrine is via a steep stone stairway that starts at Ni no Torii and takes between two and three hours depending on one's energy.) The first shrine structure that comes into view after the climb is a large wooden temple gate. Tea is available at the lodge on the left. The shrine itself is another hundred or so steps up. Invocations for protection from fire are conducted here, and various talismans are sold. In accordance with an old custom, branches of the dark-green leafed *shikimi* (*Illicium religiosum*) are given to the white-clad pilgrims who visit the shrine. Two priests perform services for a donation, and they are kept surprisingly busy, especially on weekends.

As you leave the shrine, a path to the left of the stairs leads past Tsukinowadera and returns to Kiyotaki. If you return via the main route, another path diverges from it to the right, leading to the JR Hōzukyō Station. This descent takes about an hour and a half; the Tsukinowadera route takes about ten minutes more but is the more interesting of the two. It takes about twenty minutes to reach **Tsukinowadera** (Moon Ring Temple), a Tendai temple. On its grounds is a variety of cherry tree called *shigurezakura*. The petals of this cherry are so delicate they are said to resemble a fine misty rain (*shigure*) as they float to the ground. The path down the mountain is lined with an attractive growth of *kumasasa*, a crisp, green bamboo grass. After a time, this path merges with one running beside the Kiyotaki River. Turn right here, and in about half an hour you will find yourself back at Ni no Torii. The mountainsides of this steep valley have been left uncut and, as a result, a rich variety of trees and flowers grace this stretch of the river.

A sign at the bottom of the stairs near Ni no Torii states that it is ten degrees cooler at the top. This is no exaggeration and is one reason Mt. Atago is a popular refuge from the summer heat. A special festival called Sennichi Mairi, or "the thousand-day visit" is held the evening of July 31. Hiking up the lantern-lit steps at night is supposedly worth the equivalent of a thousand visits—your supplications are multiplied a thousand-fold.

ARASHIYAMA 嵐山

嵐山

Hozugawa Kudari 保津川下り
Togetsukyō 渡月橋
Hōrinji 法輪寺
Iwatayama Monkey Park 磐田山自然遊園地
Ōkōchi Sansō 大河内山荘
Jōjakkōji 常寂光寺
Rakushisha 落柿舎
Nonomiya Shrine 野宮神社
Tenryūji 天竜寺
Hōgon'in 宝厳院
Kōgenji 弘源寺

Nestled in the western hills of Kyoto, the tree-studded gorge of the Hozu River enters the city at Arashiyama, the "Storm Mountain" that has given its name to an area that offers visitors some of the city's finest scenery. There is also plenty of action to be found in touring Iwatayama Monkey Park or shooting the Hozu rapids. Pathways along the riverbanks offer many places to stroll, sit, and people-watch. The Zen temple complex of Tenryūji, a World Heritage Site, is here, along with the beautiful garden of Ōkōchi Sansō, and Jōjakkōji, with its spectacular view. Those with literary inclinations will not want to miss Rakushisha, or the evocative Nonomiya Shrine.

There are many ways to reach Arashiyama: City Bus, Kyoto Bus, and the JR, Keifuku, and Hankyū railways all go there. But the most scenic approach is to take the regular JR train or the narrow-gauge Romantic Train to the town of Kameoka and return to Arashiyama by running the rapids of the Hozu River, a trip known as the **Hozugawa Kudari.**

Take the JR Sagano Line from either Kyoto or Nijō Station to

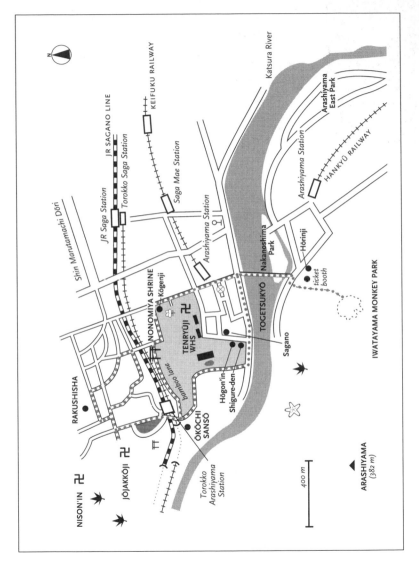

ARASHIYAMA

Saga Station, then walk to the nearby Torokko Saga Station, the starting point of the Romantic Train. (JR Saga Station and Torokko Saga Station are about a block apart.) One-way tickets are ¥600 for adults, ¥300 for children. The train winds through the spectacular Hozu River gorge to the wide, flat valley of Kameoka, terminating at Torokko Kameoka Station—a trip of about twenty-five minutes.

Those opting for the river trip should walk to JR Umahori Station (about ten minutes), catch the train to the next stop (JR Kameoka Station), and then walk about eight minutes toward the river. You will see a low building at which tickets are sold and boats launched. Fares are ¥3,900 for adults and ¥2,500 for children under eleven. Boats leave at 9, 10, 11, 12, 1, 2, and 3:30, except during January and February, when this service is discontinued. You may buy drinks there or wait until boats selling refreshments glide alongside your boat as you enter the placid waters of Arashiyama, an hour and forty minutes later.

If you did not take the Hozu River ride, but are tempted to view the scenery afloat, the blue rowboats at Arashiyama rent for ¥1,400 an hour. Large covered boats with an oarsman can be rented for ¥3,500 for a thirty-five-minute river tour during which the boatman will point out all the sights along a one-kilometer trip upriver.

One of the principal sights of Arashiyama is the famous old wooden bridge, **Togetsukyō**, which spans the Katsura River (as the Hozu River is known below Arashiyama; above Kameoka it is called the Ōi). The name means "Moon-Crossing Bridge," an allusion to the moon crossing the night sky. This bridge, with the mountains in the background, is represented in many a scroll and screen painting.

At the south end of the bridge is a narrow stairway with a white sign and black letters that reads *Jūsan-mairi*. This is the north entrance to **Hōrinji**, a Shingon temple to which many Kyotoites take their thirteen-year-old sons and daughters to be blessed so that they may face adulthood with wisdom and maturity. The semi-official dates for this ceremony are between March 13 and May 13, but at any time of the year, one may see young boys dressed in suits and girls in kimono being presented to the temple's priest for his prayers and blessing.

Besides being home to many species of birds, Kyoto has a large number of furry citizens that visitors can get a close look at in the **Iwatayama Monkey Park**. Admission is ¥500 for adults, ¥250 for children (an English pamphlet is provided). Those who make the steep ten-minute walk to the crest of Iwatayama will be rewarded with a panoramic view of the city. Iwatayama is one of several feeding stations in the city, and fifty or sixty monkeys assemble daily at 10, 11, 12, 1:30, and 3 to devour the dried soybeans scattered about by the attendants. Some of the younger monkeys have taken up an interesting activity dubbed *ishi asobi*. It looks like a version of the game played by seasoned carnival men where onlookers have to guess which container hides an object underneath while the containers are switched around rapidly. (Visitors are cautioned not to feed or touch the monkeys, nor to look the dominant monkeys directly in the eye).

There are many food stalls in the riverside area: some sell unusual varieties of Japanese sweets, such as soft green-tea ice cream cones and frozen sweet-bean-paste popsicles, as well as the usual kinds of beverages and food.

Ōkōchi Sansō [Open 9 to 5. Admission, with tea and a sweet, is ¥1,000. Tel: 872-2233] is an estate that was once the home of the famous silent-screen star Ōkōchi Denjirō (1898–1962). From the bridge, follow the walk along the north side of the river to the curving stone steps. The road enters a wooded area leading to Ōkōchi Sansō. The lush and varied garden uses a Japanese gardening conceit known as "borrowed scenery," incorporating a view of the nearby mountains into its spacious grounds. The use of roof tiles as borders around the sand-and-gravel entrance is ingenious in its simplicity. A restaurant on the grounds serves exquisitely named meals: Snow, Cloud, Moon, and Flower. Prices range from ¥4,000 to ¥12,000. Reservations are unnecessary, but it is advisable to call ahead. Tea is served in the building to the left of the exit or, weather permitting, outdoors. If this is your first taste of green tea, eat the sweet first, then take the bowl in both hands to sip the slightly bitter brew.

From Ōkōchi Sansō, turn left and walk toward a small gray-green pond with a shrine on its west bank. To the right is Torokko Arashiyama Station.

A scenic lane provides shade in Arashiyama.

The road that runs along the east side of the pond leads to the Nichiren temple, **Jōjakkōji** [Open 9 to 4:30. Admission ¥200. Tel: 861-0435]. A simple thatched gate at the top of a long flight of worn stone stairs marks the entrance. The main gate, flanked by two guardian deities (Niō) has many pairs of old faded straw sandals hanging from it. Long ago, pilgrims left them in thanks for accomplishing their goal and having prayers answered. The Main Hall, a building that once stood on the grounds of Fushimi Castle, has a small but restful garden, a landscaped microcosm of moss, stone, and azaleas. Farther up is a two-story pagoda dating to 1620, designated an Important Cultural Property. The superb view from the upper garden encompasses Sagano and Arashiyama. Tombs of past abbots dot the hilly grounds.

Exit the temple, turn left, then right. You will see a thatched house a block away. This is **Rakushisha** [Open 9 to 5. Tel: 881-1953], the "Cottage of Fallen Persimmons." One of the sites associated with the poets Kyorai and Bashō, its rural charm has endured. Many of the ornamental stones in the cottage's gardens have poems carved into them; the ¥150 admission includes a leaflet with translations.

Turn left when you exit, then right, crossing the train tracks. Ahead is a red picket fence that encloses **Nonomiya Shrine**. In ancient times, this shrine prepared imperial princesses for their duties as vestal virgins at the Grand Shrine of Ise. The main gate is of concrete, made to resemble a primitive one of bark-covered logs. Formerly, it was rebuilt when the maiden completed her three-year training, but the kind of oak used in its construction has grown scarce, forcing this practice to be discountinued. Mentioned in *The Tale of Genji*, and providing the setting for the Noh play *Nonomiya*, the shrine evokes many associations in people familiar with classical Japanese literature and is one of the most visited places in the area.

As you leave the shrine, turn right and follow the road until it emerges onto the main road. Turn right to reach the famous Rinzai Zen temple complex **Tenryūji** [Open 8:30 to 5:30; 5 in winter. Admission ¥600. Tel: 881-1235]. The path leading back to the Main Hall from this street passes many subtemples. Most are not open to the public, but some allow visitors into their front gardens. Overlooking the complex in the west is the magnificent Main Hall. Built in 1339, its garden is one of the oldest of the "borrowed scenery" type, incorporating the mountain that looms in the background. The graceful maples and the fresh green of the pines are reflected in the rock-lined pond. The temple architecture features cusp-arched windows and extensive covered walkways. Like the temple's name, which means "Heavenly Dragon," a path winds sinuously along the edge of the hill and exits on a shady, bamboo-lined road that runs along the north side of the temple.

There are two subtemples of Tenryūji that are only open several weeks in the spring and autumn but are well worth a visit. A combined visit costs ¥900, a slight saving but an appreciated gesture.

Hōgon'in [Open 9 to 5. Admission ¥500. Tel: 861-0091] was moved and reconstructed several times, a not uncommon occurrence with fires sweeping the city and civil wars destroying much property. The spacious garden dates from an earlier time than the temple buildings. It is a magnificent moss-covered stroll garden with one large boat-shaped rock that represents the vehicle one boards to cross from this world to the next.

Kōgenji [Open 9 to 5. Admission ¥500. Tel: 881-1232] has a small hall that houses the Important Cultural Property of the image of Bishamonten, the guardian of the north. Within the main building, several rooms are filled with painted sliding *fusuma* doors. The *karesansui* rock-and-sand garden in the main building is of special note. Compact and strong, the juxtaposition of rock, sand, and moss is masterfully complemented by a large crepe myrtle tree. The wooden pillars between the doors of the Main Hall bear the unusual scar of sword marks. Members of the Chōshū clan practiced their swordsmanship here during the civil war years leading to the Meiji Restoration in 1868. White strips of paper with lettering are pasted to the spots where chunks of wood were cleaved.

A sophisticated card game called *karuda* in which players complete a poem by matching it to its partner card has been recreated in the **Shigure-den** [Open 10 to 5. Admission ¥800. Tel: 882-1103], a museum that tests visitors' knowledge of the *Hyakunin Isshu*, an anthology of *waka* poems. Unless one is familiar with these poetic verses, a visit might not prove interesting.

Arashiyama is famous for *yudōfu*, considered by many the most delicate of all Kyoto dishes. This hot-pot of simmered bean curd is eaten after dipping it into a pungent soy sauce mixture. Tiny wire scoops are provided for fishing the soft cubes of tofu out of the boiling stock. *Yudōfu* eateries, identifiable by red-and-white striped lanterns and the plastic food samples displayed in their windows, can be found along the north bank of the river and near Jōjakkōji. A simple serving of *yudōfu* costs ¥1,000. Within the precincts of Tenryūji is the *yudōfu* restaurant **Seizan Sōdō** [Open 11:30 to 4:30. Tel: 882-9725], specializing in the Buddhist vegetarian cooking *shōjin ryōri*. Lunch is ¥3,000 and is served on bright red lacquer dishes in a Japanese garden. Reservations are recommended.

Another restaurant for *yudōfu* is called **Sagano** [Open 11 to 7. Tel: 861-0277]. The east garden is filled with stone statues of bodhisattvas while the north garden features sand-and-rock "waves." The restaurant interior is tastefully done in traditional Japanese style, and all rooms overlook gardens. The owner is a *shakuhachi* (bamboo flute) enthusiast, and the restful sounds of this instrument accompany the ten-dish, ¥3,500 course.

For those interested in prolonging the mood induced by the dramatic scenery, there are footpaths through Nakanoshima Park just south of Togetsukyō. This is where the flat-bottomed river boats are loaded onto trucks for the return trip to Kameoka. Arashiyama East Park also runs beside the Katsura River here, and its paths lead to the next Hankyū Railway Station at Matsuo, where you can get a train returning to the city (transfer at Katsura) or catch City Bus 3 for Shijō-Kawaramachi.

UZUMASA 太秦

Myōshinji 妙心寺
Taizōin 退蔵院
Keishun'in 桂春院
Daishin'in 大心院
Hōkongōin 法金剛院
Kaiko no Yashiro 蚕ノ社
Kōryūji 広隆寺
Tōei Movie Village 東栄映画村

Snarled with traffic and dense with shops, the bustling neighborhoods that make up Uzumasa are among the oldest settled areas in the Kyoto basin. Some of Kyoto's most important temples and gardens—Myōshinji, Hōkongōin, and Kōryūji—are located here. Amid the encroaching urbanization and heavy traffic, they remain tranquil repositories of art and history, sanctuaries for spiritual pursuits.

Many fine examples of Zen architecture can be found among the main buildings and subtemples in the precincts of **Myōshinji** [Open 9:10 to 3:40. Tel: 463-3121], the largest of all of Japan's Zen temples, which includes forty-six subtemples. To reach Myōshinji, take the Keifuku Railway from Hakubaichō three stops to Myōshinji Station (¥210), or City Bus 10 or 26 to Myōshinjimae (¥220). Either will leave you a short walk from the North Gate of the complex.

Although it is an active training center of the Rinzai school, the Hattō (Lecture Hall) and Hōjō (Abbot's Quarters), as well as several of the subtemples, are open to the public. Founded by Kanzan Egen in 1337 under the patronage of the retired emperor Hanazono, the monastery was destroyed during the Ōnin War (1467–77). Most of today's buildings date from the 1600s. Two large plaques mounted

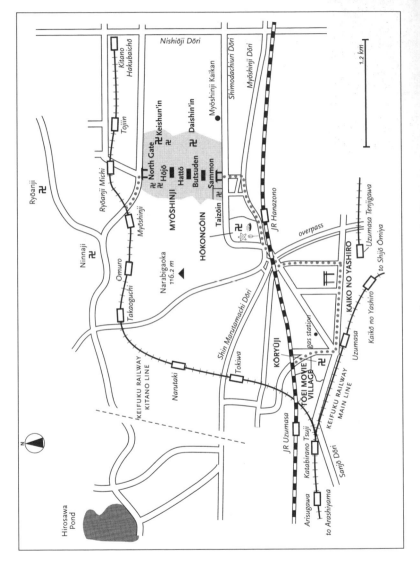

UZUMASA

under the eaves of the veranda of the Hōjō list the names of thirty-five-hundred affiliated temples nationwide, testifying to the continuing importance of this venerable institution.

Zen was one of the last major forms of Buddhism to enter Japan, and along with it came the architectural style of Sung-dynasty China. The temple precincts (*garan*) have the broad, symmetrical design found in each of Kyoto's Zen temple complexes. The Sammon, or entrance gate, faces south, and behind it in a line are the Butsuden (Buddha Hall), Hattō, and Hōjō. Besides the symmetry of the basic plan, other Chinese architectural features include window shutters that open out and upward, and the large Chinese-style abbot's chair facing the altar in the Lecture Hall, the floor of which is at ground level and paved with squares of slate. In contrast to the main buildings with their Chinese flavor, the subtemples on the outer edge of the complex are all in Japanese style, surrounded with flowering trees and shrubs reflecting the Japanese love of gardens. Although not all of the subtemples are open to the public, glimpses of their well-tended front gardens can be viewed from their gates.

Begin your tour of the Myōshinji complex at the North Gate. Two stone paths lead from it to the Hattō and adjoining Hōjō. A handsome stone *tatami*-style path (slabs of stone geometrically arranged) leads to the central precinct, as does the narrow stone path on the left that skirts the northeast side of the temple, passing a large open area that serves as the monastery's vegetable patch.

Admission to the **Hattō** is ¥500. It includes a twenty-minute tour of that building and of an old bathhouse, as well as an excellent written explanation in English. Tours are conducted consecutively from 9:10 to 11:50 and 12:40 to 3:40. Visitors waiting for the next tour can visit the Hōjō and admire the ink-wash paintings on its sliding doors, the work of Kanō Tan'yū (1602–74), and sit and appreciate the garden.

Guides announce the beginning of the tour and swing open a

gigantic wooden door to usher visitors into the cavernous Lecture Hall. Banners of bright colored silk hang from high above, adding a dramatic touch to the otherwise austere setting of unpainted walls. The banners also serve as a frame for the magnificent picture of a dragon that covers the entire ceiling. Originally painted in color with vegetable dyes, the picture has now faded to shades of black and white. This monumental work is a masterpiece by Tan'yū, one of the most talented artists of the Edo period, and has remained untouched for 350 years.

In Asia, the dragon is the king of beasts. His flights into the heavens place him above all the other animals in the Asian zodiac, and he is the most powerful. Tan'yū gave his creature the eyes of a cow, the mouth of a crocodile, the whiskers of a catfish, the horn of a deer, the body of a carp, the tail of a snake, and the talons of a falcon. Viewing it from the west side of the hall, the dragon appears to be descending, and from the east, ascending. The guide invites everyone to walk around the hall to view the painting from several angles.

In the northeast corner of the hall is a bell believed to be the oldest in Japan; it is inscribed with a date corresponding to 698. It was in use until around 1962. Designated a National Treasure, it was replaced by the replica hanging in the adjacent bell tower.

The next building on the tour is the bathhouse, or more correctly, steam-bathhouse. There is another bell tower directly north of the bathhouse whose bell was struck to announce when the bath was ready. Wooden benches immediately inside the bathhouse entrance served as places for monks to sit and meditate while they waited to enter the bath, reminding them not only to clean their bodies, but also their minds. Superiors bathed separately from monks of lower rank, and a lacquered sign indicated who was occupying the bath. Bathing, by the way, was a luxury and not a daily custom. Its infrequency was one part of the strict training postulants had to endure. Dates that contained a four or nine and New Year's Eve were bath days. In the smoke-blackened back room, water was stored in stone troughs and heated in three cauldrons. Steam filled the enclosed wooden room, and after spending a few minutes in the dense atmosphere, the monks went out to the "washing place," an area in front of the steam room where a floor of solid wooden planking slants slightly toward the center of the room, where there is a narrow opening to carry away the rinse water. Two charred spots on the floor indicate where candles burned to illuminate the bath. The steam bath was used until 1935. Since then bathing has taken place in the modernized subtemples and is no longer the communal experience it used to be.

Taizōin [Open 9 to 5. Admission ¥500. Tel: 463-2855] provides a lush contrast to the severe, formal atmosphere of the main buildings. There are two fine gardens in this subtemple: an older Zen garden associated with Kanō Motonobu (1434–1530), founder of the Kanō school of painting, who lived here; the other by the modern landscape artist Nakane Kinsaku (1917–95).

The former is Myōshinji's most famous garden. Located in front of the Main Hall of Taizōin, it is composed of low rocks and azalea bushes surrounded by white gravel, suggesting a river flowing around boulders. A replica of the painting "Catching a Catfish with a Gourd," a National Treasure, sits on the veranda. Painted by Josetsu, a master of the Sung style of Chinese painting, it illustrates a Zen allegory of trying to catch a slipper fish with a smooth-mouthed gourd. The original is now in the Kyoto National Museum.

Nakane's modern garden is to the right of the graveyard. The upper level is composed of a graceful weeping willow flanked by powerfully arranged stones and gravel. The lower level of the garden is markedly different: the ground disappears under billowy, cloud-like azalea bushes, giving its softly shaped greenery a very sensuous feeling. This voluptuousness, contrasting with the sparseness of the upper level, divides the garden into two realms—

the sacred and the secular. A Zen tradition is upheld in the fact that both sections are to be viewed rather than strolled through.

Green tea and a sweet bearing a catfish-and-gourd motif (an allusion to Josetsu's painting) is ¥500 and can be paid for in advance at the concession.

Two other Myōshinji subtemples are open to the public: Keishun'in in the northeast sector of the precincts, and Daishin'in, located to the east of the Hōjō. Compared to Taizōin, they are small and modest. **Keishun'in** [Open 9 to 5. Admission ¥400. Tel: 463-6578] has two gardens in the Zen tradition. One suggests a deep woodland setting; the other acts as a passage from the mundane world into the spiritual world of tea. The new garden of **Daishin'in** [Open 9 to 4. Admission ¥300. Tel: 461-5714] is called "A-Un," meaning alpha and omega, the beginning and the end—that which includes everything. A narrow strip of gravel along the veranda is filled with a "stream" of deeply raked gravel that cuts through moss and rock "banks."

The traditional entrance to Myōshinji is the Sammon gate near the southern end of the complex. This pale red structure was built in 1599, and, as with many other Zen temples, a rectangular pond and grove of tall pines stand to its south. The modern entrance to the temple complex lies east of the Sammon, but the original approach is wonderfully dramatic.

The new **Myōshinji Kaikan** [Tel: 467-1666] to the east of the Sammon on Shimadachiuri Dōri has a restaurant that offers temple food served in red lacquer dishes from ¥1,800.

On leaving the south entrance of Myōshinji, turn right and continue west until reaching the Hanazono JR Station. Across from the station, on the north side of the street, is **Hōkongōin** [Open 9 to 4. Admission ¥400. Tel: 461-9418]. Originally, its grounds were part of a villa of a Minister of the Right (the Heian-period equivalent of a prime minister), who lived here in the early ninth century. The grounds were turned into a temple on his death. After a pe-

A landscaped entrance to Tenryūji, one of Kyoto's largest Zen complexes.

riod of decline, it was restored in 1129 by Taikenmon'in, consort of Emperor Toba. Today, in spite of the consolidation of its buildings and grounds when Shin Marutamachi Dōri was widened in 1937, it contains a rare example of a Heian-period garden. Its Treasure House has four magnificent Buddhist statues designated Important Cultural Properties; visitors are provided an excellent English explanation of its contents and of the temple's history. The figures displayed from left to right are an eleven-headed Kannon, the guardian deity Fudō Myōō, a seated Amida Nyorai, the priest Shōjin Osho, the bodhisattvas Monjū and Jizō, and a standing image of Amida.

The temple also is known for the large variety of lotus flowers it cultivates. These lotuses, which have been assembled from many different prefectures and countries, bloom from mid-July to mid-August. (During this time, the garden opens at 6:30 a.m., when the flowers start to open with a pop.) Its hanging cherry trees, irises, hydrangeas, and maples also attract visitors. Gently masking the sounds of traffic is the oldest artificial waterfall in Japan.

The Uzumasa area was settled by the members of the Hata clan, of Chinese-Korean origin, who came to Japan in the fourth century. They were a prosperous family who brought with them the secrets of sericulture. (Coincidental or not, *hata* is the Japanese word for loom.) Not surprisingly, **Konoshima Shrine**, popularly known as **Kaiko no Yashiro** (Silkworm Shrine), has a small structure on its grounds dedicated to the god of silkworms. To reach the shrine, cross Shin Marutamachi Dōri at the light west of Hōkongōin, cross under the elevated JR train tracks, and turn right. Take the second left after the elevated road and walk in the direction of a woods, the treetops of which are visible two hundred meters to the south. At the entrance of the shrine stands a huge unpainted cryptomeria-wood *torii*.

Although it is not known when the shrine was founded, it is mentioned in a chronicle written in 701. The woods on the grounds are known as Moto Tadasu no Mori, and held to be the predecessor of the famous Tadasu no Mori in the precincts of Shimogamo Shrine (*moto* means "original"). Pure water was essential in the production of textiles, and the spring here was considered sacred. Even today, people still believe that wetting their hands and feet in its water in summer will protect them from chilblains and beriberi. The symbol of Konoshima Shrine is an unusual triple-pillared *torii* that stands in the pond in the northwest corner of the grounds. Its unique shape allows worshippers to approach it from three directions. This is one of the three unusual *torii* for which Kyoto is famous; the others are the stone *torii* of Itsukushima Shrine in the Imperial Palace Park and the stone *torii* at Kitano Temmangū Shrine.

Exit the shrine and turn right. Follow the street until it merges with Sanjō Dōri. To the west is **Kōryūji** [Open 9 to 5. Tel: 861-1461], built in 603 to house a Buddhist image presented to Hata no Kawakatsu, head of the Hata clan, by Prince Shōtoku (572–621), the imperial regent credited with promoting Buddhism. This image, still displayed, is one of the best known in Japan. The entrance to Kōryūji is on the north side of Sanjō Dōri. The white-walled Kōdō (Lecture Hall) on the right is the oldest structure in the compound. Built in 1165, it houses a trinity of immense wooden statues; an Amida (a National Treasure) flanked by the bodhisattvas Jizō (right) and Kokuzō (left), both of which are Important Cultural Properties. These images date from the ninth century. The Hondō, with an immense black roof, was built in 1713 and is the largest building on the complex. Inside, the coffered ceiling is covered with painted motifs.

A ¥700 admission fee allows entrance to the Treasure House, located at the back of the compound. No English information is given, although English labels identify many of the statues within the hall. This modern structure is one of the most attractive temple treasure houses in Kyoto. The richly colored cherrywood floor and the walls and ceiling of pale paulownia provide a soft backdrop to a world-famous collection of Buddhist statues. The main figure is of Miroku Bosatsu (the bodhisattva Maitreya, also known as the Buddha-to-Come). The crowned image is seated with its right foot resting on the left knee and right hand almost touching the right cheek—a pose of contemplation. Although originally covered with gold foil, only the natural soft luster of Miroku's red pine structure remains. Glimmerings of gold leaf can still be detected around the right ear and at the waist. (Sprinklings of gold foil are also visible on the image to the right.) The original of this delicate figure is the subject of ongoing research. Some scholars believe that the image was brought to Japan from Korea; others contend that it was made here by Korean or native artisans. Farther to the right of Miroku Bosatsu along the same wall are two seated wooden figures that represent Hata no Kawakatsu and his wife, clothed in the robes of nobility.

The huge figures opposite Miroku Bosatsu once had their own buildings and for years stood at the back of the Lecture Hall. The deterioration of some of the images provides insight into their construction. For example, the large seated figure in the middle, dating to 1012, was made in sections and fitted together, a process known as *yosegi-zukuri*.

Kōryūji also has an octagonal chapel that is considered by some scholars to be the oldest in Kyoto. It is open for viewing on Sundays in the months of April, May, October, and November.

Although one would expect to find such an august site a haven of tranquility, unfortunately this is not the case, thanks to the **Tōei Movie Village** [Tōei Eiga Mura. Open 9 to 4:30. Admission: adults ¥2,200; Jr. and Sr. high school ¥1,300; elementary school ¥1,100. Tel: 864-7716] that abuts Kōryūji on the north. The "village" is a collection of old sets readily recognizable to Japanese TV viewers. There is even a pond out of which emerges a Nessie-like creature. A favorite place for visiting students and fans of samurai dramas, the complex can be viewed in about an hour, depending on your enthusiasm. For ¥12,000, one can be dressed and made-up as a geisha or samurai.

Opposite Kōryūji's gate is Uzumasa Station on the Keifuku Arashiyama Line. Note that tickets are not sold on the platform. Instead, a ticket machine just inside the door of the train dispenses them. Board, take one, and pay when you get off. A ¥200 ticket will take you to either Shijō-Ōmiya or Arashiyama.

If you are in the mood for walking a little farther, a pleasant pond called Hirosawa Ike is about a thirty-minute walk to the northwest of Kōryūji. That scenic area is a good deal more restful than the streets traveled earlier. From the pond, City Buses 10, 26, and 59 provide frequent access to downtown.

OMURO 御室

Ninnaji 仁和寺
Ryōanji 竜安寺
Kinkakuji 金閣寺

For centuries, people have traveled to sites considered sacred due to their association with a religious figure or miraculous event. Benares, Canterbury, Lourdes, Mecca—all are famous destinations for pilgrims. Japan, too, has its share of famous holy places. As readers of The Tale of Genji *know, Kyotoites made pilgrimages to the Grand Shrine of Ise a thousand years ago. Even today, many Japanese make circuit pilgrimages to a prescribed number of temples for social and religious reasons. For those who cannot make the long journey, scaled-down versions of these rugged treks exist throughout the country. The eighty-eight temple circuit on the island of Shikoku is perhaps Japan's most famous pilgrimage route. Kyoto has its own miniature version of this route in the district of Omuro, on the grounds of the temple Ninnaji. Two of Kyoto's most famous and most visited temples are also close to this area. Ryōanji with its renowned rock garden and Kinkakuji, the Golden Pavilion, with its glittering façade both provide interesting contrasts to Ninnaji, which was originally the palace of a retired emperor.*

In 886, Emperor Kōkō started construction of a palace at Omura in the northwest of Kyoto. It was completed during the reign of his successor, Emperor Uda, who made it his retirement residence, which came to be known as Omuro Gosho (Omuro Palace). Later, the palace was designated a Shingon temple and renamed **Ninnaji**. For nearly a thousand years a prince of imperial lineage served as its abbot, and its buildings and grounds are constructed in an elegant regal style befitting a *monzeki* temple (the title given to a temple governed by an imperial prince). Ninnaji once possessed

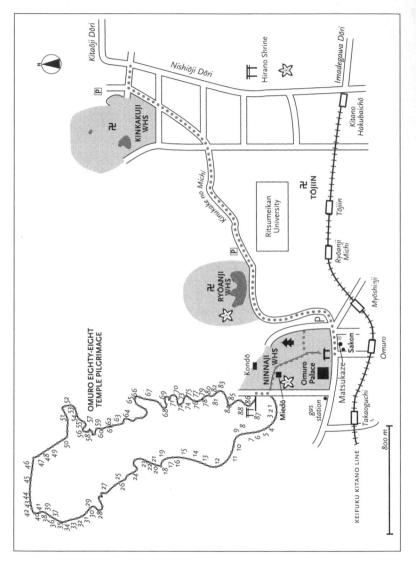

OMURO

vast tracts of land and encompassed sixty subtemples and several hills. Over the centuries fires have greatly reduced the temple's size, but its oldest buildings, dating from the seventeenth century, are among Japan's most important cultural assets.

Ninnaji is also home to the Omuro school of *ikebana*, and examples of this style of flower arrangement are displayed in the complex of buildings to the left of the main gate, the **Omuro Gosho** [Open 9 to 4:30. Admission ¥500. Tel: 461-1155], constructed on the site of Emperor Uda's original palace in a restoration of the temple carried out in the 1630s. Nowadays the temple is probably best known for the lively hordes of cherry blossom viewers who crowd the grounds in April to enjoy the two hundred late-blooming dwarf cherry trees (*Omuro-zakura*). Entrance to the temple grounds is usually free, but during the cherry blossom season a ¥200 admission fee is charged.

The **Reihōkan** [Open 9 to 4, in season. Admission ¥500], the temple's museum, is located to the east of the Omuro Gosho. Open only during the months of April, May, October, and November, it houses many Buddhist artifacts, including a number of National Treasures and Important Cultural Properties.

A five-story pagoda stands to the east of the main path. It dates to the renovation of the temple in the 1630s, as do the **Kondō** (Main Hall) and **Miedō** (Founder's Hall). The latter were originally two of the central buildings of the main imperial palace, and were reconstructed on the temple grounds (the palace itself was being completely rebuilt at the same time). The splendid square Founder's Hall, topped with a flaming jewel, is dedicated to the great teacher Kūkai (774–835), posthumously known as Kōbō Daishi. Kōbō Daishi was born on the island of Shikoku, and his followers later established a pilgrimage route on Shikoku, one of the most famous in Japan, made up of eighty-eight temples with which Kōbō Daishi is said to have been associated.

Kōbō Daishi is honored in another way at Ninnaji; the Shikoku pilgrimage route dedicated to him has been reconstructed behind the temple and is known as the **Omuro Eighty-Eight Temple Pilgrimage**. The imperial prince and twenty-ninth abbot of Ninnaji, Sainin, was a devoted follower of the Buddhist saint. The temple compound lies at the foot of Mt. Jōju, and it was here, in 1829, that Sainin decided to reproduce in miniature the eighty-eight temples of Shikoku. Completed in 1832, most of the structures were destroyed in an earthquake that struck Kyōto the following year. They were reconstructed and, ever since, religious devotees, health enthusiasts, dog walkers, joggers, and sightseers have made the approximately two-hour, three-kilometer walk. It is advisable to take along something to drink if the day is hot because there is nothing sold along the course.

The route begins at the northwest side of the Ninnaji compound beyond a small gate. After passing through the gate, about two hundred meters ahead is a conspicuous white sign with black lettering. This indicates the first "temple." (The rest will have small stone markers with their numbers written in Chinese characters.)

Temple No. 1 is to the right of the sign. The priest who lives here said that the most frequent travelers are local people who walk the route to keep in shape or to enjoy the view. In fact, about a thousand people stop at his temple every month to light a candle or incense and pray before starting off. There is also a public restroom here, which many prospective climbers take advantage of.

The pilgrimage continues from behind a large statue of Kōbō Daishi that stands between the temple and restroom. Like a paved ribbon, the path stretches ahead and veers slightly to the right through a wooded area of Japanese cypress trees (*hinoki*), but farther along the woods begin to vary. All along the left side of the path are set low stone posts with Sanskrit letters engraved near their tops. These represent the names of different deities—gods of strength, dance, poetry, and others. (Sanskrit traveled to Japan from China and Korea with Buddhism as part of the Buddhist liturgy.)

Most of the "temples" are small wooden buildings with cusped windows and wooden lattices covering glass windowpanes (though as time takes its toll, new concrete structures are starting to appear). Many of the altars have dusty plaster statues of Kōbō Daishi and Kannon, bodhisattva of mercy. Some visitors observe the tradition of leaving one yen at each stop or eighty-eight yen at the eighty-eighth temple for good fortune. Sundays from April to November, rubber stamps are available at each stop and you may notice people collecting imprints.

The ninth temple depicts the well-known scene of the death of Shakyamuni, the historical Buddha. Barely visible through the dusty glass, Shakyamuni is shown lying atop several layers of bedding, his disciples waiting nearby. To the right of this temple is a tall stone lantern, and beyond that a stone stupa almost covered by undergrowth.

From No. 13 the staired path grows steeper. It gently climbs and dips, and trees have been cleared in several places, affording visitors different views of Kyoto. Although it is only 236 meters high, it is amazing how much of the city can be seen from the slopes of Mt. Jōju.

No. 28 has a carving of waves in the front eaves, a motif that perhaps alludes to the parent pilgrimage temple on the island of Shikoku. To the left of No. 33 is a large bronze statue of Kōbō Daishi, minus the begging bowl that should be in his left hand.

No. 36 is larger than most, and one of its walls is formed of orange clay. No. 37 has a carved dragon in the front and a paneled ceiling covered with faded paintings of flowers. Many of the "temples" were given by devotees, and quirks of personal taste may have determined their appearance.

No. 41 is a lovely six-sided structure with an unframed cusped window. Between Nos. 43 and 44, a small sign hanging from a tree points to a nearby lookout where log benches in a clearing make a favorite spot for picnickers. The view is of the mountains, which stretch before you, offering their beauty in solitude and silence. Pygmy woodpeckers, varied tits, long-tailed tits, and Siberian blue-chats can been seen in this vicinity in the cooler months. Besides the sounds of the birds, pilgrims greet others on the trail with a hearty "*Konnichiwa*" or "Good day." Give it a try, and you will be greeted in kind.

Soon after No. 52, the path splits. No. 53 (to the right) has a solid rock approach that can be climbed. The path continues from behind the temple to No. 54, which enshrines a statue of Fudō Myōō, a popular Buddhist deity who is always portrayed with a fierce countenance and flames.

No. 64 faces a small overgrown pond. There are many ferns, mountain azalea, and *dodan*, a deciduous azalea, growing beneath the larger pines and cypresses in the area. No. 65 forms part of a priest's residence. An eleven-headed Kannon (not open to public viewing) is housed deep within its altar. A side path leads back to a man-made waterfall that pours forth in a single stream. Many stone statues of Fudō Myōō have been placed at the water's source. This waterfall is used in the practice of a religious austerity: practitioners stand beneath it reciting sutras in hopes that the force of the water will cleanse the spirit and awaken the Buddha nature within them.

After No. 85, the path widens. The rest of the temples are here, as well as a large iris pond stocked with beautiful carp. A stone bridge spans the pond and leads to No. 88, the last and biggest of the temples. Tiny bright orange shrines dot the grounds, and there is a large statue of Kōbō Daishi in traditional pilgrim garb, complete with cotton leggings. The wide road leads back to the side gate of Ninnaji, the same gate you emerged from two hours ago. Beverages are available at the temple's concessions.

Across from the main gate of Ninnaji are several restaurants. One called **Sakon**, directly south of the main gate, features French food served Japanese-style. Lunches start from ¥4,700. Although reservations are not necessary, on weekends or holidays it is advised. Next door is the noodle shop **Matsukaze** [Open 11 to 3. Closed Tuesdays. Tel: 462-7272]. There are also a number of coffee shops along Kinukake no Michi, the road that leads to the next major temple, Ryōanji, about a ten-minute walk east.

Ryōanji [Open 8 to 5. Admission ¥400. Tel: 463-2216] has the most famous Zen rock garden in the world. A picture of it is included in textbooks and, for this reason, it is almost always included on high-school trip itineraries. The garden is not really for the

A two-tiered pagoda on the grounds of Ninnaji.

young, and children are not admitted unless accompanied by an adult. Viewed from the hall's veranda, a scattering of rocks nestled in beds of moss appear on a flat surface of white raked gravel enclosed by a rustic earthen wall. The deceptive simplicity of this tableau reveals the austerity and discipline of the Zen mind. It is said that the garden has nothing but has everything. It takes a mature mind to appreciate this minimalist beauty and restrained aesthetic. Except for a light dusting of snow, a few scattered cherry blossoms, or fallen maple leaves, the seasons do not play a significant part in this garden's attractiveness. It is a contemplation garden, one that requires time and silence to appreciate. In contrast, the outer grounds are as lush as the rock garden is severe. Every seasonal flower is represented in this thousand-year-old garden, for this was the estate of a nobleman who lived here long before the influence of Zen came to Japan. The path runs by a large pond called Kyoyochi, and the flat-bottomed boats near the water's edge are replicas of ancient craft used by this aristocrat. Clearings along the paths that lead up the mountain to imperial tombs behind the temple offer fine views of the city. On the Ryōanji grounds, just beside the pond, is a reasonably priced *yudōfu* (bean curd hot-pot) restaurant with outdoor seating called **Saigen'in**, the servings as minimalist as the garden [Open 10 to 5. Tel: 462-4742].

Another twenty minutes' walk east on Kinukake no Michi is **Kinkakuji**, the Golden Pavilion [Open 9 to 5. Admission ¥400. Tel: 461-0013]. The villa of the nobleman Saionji Kintsune stood here in the early thirteenth century. A little over a century later, the third Ashikaga shogun, Yoshimitsu (1358–1408), built the pavilion here as part of his sprawling retirement estate. The complex within which it stands is known as the Zen temple Rokuonji, for Yoshimitsu bequeathed his estate to the famous priest Musō Kokushi, who because its first abbot. For centuries the Golden Pavilion was the jewel of the temple until it was burned to the ground in 1950 by a young priest, an incident retold as fiction in Mishima Yukio's novel *Kinkakuji*. The present building is an exact replica of the original, completed in 1955.

The main approach to Kinkakuji is broad and shaded by a dense covering of maple trees. After passing through the temple's gate, the view expands to include the pond and pavilion. It may seem a typically Japanese piece of architecture, but in 1394 when Yoshimitsu combined several different architectural styles in its construction, the three-story building was considered innovative. The pavilion was renovated in 1987, and regilded with gold leaf five times thicker than that used on the original. The dazzling roof is reflected in the aptly named Kagamiike, or Mirror Pond.

None of the temple buildings may be entered, but the stroll garden offers plenty of views on this elegant structure and the gardens of other buildings on the grounds. To the right (or north) of the pavilion is a remarkably shaped pine tree, its extended branch pruned and supported to resemble a boat.

Along the way to the three temples on this walk are shops that sell pottery, prints, and assorted crafts, so there is ample opportunity for window-shopping. Many buses are available on Nishiōji Dōri, the thoroughfare just east of the Golden Pavilion.

ŌHARANO 大原野

Ōharano Shrine 大原野神社
Shōhōji 勝法寺
Hana no Tera (Shōjiji) 勝侍寺
Gantokuji 願徳寺
Chikurin Kōen 竹林公園

Ōharano, in the southwest corner of the city, is home to a temple so famous for its trees that local residents refer to it as Hana no Tera (Cherry Blossom Temple), instead of Shōjiji, its formal name. Its next-door neighbors, Ōharano Shrine and the temple Shōhōji, with lovely cherries of their own, are also worth a visit.

Buses leave Higashi Muko Station (a fifteen-minute ride from downtown Kyoto on the Hankyū Railway) approximately every thirty minutes. Just outside the station's only exit, catch Hankyū Bus 5, bound for Minami Kasugachō (¥270). Take the bus to the end of the line (a twenty-minute ride). Ōharano Shrine is a seven-minute walk from there. A sign at the bus terminus points the way. When the road forks, bear right, and in a few minutes you will see a large stone *torii*, the entrance to the shrine, on the right.

Ōharano Shrine dates from about 784, when nearby Nagaoka became the site of the imperial court. When the decision to move the court here was made, along with the emperor came the influential Fujiwara clan, many of whose members were government ministers. The head of the clan invited the family's tutelary god to relocate with them and the god accepted, it is said, riding into the new capital on the back of a deer. Because of the area's associations with the Fujiwara, a bronze deer, several stone ones, and even four live ones are found at this shrine. Fortunes sold here

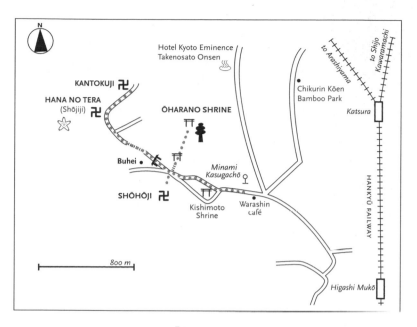

ŌHARANO

come as tightly rolled slips of paper held in the mouths of tiny wooden deer. Another interesting feature is that, instead of the usual guardian gods, male and female deer keep watch at either side of the main shrine. On its right is a towering fir, 450 years of age, the oldest tree in the shrine. Beyond the lily pond is a spring enclosed by stone posts, water from which was used in 851 for the infant emperor Seiwa's first bath.

The path to **Shōhōji** [Open 9 to 5. Admission ¥300. A bowl of tea with a sweet is ¥300. Tel: 331-0105] starts almost directly across from the entrance to Ōharano Shrine. None of the original buildings of this Shingon temple, founded in the Tempyō era (729–49), remain. A lovely hundred-year-old hanging cherry presides over a new rock garden made up of a menagerie of stones collected by parishioners from different prefectures in Japan. Among them you can pick out stones resembling all kinds of animals—even a penguin! Some of the garden's other features have been given more spiritual attributes: Pond of the Heart, Rainbow Bridge, and the Goddess of Mercy Waterfall. Also on the grounds are two large statues of the bodhisattva Jizō, protector of children. Prayers for aborted children are directed to these images in hopes that the souls will receive Buddha's heavenly guidance in the next life. Placed before some of the smaller statues are offerings of candy or other treats that a child would enjoy.

Shōjiji, or **Hana no Tera** [Open 9 to 4:30. Admission ¥400. Tel: 331-0601], is a ten-minute walk in the direction of the mountains from either Ōharano Shrine or Shōhōji and can be identified by a large stone marker by the roadside. Uneven stone steps lead up to an unpretentious, faded red gate that houses images of a pair of temple guardians called Niō. One has his mouth open to utter the first letter of the Sanskrit alphabet, *ah*, welcoming goodness. The other has his mouth closed as he pronounces the last letter, *un*, shutting out evil.

Because the temple is so isolated, the walk to it seems long. Perhaps this remoteness is what attracted Saigyō (1118–90), a famous poet-priest who composed many verses about Hana no Tera while he lived in a hut on the grounds. His love of the cherry blossoms was so great that he expressed a longing to die beneath these trees bathed in the light of a full moon. During a remarkably full and varied life as an imperial palace guard, then as a Buddhist priest, and lastly, as a poet, he traveled throughout the country writing about his travels and exploits. Centuries later, these trips were emulated by his admirer, the famous poet Bashō.

Among the temple's approximately two hundred cherry trees are a variety named *Saigyō-zakura* in his honor, many *somei yoshino* trees, and a number of weeping cherries. When the flowers

The Buddhist images at Shōhōji are dedicated to lost children.

are open, the pale pink billowing blossoms add a softness to the hilly grounds; later, the little pond and paths are covered with their petals. In the fall, the leaves turn a rich golden peach color, bringing a vividness to the grounds that is heightened by the deep blue autumn sky.

On the porch of the temple's main building sits a small carved figure of Binzuru, a disciple of Buddha said to have the power to heal sickness. Generations of worshippers have rubbed off the red lacquer that once covered him in the hope that their illness would be healed. On the other side of the porch is a turn-of-the-century wooden water pump.

The temple's concrete storehouse contains several treasures that are well worth seeing. The tiny Yakushi Buddha on the center pedestal was originally found inside the bronze seated image that now sits behind it. At the back of the storehouse stands a venerable set of twelve statues, one for each year of the Asian zodiac, starting on the left with the rat, followed by the ox, tiger, rabbit, dragon, snake, horse, ram, monkey, rooster, dog, and boar.

A few minutes' walk beyond Hana no Tera is a much smaller Tendai temple, **Gantokuji** [Open 9:30 to 4:30. Admission ¥400. Tel: 331-3823], which houses a seated Goddess of Mercy image, a National Treasure, in its concrete storehouse.

Although well known to Kyotoites, Hana no Tera's relative inaccessibility means that in April crowds here are smaller than elsewhere. This part of Kyoto is truly rural, and many unmanned wayside stalls offer vegetables fresh from the nearby fields. They operate on the honor system, so just take your pick and leave the amount specified.

Dense bamboo forests provide the district with the main ingredient for the delectable spring dish *takenoko gohan*, rice cooked with succulent slivers of bamboo shoot. A luxurious Japanese restaurant called **Buhei** [Open 11 to 9:30. Tel: 331-2248] is situated five minutes from the main entrance to Hana no Tera. Box lunches (*obentō*) served in a *tatami* room start from ¥3,000. During bamboo shoot season, local eateries also offer less elaborate dishes based on this delicacy. One is **Warashin**, a small coffee shop and eatery next to the Minami Kasugachō bus stop. Open during lunch and after 6, bamboo dishes are available in season.

A two-kilometer walk from Ōharano Shrine is the impressive bamboo park, **Chikurin Kōen Bamboo Park** [Open 9 to 4:30. Free admission. Tel: 331-3821; www.5.ocn.ne.jp/~rakusai/kyoto.html]. While difficult to reach, it is worth a visit, particularly for those interested in bamboo. The walk through rural housing and fields will take about 45 minutes but finding Fukunishi-Higashi Dōri is difficult, so catching a taxi would be an easier means of getting there. Planted with 110 varieties of bamboo, the spacious garden uses bamboo grass as a ground cover while the pathways are lined with lush groves of multiple varieties. The focal point of the layout is a 450-year-old stone bridge of historical interest, as it divided two warring factions during the Ōnin War (1467–77). The stone images of Buddha are ones unearthed during the construction of the subway and given a new home here.

In the museum is one of Thomas Edison's original bamboo filament light bulbs. Searching for an ideal filament for his invention, he tested over 6,000 kinds of plant material fiber. Thin strips of bamboo proved the best, and of the three varieties, the best was found in Jōyō, a city a little south of here. The two species of bamboo favored by the giant panda, *yadake* and *sochiku,* are also displayed here.

Walk five minutes from the Minami Fukunishi Chō City bus stop to take bus Nishi 3 or Nishi 8 to Hankyū Katsura Station.

Takenosato Onsen is a refreshing way to end a day of sightseeing. Appropriately enough, *take-no-sato* means bamboo village. [Located in the Hotel Kyoto Eminence. Open 10:30 to 9:30. Closed January 1–3. Admission ¥1,000. Tel: 332-5800; www.k-eminence. com.] Located in Rakusai New Town, it's a fifteen-minute walk from Chikurin Kōen and City Bus Nishi 1, Nishi 2, and Nishi 5 from the Sakaidani Ōhashi bus stop to Hankyū Katsura Station.

YOSHIMINE 善峯

Yoshiminedera 善峯寺
Jūrinji 十輪寺

*The jewel of this southwest area is Yoshiminedera,
one of Kyoto's vast mountain temple complexes. Its
inaccessibility is part of its charm, along with the
views it offers of the wide basin that extends south of
the city. Nearby Jūrinji is associated with a romantic tale from
Heian literature.*

To get to Yoshiminedera and Jūrinji go to the Hankyū Line's Higashi Mukō Station and take Hankyū Bus 6 to Oshio, the last stop.
Buses depart at 7:33, 9:27, 12:26, and 4:40. The twenty-minute trip
costs ¥300. Because it is a thirty-minute walk from the Oshio bus
stop up a steep incline to Yoshiminedera, you may be tempted to
take a taxi from the station. The ride costs approximately ¥1,800
one way. Return buses leave Oshio for Higashi Mukō Station at
9:51, 12:50, 5:03, 6:03, and 7:30.

The Tendai temple of **Yoshiminedera** [Open 8 to 5. Tel: 331-
0020] was founded in 1029 by the priest Gensan. It was bestowed
imperial rank by Emperor Go-Ichijō in 1034, and in 1042, Emperor
Go-Suzaku gave the temple its principal image, a thousand-armed
Kannon, bodhisattva of mercy. Over the ages, Yoshiminedera enjoyed imperial patronage, and the princes who lived here were
known as the "Princes of the Western Hills." The temple was destroyed in the Ōnin War in 1467 and lay in ruins for two centuries
until it was rebuilt by Keishōin, mother of the fifth Tokugawa shogun. For this reason, many of the temple's buildings date from the
end of the seventeenth century.

Tall cedars line the steep and curving approach to the temple.
The air, decidedly cooler than in the city below, is refreshing and

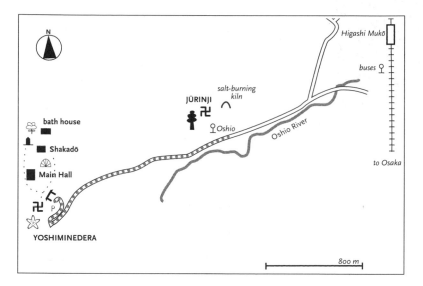

YOSHIMINE

invigorating. Yoshiminedera is a typical mountain temple, with its halls spread across the mountainside rather than grouped in a symmetrical courtyard on a north–south axis. Most face east, and are separated by beautiful stone-inset stairways, landscaped pathways, and panoramic views. Besides pilgrims, Yoshiminedera draws a fair share of hikers because of its location and the beauty of its setting. Mountain paths lead from here to Arashiyama, though they are not well marked.

A ¥500 admission fee will be collected at the ticket office in the massive **Main Gate**, where an English pamphlet is available. Yoshiminedera is the twentieth stop on the thirty-three-temple Kannon pilgrimage of western Japan, and the thousand-armed Kannon given by Emperor Go-Suzaku is housed in the **Main Hall**. Off to one side, priests in the concession sell postcards and amulets, and also impress the temple's seal on the scrolls brought by pilgrims, who can be seen carefully drying the freshly written script with hair dryers made available for that purpose.

Yoshiminedera is renowned for its elegantly tended plants and trees, the most famous of which is a six-hundred-year-old white pine. From the Main Hall, stone steps to the left lead up and under a twenty-meter-long branch of the "Frolicking Dragon," as this prized tree is known. Trained to grow horizontally, the pine extends its two limbs as though in supplication to the temple's deity, and is the source of the temple's nickname, Matsu no Tera, or Temple of the Pine Tree. In 1994, a fifteen-meter piece of one bough was severed in an attempt to halt the infestation of pine weevils, but this life-saving operation has not diminished the tree's beauty. Directly west of the pine is another horticultural marvel, a dome-shaped maple out of which sprouts a hanging cherry, said to have been modeled on the flowered parasols used in processions and festivals in Japan. Both trees are about three hundred years old.

Numbered signs indicate the way to the bell tower and the sutra tower, the latter a small building which houses an image of Fudō Myōō. On the next level up is the **Shakadō**, a more recent building with a stone image of the Buddha carved in the eleventh century by the temple's founder, Gensan. It was removed from the its rocky perch on nearby Mt. Shaka and placed inside the compound in 1885. To the right of the Shakadō is a medicinal bath that is open from 8 to 3 on the second Sunday of the month from May through September. Those interested in taking a dip need only make a small contribution to enter. The clear room-temperature water is for rinsing off, the dark herbal water is for soaking in. Soap is neither allowed nor necessary. This is a bath to alleviate the aches and pains of old age (or those acquired while walking to the temple). A towel bearing a picture of the splendid long-limbed pine tree can be purchased at the Main Gate. In the compound's

The famous pine tree at Yoshiminedera stretches across supports.

uppermost reaches lie the tombs of imperial princes, surrounded by lush hydrangea bushes and towering cryptomeria.

Just outside the Main Gate is a tiny eatery that serves simple fare and drinks, and in a fifteen-minute walk downhill there is a pickle shop that also sells noodle dishes. East of the pickle shop is an outdoor eatery called **Yoshimine no Sato**, which operates in season. It serves two local delicacies, *takenoko gohan* (rice with bamboo shoots) in the spring, and in late autumn, *matsutake gohan* (rice with fresh mushrooms). Farther down is a shop selling wares made from bamboo that grows in this part of southeast Kyoto.

About a kilometer down the road from Yoshiminedera is **Jūrinji** [Open 9 to 5. Admission ¥500. Tel: 331-0154]. Jūrinji is also known as Narihiradera, in memory of the Heian-period poet Ariwara no Narihira (825–80). One of his pastimes was making salt by boiling seawater, an indulgence enjoyed by ninth-century aristocracy. When his lover Nijō no Kisaki visited the nearby Ōharano

Shrine, Narihira supposedly colored the smoke purple as a sign of his love. To commemorate this gesture, seawater is boiled here every year on November 23. Waving one's hands through the steam is said to guarantee believers a long and successful marriage.

Inside the grounds on the left stands a towering camphor tree. Legend has it that when this revered tree was planted eight hundred years ago, it grew to its present size overnight. It is considered one of the ten oldest trees in Kyoto. The 250-year-old Main Hall has a distinctive roof, one which is rounded and domed and is said to resemble that of a *mikoshi*, or portable shrine. The main image, shown only once a year, is a Jizō figure that is said to facilitate childbirth. Bolts of cotton, used in Japan by pregnant women as a midriff support, are piled in the back of the room. These offerings represent the prayers of expectant mothers and thanks for a successful birth.

The covered walkway from the Main Hall leads past a simple meditation garden and several rooms where some of the temple's treasures are on display. A narrow path that circumvents the Main Hall leads to the back of the temple and a bamboo grove, in the center of which is a concave depression, the site of the salt-making kiln.

DAIGO 醍醐

Zuishin'in 随心院
Daigoji 醍醐寺
Sambōin 三宝院
Kami Daigo 上醍醐
Shimo Daigo 下醍醐

Daigoji, one of the largest Shingon temple complexes in Kyoto and a World Heritage Site, occupies this part of the city. Divided into upper and lower compounds, the precincts of this temple are graced by magnificent buildings that require several hours to fully appreciate. Its principal subtemple, Sambōin, is an excellent example of the handiwork of the extravagant warlord Toyotomi Hideyoshi. Nearby, in contrast, is Zuishin'in, the humble residence of the Heian-period poetess Ono no Komachi.

Daigo and Zuishin'in can both be reached by Keihan Buses 22 and 24 from Yamashina Keihan Station, bound for the Ono and Daigo Sambōin stops, and the Tōzai (East line) subway, which runs along Ōike Dōri. The subway ride takes seventeen minutes from downtown to Ono Station for Zuishin'in and Daigo Station for Daigoji. Both temples are about a fifteen-minute walk from their respective subway stations.

Ono no Komachi was a woman famous for her beauty, literary accomplishments, and eventual misfortune. She lived in the middle of the ninth century and served as a lady-in-waiting in the Heian court. A central figure in the literary life of the capital, Ono no Komachi corresponded with other well-known writers and was ranked among the Six Poetic Sages (Rokkasen) of the ninth century. The eighty or so poems with which she is credited deal with such themes as nature and unrequited love, and reflect the then-prevalent influence of Pure Land Buddhism.

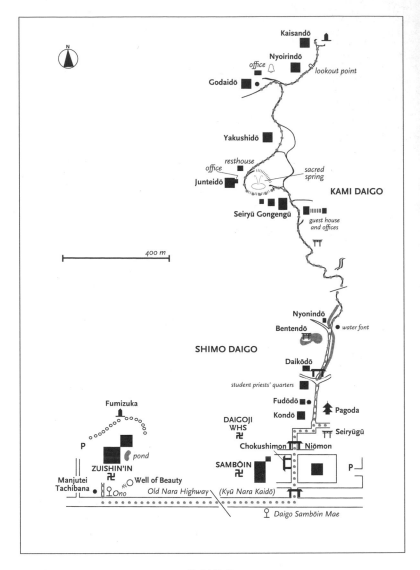

DAIGO

Perhaps her beauty and talent made her too conspicuous at court, for she was sent down to a district southeast of the capital called Yamashina. Various places in the area claim to have served as her residence, but one site considered authentic is **Zuishin'in** [Open 9 to 4:30. Admission ¥400. Tel: 573-3191], established in 991 as one of the main temples of the Shingon sect. Devastated by fire and rebuilt in 1599, the temple and its grounds are beautifully maintained, making this one of the more elegant temple compounds located in this area. Surrounded by tall trees, the inner garden has a dense, rich feeling, and offers one of the best examples of Japanese gardening techniques to be found anywhere.

The main building, constructed in 1599, is an example of Momoyama-period (1568–1600) architecture. Gorgeous *fusuma* (sliding doors), painted twenty years ago by Higuchi Tomimaru of the Kyoto Kanō school, enclose an altar to Ono no Komachi housing an image of the poetess. Portraying a woman wizened with age, it was supposedly carved at her request—a reminder of the passing of youth and beauty. One of her most famous poems (in a translation by Nicholas J. Teele) tells of this universal fate:

The color of the blossoms
Has faded
Vainly
I age through the rains of the world
Watching in melancholy.

Some of the other *fusuma* on display are decorated with portraits of thirty-two Chinese sages, and scenes of sixth-century *bugaku* dancers and imperial horse races. A renovated back room houses a display of Buddhist statuary, some of which have been designated Important Cultural Properties.

Near the Old Nara Highway (Kyū Nara Kaidō), but still on the outer temple grounds, is a shady bamboo grove that supposedly marks the site of Ono no Komachi's cottage. A thicket fence encloses stone steps that lead down to the cottage's well, known as the "**Well of Beauty**." Behind the temple is a landscaped walk that includes a memorial stone that honors her lovers, as well as the poems that they inspired.

North of the entrance to Zuishin'in is a four-hundred-year-old building called **Manjutei Tachibana** [Open 11 to 3. Closed every Thursday and third Friday. Tel: 572-7001], that according to the owner was once part of the temple complex, and at another time, the home of a samurai. Now it is a restaurant, serving noodles, tempura, and various other reasonably priced dishes in a beautiful setting of exposed beams, earthen walls, and *tatami* rooms.

Three bus stops down the road from Zuishin'in is Daigoji and its famous subtemple, Sambōin. Keihan Buses 22 and 24 both use the same stop, and the fare from Zuishin'in is ¥180. Walking would take about fifteen minutes but be aware that this is a narrow, busy road. **Daigoji** [Open 9 to 4:30. Tel: 571-0002] owes much of its present shape to the patronage of warlord Toyotomi Hideyoshi (1535–98), who is credited with uniting all of Japan by sheer force of will and ingenious political manipulation. From humble origins, he rose to the titular rank of *kampaku*, or imperial regent, and was in fact military dictator of the entire country. On his way to securing a place for himself in history, Hideyoshi made sure that all of the buildings associated with him were as ostentatious as possible. No one would be allowed to ignore him.

The monk Shōbō, posthumously known as Rigen Daishi (832–909), founded Daigoji in 874. Two centuries later, the complex covered the mountainside. By the time Hideyoshi, drawn to the temple by the fame of its cherry trees, saw it in the sixteenth century, all of Daigoji's buildings except for its five-story pagoda (built in 951) had fallen into disrepair. The warlord was persuaded by the head abbot to help restore the temple, and in doing so, he fashioned one of the subtemples, Sambōin, to his own taste.

Today, within the compound walls, the famous Daigo cherry trees attract many spring visitors. **Sambōin** [Open 9 to 5; 4 in winter. Admission ¥600. A ¥1,500 admission fee allows access to the Daigoji grounds and the museum. Tel: 571-002] is just inside the main entrance to the Daigoji complex, on the left. All the displays have English explanations. Unfortunately, no photos are allowed, but postcards and other items are on sale in the souvenir shop.

Although the other buildings at Daigoji maintain a more orthodox religious atmosphere, Hideyoshi recreated this subtemple to accommodate more secular pursuits, such as cherry blossom viewing and tea ceremony parties. Sambōin has the feel of an aristocratic villa rather than a temple, with its layout of detached raised buildings with garden views and covered passages spanning flowing streams. As befitted military rulers, the taste of Hideyoshi, and that of the Tokugawa shoguns who ruled after him, ran toward the opulent. Not surprisingly, all of Sambōin's interior surfaces are covered with pictures executed with powerful brush strokes and utilizing generous amounts of color and a liberal sprinkling of gold dust.

The garden, like that of Nijō Castle (another display of military taste) is studded with rocks, supposedly eight hundred in all. Two ancient dwarf pines that straddle the island in the carp-filled pond barely manage to soften the garden's rugged quality.

The rooms in the Junjōkan (Pure View Hall) were repainted in 2001 by Hamada Taisuke, and provide an interesting comparison to the older works. An intriguing scent wafts from the Main Hall of Sambōin, where an image of the bodhisattva Miroku sits. The source is a flaked incense called *jūshūkō*. A blend of about ten ingredients, it is sold only in the shops on the complex. This mixture, as well as the three varieties of coil incense on display, has exotic wood-resin undertones, evocative of the nearby woods, which add a rich and fragrant dimension to the temple.

One of Sambōin's most interesting features must be viewed

from outside the grounds; the large wooden gate called the **Chokushimon**. On it, two huge imperial chrysanthemum crests are arranged side by side with two of Hideyoshi's paulownia-leaf crests—Hideyoshi's rather unsubtle reminder of his own importance.

South of Samboin is the Reihōkan [Open 9 to 4:30 from the third Saturday in March to the second Sunday in May. Admission ¥600]. It is a sleek modern structure that houses several National Treasures. The front hall provides a space for contemporary artists to exhibit their works. An English pamphlet is available.

The vast Daigoji [Admission ¥600] complex is divided into Kami and Shimo—Upper and Lower—Daigo. The **Niōmon**, a large gate that houses two Niō, or guardian kings, is the entrance to the complex of buildings that make up **Shimo Daigo**. The Main Hall was built in the Kamakura period (1185–1333), and is believed to have been moved here from the famous Shingon temple of Manganji Yuasa in Wakayama when Hideyoshi defeated its warrior-monks.

Lower Daigo's most valuable structure is the thirty-eight-meter five-story **pagoda**, built in 951. A National Treasure, it is the oldest wooden structure in Kyoto. (The oldest wooden buildings in the world are found at Hōryūji in Nara, dating to 701). Across from the pagoda to the west is **Seiryūgū**, a Shintō shrine dating to 1097. The present elegantly detailed buildings are from 1517. The hall dedicated to Fudō Myōō has a large stone statue of that deity near an outdoor firepit used for religious ceremonies. The **Dai-kōdō**, (Great Lecture Hall), built in 1930, houses a statue of Amida. Next to that, a small shrine dedicated to Benten, the goddess of music, perches on an island in a pond surrounded by cherry and maple trees.

While these buildings comprise most of Shimo Daigo, there are many noteworthy buildings in **Kami Daigo** that rival them in size and historical value. From the wooden gate, the walk up takes

The one-hour path up to Daigoji cuts through a densely wooded mountainside.

about an hour, depending on your gait and the number of rest stops you take. The first building you encounter is the **Nyonindō**, which literally means "Hall for Women." Forbidden to climb sacred mountains and arouse the ire of the gods, women worshipped here and not higher. The stepped climb winds through woods of dense and varied growth. A little over a third of the way up, you will come to a man-made waterfall that flows from beneath an image of Fudō Myōō. The water here is potable and delicious and also suitable for performing a religious austerity; those who wish to do so can sit beneath it! About halfway up is a pair of towering cryptomeria ringed with sacred straw ropes and a small shrine.

At the top, the path levels off as you approach a grove of lush, green bamboo. All of Daigo's buildings are very large and all the more stunning when one considers the steepness of the mountain on which they were constructed centuries ago. The first building on the right, an impressive one with a copper-covered tile roof, is a guesthouse for pilgrims, closed to the general public. The Haiden, or Worship Hall, of the **Seiryū Gongengū**, a Shintō shrine, was built in 1434 and is designated a National Treasure. Viewed from a higher vantage point, its powerful, swooping cypress roof conveys the image of a majestic bird at rest among the tall conifers and full-branched maples. The next building on the left shelters a **sacred spring**. Lift the aluminum cover and draw out some water with one of the dippers. The cool, delicious water is considered restorative. The stairs on the left pass the imperial tomb of Seiryū no Miya and another small Shintō shrine. At the top of the stairs is the **Junteidō**, in which an image of the bodhisattva of mercy known as the Juntei Kannon is enshrined. Although the other buildings also have sacred images, these can only be viewed through slats in the lattice windows. The Junteidō, however, can be entered and offerings made, a satisfying act after the long climb. Daigoji is the eleventh stop on the thirty-three Kannon pilgrimage in western Japan, and groups of white-clad pilgrims come to this hall to have their scrolls or accordian-folded books stamped and inscribed. A small rest house with benches provides hair dryers to dry the fresh inscriptions.

The **Yakushidō**, a National Treasure built in 1121, is uphill from the rest house. Barely visible through a small opening is the priceless image of Yakushi Nyorai, also a National Treasure dating from about 907. A five-minute walk along the path leads to the next peak, where there are three more buildings. Where the path divides, take the left fork, passing the bell tower and office to reach the **Godaidō**. This hall is the twenty-third temple on a thirty-six-temple Fudō Myōō pilgrimage in the Kinki region, and stamps and inscriptions verifying one's visit can be requested at the office.

Retrace your steps and follow the path around to the left where the highest buildings in the Daigo complex stand at the elevation of four hundred meters. Both of them were rebuilt in 1698. The

Nyoirindō, with its cypress-bark roof, is an elegant elevated structure supported by pillars and crossbeams. Unfortunately, it cannot be entered, nor may its famous image, the Nyoirin Kannon, be viewed. The **Kaisandō** (Founder's Hall), also with a cypress-bark roof, is located in the same clearing. A view of the plain that stretches south of Mt. Daigo can be viewed from this peak, and on clear days, the Osaka skyline is visible in the distance.

Because it gets dark quickly in the winter months, plan your walk accordingly. The descent takes one hour.

FUSHIMI 伏見

Chūshōjima 中書島
Chōkenji 長健寺
Jukkokubune 十石舟
Ōkura Kinenkan 大倉記念館
Teradaya 寺田屋
Aburakake Jizō 油掛地蔵
Kizakura Kappa Country 黄桜カッパカントリー
Gokōnomiya Shrine 御香宮神社

Robust, hearty, full-bodied. Does this sound like an ad for sake, *the rice wine that is Japan's national drink? It could just as well describe the structures of the* sake-*making district of Fushimi themselves. The strong, handsome architecture of the* sake *warehouses; the sturdy, wooden barrels that contain the mash; the compact, beautifully wrapped* sake *casks that decorate shrines throughout the country; right down to the bushy cedar balls that hang above the brewery doors—these are the images that describe Fushimi.*

Fushimi is one of Japan's many former castle towns. The great warlord Toyotomi Hideyoshi built Fushimi Castle here in 1594. After Hideyoshi's death, Fushimi languished as a seat of power and the castle was completely dismantled by 1623 (today's Momoyama Castle is a modern replica), but the region continued to be known for producing fine-tasting *sake*. The three rivers that converge (the Uji, Kamo, and Katsura) in Fushimi made it a natural production center. Rice could be easily brought in and *sake* barged out. Moreover, bubbling springs of sweet-tasting water, another indispensable ingredient of *sake*, existed in abundance. Approximately twenty-five brands of *sake* are still produced locally. The largest and most famous brewery, Gekkeikan, has turned one

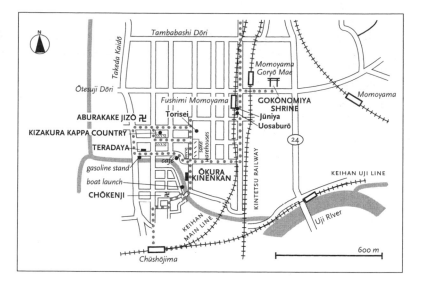

FUSHIMI

of its warehouses into a museum of the history and techniques of *sake* making.

More than *sake* flourished here. Take the Keihan Railway (either an Osaka- or Uji-bound train will do) to **Chūshōjima**, an old pleasure quarter which blossomed about four hundred years ago in the shadow of Fushimi Castle. The goddess of water and music, Benten, became the patroness of the ladies who graced this district, and a wooden image of her is housed in the temple **Chōkenji** [Open 8 to 5. Donation requested. Tel: 611-1039]. A large stone pillar opposite the exit from Chūshōjima Station serves as a signpost for the temple. Walk two blocks down the street immediately to the right of the pillar, past the various "snack bars" and similar establishments—modern-day versions of the nightlife of yesteryear. You will see huge gingko trees which reveal the temple's whereabouts long before you can see the red wall enclosing its compound. A distinctly Chinese tile-roofed gate is flanked with cherry trees brought long ago from Chōkenji's famous parent temple, Daigoji. Enormous *sake* casks—contributions from local breweries—line the walkway. Another prominent feature of the compound is a circular stone pit in which wooden prayer sticks (*gomagi*) are burned during colorful, periodic ceremonies, the biggest taking place in July. The temple also sells an unusual amulet shaped like an antique coin, but with an engraving on one side of an explicitly sexual nature. The paper wrapper states that seashells once were valued as money; hence, the clam-shaped picture. (It does not explain that clams also have an erotic connotation in Japanese art.) Ring the bell by the Main Hall for assistance. The amulet costs ¥700.

The **Jukokubune** [Open from 10 to 4:20, leaving approximately every twenty minutes. Admission ¥1,000. Tel: 075-321-7696] is a fifteen-seater shallow-bottom boat, the likes of which used to ply these canals and beyond, taking rice from the neighboring Shiga Prefecture via the Lake Biwa Canal and charcoal via the Takase River, out to the greater Yodo River to Osaka. The forty-minute ride, which operates from April through early December and which includes a stop at a clock tower and small museum in the Harbor Park, is a pleasant way to learn more about the water system that contributed to this area's growth and wealth.

After leaving Chōkenji, turn right at the river, then left to cross the Benten bridge and go down the stairs immediately on the right. The ride's cost comes with a small bottle of *sake* or *sake*-flavored cake.

From the bridge, follow the gently curving road left until you spot the imposing façade of the **Ōkura Kinenkan** [Open 9:30 to 4:30. Closed at year end. Admission ¥300. Tel: 623-2056], a *sake* warehouse that Gekkeikan has turned into a museum. This impressive structure has been rebuilt, using many of the original wood beams and pillars. Just above the sliding paper doors of the entrance hangs a large ball of cedar twigs (*sakabayashi*), a sign welcomed by *sake* drinkers because when fresh and green, this fragrant bundle is the traditional way to announce that the new year's *sake* is on the market. The tradition of making the *sakabayashi* with cedar is related to the huge sacred trees that stand in one of Japan's oldest shrines, Ōmiwa Shrine in Nara Prefecture, whose resident deity, Miwa Myōjin, is the god of *sake*.

The visitor receives a tiny bottle of Gekkeikan's well-known brew on payment of the ¥300 entrance fee. In addition, free samples of crisp new *sake* (*namazake*) or fruity plum wine (*umeshū*) are available at the counter in the waiting area. Depending on the type, *sake* can be drunk hot, at room temperature, or chilled. Inside the museum is a comfortable rest area, near which is a fifty-meter-deep well that provides some of the delicious water for which Fushimi is known. The museum retains the atmosphere of an old-style brewery and displays everything to do with this business: woodblocks used in the printing of labels, *sake* containers of various shapes, the many tools for making *sake*, from wooden barrels to complicated machinery, and even the work clothes worn by the brewers. (There is also a thirty-minute film in English on request.) Background music consists of work songs that complemented the rhythm of the task at hand, chants that predate the modern production of *sake* in the immense stainless-steel vats that Gekkeikan uses today. Many of Fushimi's small *sake* breweries still rely on some of the equipment shown.

Exit the museum, turn left, then left again, and follow the street as it jogs right, then left. The handsome, black-walled building along the way is part of the Gekkeikan offices, now converted into the **Fushimiyume Hyakushu Café** [Open 11 to 5 weekdays; 10:30 to 6 on Saturdays and holidays. Closed Monday. Tel: 623-1360]. The building, with its high ceilings and spacious rooms, was built in 1919, and is worth a look. Maps and local information are available. The willow-lined Uji River can be glimpsed on the left. Just ahead is a gas station, and across the street on your right is **Teradaya** [Open 10 to 4. Tel: 611-1223]. This inn is the site of a famous attack on Sakamoto Ryōma, a loyalist and martyr to the imperial cause in the years leading up to the Meiji Restoration. Swords bared, forces supporting the shogunate stormed into the inn one night in 1866. Sakamoto escaped, but just barely. A year later, he would not be so lucky. The inn has a print-out in English, but unless you are a real Meiji Restoration buff, you may not want to pay ¥400 to view room after room of unreadable memorabilia.

From Teradaya, continue west past the gas station and take a right at the next street. Walk two short blocks to Aburakake Dōri (Oil-Covered Street) and turn right. This bustling street and others like it in this area have a full array of every kind of shop imaginable. Unlike the upscale stores of downtown Kyoto, these small shops operate more like an open-air market. Continue along Aburakake Dōri to the narrow entrance on the first left to **Saiganji**, a Jōdō sect temple. The Main Hall houses an image of Amida and the small hall near the street was rebuilt to house the famous Kamakura-period (1185–1333) stone image of **Aburakake Jizō**. Fushimi was a hub of commerce and trade. Inbound cargo was unloaded on the wharves at Chūshōjima, then carried by porters another two kilometers into Kyoto. One day, an oil vendor from Yamazaki (a place to the southwest of Kyoto known for its sesame oil) was making his way down Aburakake Dōri when he tripped and fell, spilling his precious load. He scooped up what was left and offered it to this wayside Jizō. Thereafter he prospered, and as word spread of his good fortune, others came to pray for success. When they achieved it, they gave thanks by pouring a little bit of oil over the image. Today, shopkeepers and businessmen continue the tradition of pouring oil over the glistening 1.7-meter-high image, and offerings of ten-liter cans of oil are stacked inside the hall.

Walk east on Aburaka-ke Dōri to **Kizakura Kappa Country** [Open 11:30 to 2 and 5 to 10; 11 to 10 on weekends and holidays. Tel: 611-9919], a renovated *sake* warehouse that is a gallery, shop, beer and *sake* brewery, and restaurant offering affordable dishes. Continue east to the end of the street, turn right and walk south. The traditional building on the left is the *yakitori* restaurant, **Torisei** [Open 11:30 to 10. Closed Mondays. Tel: 622-5533]. *Yakitori* consists of seasoned bits of chicken and vegetables grilled on bamboo skewers. The charge usually is

The lantern at the famous Teradaya inn.

by the skewer. Locally brewed *sake* is available and although there is no English menu, if you see tasty dishes at the other tables you can ask for the same. (Point and say, *Onaji mono o kudasai*).

A block southwest of Torisei are attractive rows of *sake* warehouses. Continue south to the black-walled Gekkeikan offices. Turn left and cross the tracks to Kyōmachi Dōri, the first street after the tracks. Walk to **Uosaburō** [Open 11 to 7:30. Tel. 601-0061], a well-known *kaiseki* restaurant with an old-fashioned copper-and-glass lantern above its curtained entrance. *Kaiseki* is classic seasonal Japanese cuisine exquisitely presented in a traditional setting. Reservations are necessary. The menu is set: even the order of serving the seasonal delicacies is decided. As is typical of *kaiseki* restaurants, prices are high (lunches are ¥4,000 and ¥6,000, dinners can run from ¥8,000 to ¥20,000). The building itself bears the scars of the fighting that destroyed much of the town in January 1868, when imperial and shogunal forces clashed in its streets. The wooden lattice "window" to the right of the door still shows bullet marks from that day.

Next door is the attractive townhouse-style restaurant, **Jūniya** [Open 11 to 11. Tel: 612-7666]. Lunch courses are ¥1,100, ¥1,380, and ¥2,100, but they also serve a large selection of à la carte items.

Continue north to the wide street, Ōtesuji Dōri. Turn right and pass under the Kintetsu Railway tracks. The street slopes slightly uphill as it approaches **Gokōnomiya Shrine**, a large compound filled with trees, *sake* casks, weatherworn wood carvings, and a beautiful outdoor Noh stage. Legend tells of a fragrant spring that bubbled to the surface here one day in 862. It attracted people not only because of its sweet taste, but because of its efficacious powers. Many miracles were attributed to it and its fame grew. Centuries later, warlord Toyotomi Hideyoshi drank its water, as did those who lived in the imperial residences that dotted the area. People still come to fill their water containers to the left of the Main Hall of the shrine.

Not far from the shrine is Fushimi Momoyama station on the Keihan Main Line. If you want to take the train to visit Fushimi Inari Shrine, Fushimi Inari Station is five stops to the north on this line.

On foot, it will take about an hour to reach, and if you are up to it, the walk is a pleasant one. A path has been constructed along the Lake Biwa Canal from the Fushimi Incline to Fushimi Inari. The twenty-minute walk north from the vicinity of Fushimi Momoyama Station to the Incline along Kyōmachi Dōri passes through a residential area and provides an alternative to Fushimi's busy shop-filled streets. (Hideyoshi's retainers and samurai lived near the castle and their homes [*bukei*] represent a style of architecture representative of this class. Wandering through the old streets may still reveal a grand old structure that has been lovingly maintained.) Cross Route 24 on Kyōmachi Dōri, take the first right and go up the slope toward the canal and adjoining waterworks. The path leads north to Fushimi Inari and the famous shrine.

FUSHIMI INARI 伏見稲荷

Fushimi Inari Shrine 伏見稲荷神社
Mt. Inari 稲荷山

One of Kyoto's most beloved shrines, the thousand-torii-gated pathways of Fushimi Inari Shrine are a favorite haunt of photographers, business people, and local residents asking the gods to bless their homes, companies, and destinies.

Rice is an integral part of Japanese culture. The emperor plants rice in a sacred field every year, symbolic of his traditional role as the link between the Japanese people and the Shintō gods. Given the centrality of this grain to Japanese life, it is not surprising that a deity presides over it: Inari, whose name is thought to come from the words *ine* (rice plant) and *nari* (to become). Inari shrines number in the thousands and are located throughout the country. **Fushimi Inari Shrine** [Tel: 641-7331] is the most famous of them all, and traditionally thought to be the one from which all the others derived.

Founded in 711, the shrine was given imperial rank after it became associated with Kūkai, founder of Shingon Buddhism in Japan and head of the great temple Tōji. The wood used to build Tōji was taken from Mt. Inari, the peak behind the shrine. Subsequent rituals were performed to appease the gods of the denuded mountain and ties were established between the two sacred places. Even today, in May, a portable shrine leaves Fushimi Inari Shrine and travels to Tōji, where it is blessed by the Buddhist priests.

Local businesses incorporate the symbols of Fushimi Inari Shrine into their decorative motifs, and the nearby Keihan and JR railway stations are painted the same cinnabar red as the shrine.

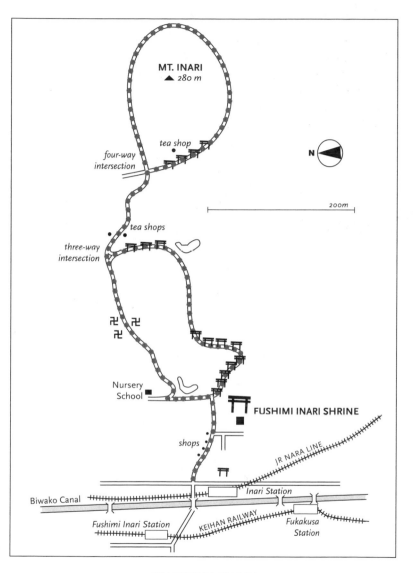

FUSHIMI INARI

You will also notice the many pairs of white fox statues adorning shops and stations in the area. One fox holds a sacred jewel in its mouth that represents the spirit of the gods, while the other holds a cylindrical object that represents the key to the rice storehouse. Foxes, especially the rare white ones, have long been associated with Inari, and various legends account for this. One says that a dandy-looking male fox and his attractive mate visited the shrine so frequently that local people believed them to be messengers of Inari and enshrined their images. Another tale says that a pair of foxes was often seen romping in a nearby rice field. Their playful union produced a healthy litter, a sign of fecundity related to a bountiful rice harvest, and an association between foxes and rice was born.

Today, the shops lining the road that leads to the shrine sell an amazing variety of fox-shaped trinkets, toys, amulets, cakes, and cookies. Eateries feature delicious fox-related foods such as *inarizushi,* a rice-stuffed pouch of deep-fried bean curd, said to be a favorite food of foxes. *Kitsune soba* ("fox noodles") is a dish made by adding the same fried bean curd to a bowl of hot noodles in broth, and is popular throughout the country. Other culinary tidbits offered in the shops here are small birds marinated in soy sauce and roasted on bamboo spits. A tiny sparrow costs ¥420, a quail ¥700.

The main shrine buildings are among the most massive and stately in the city. Approximately 130 people are employed here. Weddings are not conducted but newborns are blessed and other ceremonies are held. The courtyard is spacious enough to accommodate the thousands who visit during the New Year holidays. The money coffers placed before the sacred halls may be the largest of any shrine in Japan, testimony to the number of patrons or perhaps the effectiveness of Inari in granting wishes. As at other major shrines in Kyoto, you toss a coin into the coffer, ring the bell, say a prayer, bow, and leave. For serious devotees, however, visiting

Fushimi Inari means doing the aforementioned, then hiking up the mountain and doing the same at every subshrine. This takes about an hour and a half or two hours, depending on the length of your prayers and the number of times you drop into the many tea shops along the way. Without making the trek to the top of 233-meter **Mt. Inari**, you really cannot claim to have seen the shrine.

The path up begins at the stone stairs you see as you face the mountain. Take the path on the right. A long row of red votive *torii* (as pictured on the cover of this book) forms a tunnel of stunning simplicity. Whether dappled in sunshine or exuding a feeling of warmth on a cold day, this often-photographed winding tunnel of *torii* is one of the most inviting features of Fushimi Inari Shrine. The *torii* at the bottom of the hill are more massive than those farther up. You might even see a crew of workmen replacing deteriorated *torii*. A thin piece of wood bearing the name of the donor of the new *torii* is inserted in the spot where the old gate had stood and will remain there until the new *torii* has been completed: thereafter the patron's name or that of his or her business will be painted in black on the new gate.

The purchase of a *torii* is considered an offering to the guardians of the rice storehouse. Long ago, rice was collected as taxes from peasants and used as payment to those who served the local lord. A rich harvest, therefore, secured one's wealth. As the nation shifted from an agrarian base to an industrial one, wealth became associated with business acumen. Today Fushimi Inari Shrine is an important place not only for rice farmers, but for shop owners and businessmen, who offer prayers for success or increased prosperity. (It is still a custom among the shop people in neighborhoods throughout the city to make a pilgrimage to Fushimi Inari Shrine in the wee hours of the morning on the first day of the month.) The *torii* do not come cheap. Depending on size and location, a votive *torii* can cost between ¥500,000 and ¥20,000,000 (roughly U.S. $4,500 to $185,000 at the present exchange rate). Apparently, those in damp sites deteriorate quickly and must be replaced every five or six years! More modest *torii* offerings, however, are possible. At one subshrine farther up, small *torii* run ¥2,500, ¥5,000, and ¥10,000. These miniature *torii* are everywhere; stacked up on fences or resting askew in many of the small subshrines that line the path.

Fushimi has long been renowned for the quality of its water, and as rice and pure water are essential ingredients of *sake*, the area is famous for its *sake* makers. Many of the sets of offerings on sale at the subshrines include a tiny bottle of *sake* and rice crackers for ¥1,000. More elaborate offerings of sweets, fruit, and snacks also are combined with the ubiquitous bottle of spirits. Japanese gods like to have fun and drinking is high on their list of pleasures. They are known for their festive ways rather than their theology, so do not be surprised if some of their worshippers are a little red-faced—and not from the effects of the climb. Those who walk up Mt. Inari usually are a jolly lot. Greetings and shouts of encouragement are bantered back and forth. Older climbers, bent with age and clutching their bamboo walking sticks, are among the friendliest. Offer them a "*Konnichiwa*," and you will receive a response.

After passing a pond on the right, continue to a three-way intersection marked on the signboards in Japanese. Continue right and go past the store selling bamboo canes and the two restaurants [Open 7 to 5] that offer fine views of the wooded hillside and simple fare consisting of noodle and rice dishes. It is remarkable that all shop supplies still must be carried up on people's backs. Farther on, a four-way intersection is wide enough for benches upon which to sit and enjoy a view of the city. Although vending machines are everywhere on the mountain, the eatery at this intersection [Open 9 to 5] cools its soft drinks in an old stone basin filled with water, another reminder of the days when there were no delivery trucks, electricity, or refrigerators. From here it is ten minutes to the mountain peak.

Expressing wishes for wisdom, wealth, or a wonderful partner, these prayer plaques adorn one of the subshrines on Mt. Inari.

On the way down are two "waterfalls," places where water pours forth from an overhead trough. Supplicants stand beneath and test their faith by praying in the cold downpour, a religious austerity that I am told is common on Mt. Inari, but which I have yet to see practiced. Although this mountain is a sacred Shintō site, there are images of the Buddhist deity Fudō Myōō in both spots as well as other places on the mountain, a reminder of its ties to Shingon. Fushimi Inari is a good place to witness the active integration of Shintō and Buddhism. Farther along the path are many small Buddhist temple buildings sheltering images of Kannon, bodhisattva of mercy; Jizō, guardian of travelers and children; and more images of Fudō Myōō. In these places, incense is burnt and candles lit in typical Buddhist fashion. Outside one temple on the north side of the path a new Buddhist sect has erected a large gold-colored statue of Kannon holding two babies. Inside the building are row upon row of *Mizuko-san*, small clay images of a childlike figure in brown-and-white monk's clothing and wearing a broad-brimmed straw hat. These figures represent the spirits of aborted or miscarried infants, and may be purchased from the two attendant women priests by anyone who has lost a child and wishes to offer prayers to it. Other buildings and altars on the shrine grounds serve those asking a blessing on their search for a mate, or students seeking success in their entrance examinations. At still others, people pray for fertility and the birth of a healthy baby. But here, even those who seek aid from the Shintō gods light incense and candles in the hopes that the Buddhas and bodhisattvas will also take heed of their supplications.

The enterprising nature of the Fushimi merchants is evident everywhere. There is something sold at almost every stop along the mountain path, including books on Buddhism, altar accessories, and even flints and metal strikers used for purification rites. One of the items for which Fushimi is best known can be found in several stores at the entrance to the shrine and on the top of the mountain. These are the small, brightly painted plaster dolls known as *Fushimi ningyō*. The making and selling of these dolls is said to have started here and spread throughout Japan with the Inari cult. Shops close to the station also offer these simple folkcraft dolls, incongruously seated on shelves crammed with rubber alligators, plastic Godzillas, and even cuddly stuffed foxes.

As the path nears the bottom, it veers through a residential area, passes a nursery school, and curves left toward the main shrine. There is one spot often overlooked by visitors, but central to the nature of this shrine: its sacred rice paddy. It is at the top of the stairs behind the main shrine building, in a park-like setting near a pond. Its isolation and simplicity add an unexpectedly contemplative aspect to the shrine.

The shops along the road to the station offer a visual excursion of another kind, filled as they are with charming folkcraft items or outrageous kitsch.

SENNYŪJI 泉涌寺
and TŌFUKUJI 東福寺

Sennyūji 泉涌寺
Sokujōin 即成院
Unryūin 雲龍院
Raigōin 来迎院
Imakumano Kannonji 今熊野観音寺
Kaikōji 戒光時
Tōfukuji 東福寺
Sesshūji 雪舟寺

Despite the busy and crowded streets of this southeastern part of the city, the wooded precincts of Sennyūji are peacefully quiet. Imperial tombs set amid the hilly grounds accentuate the stillness of this Shingon temple. Just over the hills to the south is Tōfukuji, one of Kyoto's five most important Zen monasteries. Noted for its fine gardens and fall scenery, the temple has an assembly of impressive buildings, including a picturesque covered bridge spanning a narrow gorge filled with maples.

Both temples may be reached by the Keihan Railway or the JR Nara Line; get off at either railway's Tōfukuji Stations. By bus, City Buses 202, 207, and 208 all stop at both the Sennyūji Michi and Tōfukuji bus stops near the First Red Cross Hospital (Sekijūji) on Higashiōji Dōri. Tōfukuji is one traffic light south of the hospital, on the east side of Higashiōji. Sennyūji is located two traffic signals north of the hospital on a street that runs uphill past shops and homes.

Start this walk at **Sennyūji** [Open 9 to 4:30. Admission ¥300. Tel: 561-1551]. For centuries a mortuary temple for the nobility,

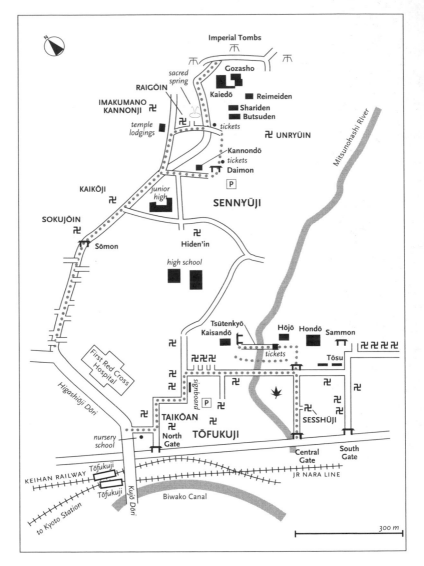

SENNYŪJI and TŌFUKUJI

Sennyūji has a solemn, remote feeling. Time seems to have consigned it to the role of passive observer of Kyoto life and dignified keeper of the ancestral spirits. Its name, "Bubbling Spring," derives from a spring in its precincts, located near what is said to be a ninth-century hermitage of Kūkai, founder of the Shingon sect of Buddhism. Founded in 1218 by the monk Shunjō, Sennyūji is headquarters of one of the subsects of Shingon.

The precincts of the present temple begin at the Sōmon. Near this gate, on the left, is the subtemple **Sokujōin** [Tel: 561-3443], dedicated to the worship of Amida. A phoenix sits astride its gate, and the building beyond it on the right is this subtemple's Main Hall, where the statue of Amida sits, surrounded by twenty-five attendant bodhisattvas. Bodhisattvas are beings who have postponed their entrance to paradise and stayed in the corporal world to help save others. All twenty-six of these delicate late-Heian-period (794–1185) wooden images are Important Cultural Properties. One unusual feature of these carvings is that the two bodhisattvas, Kannon and Seishi, which flank Amida, are seated in Japanese style, indicating that they were made by a native artisan. In the corridor of the Main Hall are color photos of an annual parade on the third Sunday of October in which children are costumed as the twenty-five bodhisattvas attending Amida.

Illustrations of a boat with billowy sails and the names of nine subtemples within the Sennyūji complex are sold for ¥1,300. The boat represents the one that carries the Seven Gods of Good Fortune. Devotees present this paper at the listed temples to have auspicious calligraphy inscribed. January 15 is the most popular day for making this "pilgrimage," but it can be done at any time.

Beyond the Sōmon, a wide, paved road leads uphill to the **Daimon**, the main gate of the Sennyūji complex. Located at the base of Mt. Tsukinowa, the present precincts cover fifty-seven acres, and an hour or more can be spent strolling around the quiet and beautifully maintained grounds. The ¥500 admission fee, collected at the north or west ticket booths beside the Daimon, grants access to the buildings in the courtyard.

Immediately to the left of the Daimon is a tiny **Kannondō**. Through a complicated set of historical and literary circumstances, this temple is dedicated to the (in)famous Chinese consort Yang Kuei-fei, a famous beauty of the Tang dynasty whose loveliness unwittingly sparked civil war and the decline of the great Tang empire. Here she is seen as a feminine manifestation of Kannon, the bodhisattva of mercy, and called Yōkihi Kannon, an unusual twist for a woman who in China is known for her tragic beauty but not the compassion she is attributed here.

Across from the Kannondō, up the uneven stairs, is **Unryūin** [Open 9 to 5. Admission ¥200. Tel: 541-3916], which has a Yakushi Buddha as its image and a lovely, compact garden of sculpted azalea bushes and aged pines. In a dell at the bottom of the slope, in the center of a graveled courtyard, stands the **Butsuden**, or Main Hall, an immense Chinese-style building containing three seated images: Amida on the left, Shaka Nyorai in the center, and Miroku on the right. Softly glimmering in the natural light, the gold-lacquered seventeenth-century figures almost seem to float in the dark and cavernous hall. The ceiling has a painting of a dragon flying among swirling clouds done by the famous Edo-period artist Kanō Tan'yū (1602–1720). Unfortunately, the netting that covers it makes it difficult to see well. The usual candles and incense for sale are supplemented here by packages of walnut-shaped metal objects that are reputed to stimulate the pressure points of the hand when grasped. They come complete with illustrations identifying the acupuncture meridians of the body.

The graceful, massive roof of the **Reimeiden** (Spirit Hall) is covered with cedar bark like the imperial palace. The Reimeiden holds 130 memorial tablets of emperors, imperial consorts, princes, and princesses. The large **Shariden** houses relics of the historical Buddha, Shakyamuni. Neither of these halls is open to the public. Farther back in the complex are the **Kaiedō** and **Goza-sho**. The latter is decorated with many delicate ink-wash paintings, as well as several paintings on wooden doors. Admission to the rooms and garden of the Gozasho is ¥300.

A well-landscaped gravel road leads back to the impressive imperial tombs, among them those of Emperor Kōmei and Emperor Go-Horikawa. Across from the north ticket booth are stone stairs that lead down to a path by a bridge. **Raigōin** is on the other side of the arched stone bridge. This temple is dedicated to Hotei, the jovial-looking, pot-bellied God of Fortune (also seen as an incarnation of the future Buddha, Maitreya) identifiable by a sack slung over his shoulder. In the back of the temple grounds are many statues of Hotei piled on the stone arch of a former *torii*, now resting on the ground. On sale for ¥1,000 is a smooth white stone on which one writes his or her wishes, and then leaves it on a pile near the statue of Kūkai, the founder of the Shingon sect in Japan. Legend claims that Kūkai named the temple for a spring that bubbled up here some twelve hundred years ago. This spring is under the altar of the building beyond the statue of Kūkai. The rusting metal doors under the altar open to this spring, and the long-handled dipper hanging from one of the beams is used to draw the water. Near the entrance is a more accessible source of Sennyūji's sacred spring water: mugs are set out beside the faucet for those who wish to sample it.

The road that passes in front of Raigōin continues downhill and joins another road spanned by a bright orange bridge. This leads to **Imakumano Kannonji**, the fifteenth stop on the well-traveled thirty-three Kannon pilgrimage route. Pilgrims are usually seen bearing scrolls on which the temple's seal and auspicious calligraphy will be artistically inscribed by the resident monk. To the right of the temple is a tiny structure, in front of which are numerous seated statues of old men and women. These figures, placed here by elderly visitors or their relatives, are part of a recent religious practice to ward off senility, an affliction much feared by Japan's aging population.

Behind the Main Hall of Imakumano Kannonji is a bright two-storied pagoda. Zigzagging through a dense bamboo forest, the path to it is lined with thirty-three small statues of the bodhisattva of mercy, a miniature version of the Kannon pilgrimage.

Kaikōji is a small subtemple on the road leading out of the precincts. Inside to the left is a colorful Benten shrine, dedicated to the goddess of music. On the right is the Main Hall, which houses a ten-meter-tall image of Shakyamuni. Carved in the Kamakura period (1185–1333), faint traces of the lacquer work are still visible. The graceful folds of the robe, the exquisite hands, and the delicate scrolling cloud design on the halo-like background make this image an impressive piece of Buddhist art. Packages of flour and cans of fruit set out among the other offerings add an incongruous touch to this Important Cultural Property.

A sign near the subtemple Hiden'in, which is close to a sports ground, points in the direction of the temple complex **Tōfukuji** [Tel: 551-0334]. However, the surest way to arrive at Tōfukuji is to return to Higashiōji Dōri, turn left at the traffic light, pass the Red Cross Hospital, and turn left at the second light, following the road until you reach the temple wall. The temple with the Jizō image to the right of the path is **Taikōan**. Established in 1346, it is one of the subtemples of this Rinzai sect temple. Just inside the entrance to the right is a small hall with another image of Jizō, one in which numerous love letters to Ono no Komachi, a famous poet of the Heian period, were discovered. The zigzag path passes a signboard of a map located in front of the temple's parking lot. Pass this signboard and turn right onto a straight path with a wall running on either side, which leads to a covered bridge spanning Tōfukuji's famous maple-filled ravine. Beyond the wooded slopes, the massive, curving roof of the Hōjō, or Abbot's Quarters, is visible.

In contrast to the stately ambience of Sennyūji, Tōfukuji, one

Jolly statues of Hotei, one of Japan's Seven Gods of Good Fortune, have been left by petitioners in hopes of bettering their luck.

of the largest Rinzai Zen monasteries in Kyoto, is characterized by activity. It is filled with sightseers and local residents cutting through the temple on their way to shop or to walk their dogs. The complex is famous for the gardens of its subtemples, the most dynamic of which are on the grounds of the Abbot's Quarters. Redesigned in 1938, the four gardens of the Hōjō [Open 9 to 4. Admission ¥400. Tel: 561-0087] reflect innovations in Japanese gardening techniques. Designed by Shigemori Mirei, the results are exciting. The east garden, the first one seen on entering, has old granite foundation pillars set within a bed of raked gravel in the shape of the Big Dipper. The south garden is a powerful rock garden. The dynamic shapes of the rocks are indicative of the strength and discipline required of students of Zen. The west garden has a checkerboard design of white gravel and squares of pruned azalea bushes. This checkerboard design continues around to the north garden where it acts as a foil to the natural hillside beyond.

On exiting the Hōjō, there is another covered bridge on the right that spans the ravine. An admission fee is collected here to cross the bridge and enter the **Kaisandō** [Open 9 to 4. Admission ¥300], or Founder's Hall. In mid-November it is sometimes difficult to see the maples for the people, but at most other times of the year it is not crowded. The entrance to Kaisandō, built in the 1600s, is through a large wooden gate. The main attraction is its garden, which features gravel raked in a checkerboard pattern and a tree with low rocks and bushes comprising the traditional crane and tortoise motifs. Opposite, a hill of azaleas and large stones overlooks the water-lily pond. A path near the bridge leads down and across the stream that cuts through the ravine, offering a view of the graceful **Tsūtenkyō** (Heavenly Way Bridge) from below.

Located diagonally across the courtyard from the Hōjō is the **Tōsu**. Although it cannot be entered most of the time, the interior can be glimpsed from outside, and it is worth a peek. This long building—once the temple's latrine—has wooden slats on the upper half and two straight rows of shallow holes inside. Long ago, it was the head abbot who cleaned these toilets as part of his religious duties, and it stands as a reminder of the sacredness of all facets of life as well as the duties of superiors. (In days before soap, hands were washed with ash, then rinsed and made fragrant with the powder of the *tachibana* flower.)

The quiet Funda'in [Open 9 to 5. Admission ¥300], a subtemple better known as **Sesshūji**, after the famous ink-painter Sesshū (1420–1506) who is supposed to have designed its garden, is down the road leading away from the courtyard. The forms in the garden allude to famous legends in Chinese mythology. Two lovely tearooms are located around the back, just off of a wooden veranda (*engawa*). Visitors can enter the four-and-a-half mat and the adjoining two-mat rooms, and experience something of the intimacy the tea ceremony evokes.

INDEX

Boldface names are those of the principal walks in this book; asterisks indicate restaurants and other commercial establishments.